THERE'S A TSUNAMI OF
GOD'S HOLY SPIRIT COMING

WILL YOU BE SWEPT UP IN IT
OR SWEPT AWAY BY IT?

REVIEWS
Does God Have a Gay Agenda?

This book is critical for those desiring to be positioned for the next move of God! King's depiction of today's Evangelical Church and God's urgent call for change will bring the Church into her glorious calling. This is a must-read book for every pastor. This revelation gives the full picture of the next movement of God through His people. It is vital that church leaders heed this forecast so that we will be like the five wise virgins who were prepared with their oil (anointing and alignment) and ready when Jesus arrives as He will in this next move of the Spirit."

> Pastor Tom Cash
> Jesus People Church of Asheville

Immediately, upon finishing *Does God Have a Gay Agenda?* a story from the Gospel of John flooded my mind and heart. In the story, Jesus had given sight to a man blind since birth. When certain of the religious authorities heard about the miracle, they called the man in for questioning. Ultimately, the authorities wanted him to disavow his experience. Ostensibly, they were angry Jesus had performed this miracle on the Sabbath. Truth was, they were threatened by his burgeoning influence. Fortunately, in spite of their "best" efforts, these bully leaders could not convince the man to change his testimony. He simply would not diminish himself or Jesus by denying the plain fact — for the first time in his life he could see. Furious that the healed man refused to acquiesce to their demands, the leaders cruelly "drove him out," essentially expelling him from the temple.

Thankfully, though, the story doesn't end there. When Jesus heard what had happened to the man, He went looking for him. Upon finding the fellow, Jesus asked him, "Do you believe in the Son of Man?" The man answered, "And who is he, sir? Tell me, so that I may believe in him." To that sincere appeal, Jesus responded, "You have seen him, and the one speaking with you is he." And at that very moment, another even more important pair of the man's eyes were opened, causing him to cry out, "Lord, I believe." In the loveliest of conclusions, the gospel writer then tells us the man "worshipped Jesus."

Earlier in the story, the man had referred to Jesus as "a prophet." And I now know that is one of the reasons this story came to me unprovoked in the instant I finished Brian's manuscript. You see, by John 9's very apt definition, Brian King is a prophet and this book, *Does God Have a Gay Agenda?* is a prophetic work. After the manner of Christ in John 9, this book is actively searching for those who have been expelled and excluded from the temple, it has been written as a Divine love-letter to those who have been pressured by religious authorities to deny their undeniable experiences of God. And for those precious children of God, those who have so desperately missed worshipping Jesus, this book will provide the sweetest of release.

Finally, in answer to the book's title, I offer a resounding yes. Yes! God does indeed have a gay agenda. Always has actually. It is just that we are now finally ready for it to unfold.

> Stan Mitchell
> Founding Pastor,
> GracePointe Church
> Nashville, TN

I started *Does God Have a Gay Agenda?* one evening and couldn't lay it down until I finished it! This book is definitely one of best books written on the subject of LGBTQ inclusion, as well as being a prophetic word to both the Evangelical Church and the LGBTQ community.

I plan on giving it out to the churches I'm affiliated with all around the world.

God bless you Bishop Brian and this wonderful book.

May it be used to God's glory here in America and around the world.

> Apostle Dylan David Crozier
> Lighthouse of Hope Network

Moshe says in Deuteronomy 18:15: "Yehovah your God will raise up for you a prophet like me from your midst — from your brothers. To him you must listen." God did not leave His people without a prophetic voice. He raised a line of prophets, beginning with Moshe until this present day. As I read *Does God Have a Gay Agenda?* I distinctly heard the strident voice of the prophet in the words that Pastor Brian wrote. He does in this book what God's prophets have done down through the ages — let God's people know what God was going to do next, called the church on the carpet for her sins, and issued a clarion call for repentance. Like Elijah he has called the church to abandon its worship of Baal which today takes the form of pursuit of wealth, prestige, and political power and in its place to do justice wholeheartedly, love mercy in the same measure they have received it, and walk humbly with the living God. Jeremiah wept over God's people but still spoke of hope and a future. I have seen firsthand Pastor Brian weep over the LGBTQ community but like Jeremiah, he offers them hope for the future when the church fully embraces the "whosoever" of the Gospel. The last sentence in Deuteronomy 18:15 says "To him you must listen." To which I add a heartfelt "Amen."

> Roi Hudson-Anaya
> Messianic Rabbi
> Reignite Ministries International

I highly recommend Pastor Brian King's Book *Does God Have a Gay Agenda?* In our current times it seems conservative voices are rebelling against education and research. The Holy Spirit is alive in the world bringing God's people back to God. I appreciate Pastor King's attention to detail while being able to explain complex theological concepts in easy to understand language for those not well versed in Master's level Christian Theology. God's truth trumps old understandings of Christian thought. Grace and Peace.

> Ken Anderson
> Pastor, Henson Chapel/ Mabel Charge
> Vilas, NC 28692
> United Methodist Church
> Chief Petty Officer, United States Coast Guard, Retired

Does God Have a Gay Agenda? Growing up in the 1960s and 70s, I attended a conservative Presbyterian church in Orange County, and as a teenager, went to Wednesday night services at Calvary Chapel in Costa Mesa, CA, with my mother and younger siblings. I remember the excitement of guitars and drums being played in worship; the young hippies with long hair, wearing jeans, fringed vests, long dresses, sandals, and even bare feet! At church! The open, enthusiastic preaching that spoke to God's interest in our everyday life was so different from my Sunday morning experience, and I wanted more! One thing we never heard, at either church, was a condemnation of people who were in the sexual minority. The word gay never passed our pastors' lips. It certainly wouldn't have occurred to anyone back then that God might have a "gay agenda!" Unfortunately, in the 1980s, many congregations began to hear preaching against homosexuality, equating it with depraved behavior, rather than an attraction or romantic interest, and condemning those whose natural attraction was for the same sex. This preaching has poisoned the modern church, and this book declares that the poison will be removed by God's Holy Spirit.

Using biblical references and church history to build his case, Pastor Brian King makes an impassioned plea to the modern church to pay attention to what God is doing among the people who have been ignored, rejected, spurned, and excommunicated from the fellowship of the saints. The research and care with which King approaches the subject is clearly a labor of love, both to the church who has gone astray from the greatest commandment, and to those who have been hurt by the church's recent teachings. King's message to the modern church, backed by scripture and prophetic word from multiple sources, is that God is ready to move in a way we haven't seen, bringing revival and salvation using His people in the lesbian, gay, bisexual, transgender (LGBT) Christian community. As a gay man of God who has sought His face through many trials, including conversion therapy to try to become straight, King brings a strong, authentic voice to the wilderness of the judgmental and lost sheep in the dwindling congregations. The reader is left with the message that whether or not an individual church or member repents of the damage done to LGBT people by those who call themselves Christians, this movement the

Spirit is coming to bring revival and much-needed acceptance of all to the Christian church.

> Wendy Prell Danbury
> Professional Freelance Editor

One Printers Way
Altona, MB, R0G 0B0
Canada

www.friesenpress.com

Copyright © 2021 by Brian King
First Edition — 2021

Foreword by Kathy V. Baldock

Edited by Wendy Prell Danbury and Jenny Rain

All rights reserved.

No part of this publication may be reproduced in any form, or by any means, electronic or mechanical, including photocopying, recording, or any information browsing, storage, or retrieval system, without permission in writing from FriesenPress.

ISBN
978-1-5255-8662-0 (Hardcover)
978-1-5255-8661-3 (Paperback)
978-1-5255-8663-7 (eBook)

1. RELIGION, CHRISTIAN CHURCH

Distributed to the trade by The Ingram Book Company

DOES GOD HAVE A GAY AGENDA?

BRIAN KING

TABLE OF CONTENTS

Foreword	13
Introduction	17
About the Author	19

Section I—Where We Are NOW — 21
- A Spirit of Stupor — 21

Section II—Here's What You Need to Know — 29
- Laying a Scriptural Foundation — 29
- The Word "Homosexual" and the Lesson of Sodom — 32
- Clobber Passages in Leviticus — 44
- Clobber Passages in the New Testament — 48
- Combining Two Greek Words — 58
- God Is Not Done with Israel — 71
  - *Replacement Theology—A Doctrine of Devils* — *72*
  - *In-Grafted Branches* — *77*

Section III—A Look at Twentieth-Century Church History — 83
- The Start of Something New: Azusa Street — 83
- The Great Charismatic Renewal — 94
- Lonnie Frisbee and the Jesus People Movement — 101

Section IV—Where the Church Has Missed the Mark — 124
- The Religious Right: A Study in Hypocrisy — 124
- Love Lost — 132
- Pro-Life vs. Pro-Birth — 139

Methinks the Lady Doth Protest Too Much: A Study of
Homophobic Men 146
The Dangers of Reparative Therapy, #NotChanged 154
Like Israel, the Church Plays the Harlot, and Makes God Jealous 170
   The Correlation between Natural Israel and the Church ... *171*

Section V—The Reality of it All ... 177
God's Presence Is What Sets a People Apart 177
The Condition of the LGBTQ Community 184
   The Gay "Lifestyle" *184*
A Call to Repentance for Affirming Leaders 189

Section VI—A Wake-Up Call! ... 200
God's Gay Agenda: His Plan for the LGBTQ Community ... 200
   God's "Heads-Up" *205*

Section VII—Something to Think About ... 212
One New Man? 212

Section VIII—What's Next? ... 217
A Word from an Intercessory General 217
The Dinner Bell to Salvation 224
Same Spirit, Different Administrations 229
   Bishop Randy Morgan and the Covenant Network *230*
   Matthew Vines and The Reformation Project *232*
   Pastor Stan Mitchell and the Everybody Church *239*
   Kathy V. Baldock and Canyonwalker Connections *246*
   Reignite Ministries International, Reignite Palm Springs,
   and RISSM *249*

Section IX—Going Forward ... 254
The Cry of the Father's Heart 254
   To the Evangelical Church—Repent *254*
   To the Affirming Church—Press in and Rise up *259*
   To the LGBTQ Community—Come Home *261*

Foreword

IN 2013, I spent a weekend at an LGBTQ Christian conference in a place aptly named Wonder Valley, hidden in the high desert region of Southern California. I had already established growing friendships with some of the attendees, many of whom had been meeting yearly since the 1990s. This was a community of dedicated, Spirit-filled believers in Jesus who happened to be gay and lesbian. I knew most of the yearly attendees by then.

After a ten-hour-long drive from Reno, I arrived at the retreat center just as the group was finishing dinner. I rushed to grab some food and sat with friends to catch up on the past year's events. I knew most attendees, but during dinner, I spotted a man with a gorgeous smile whom I didn't know. "*I need to go find out who that is,*" I thought. I sat next to Devin and asked him to tell me about himself.

I've been privileged to hear many stories shared by LGBTQ people during the almost fifteen years of my advocacy work to help repair the damage exacted by the conservative Christian church. As a straight Christian, no church leadership has ever actively attempted to pressure me to leave a faith community for any reason. Yet I am often amongst those who share this sad circumstance as a common part of their story.

Even in telling his disappointment-filled story of family rejection, Devin shone. He told me about the group of believers he fellowshipped with in Palm Springs, California. He described a dedicated group, and I was intrigued to someday meet them.

Over the next few years, Devin introduced me to those friends and fellow Christians in his Palm Springs church. It was through Devin that I met Brian King. Even from the start, I knew that Brian's fervor for the things of God and His Kingdom were genuine and deep. Every aspect of Brian's life was filtered through how he might best serve and please God.

I had the opportunity to do a presentation at Pastor Brian's church in 2016, which allowed me to spend extended time with him. Each conversation consistently centered on wanting to be an accurate reflection of Jesus in his relationships, his family, his work, his ministry, and his community.

When you read of Brian's love of God and desire to do His will in this book, it is genuine. In John 1, we read an account of Jesus' words as He saw Nathanael approaching Him. Jesus said of Nathanael that he was a man in whom there was "no guile." Jesus sized up Nathanael as a man without hypocrisy or pretense, a man who was transparent in his words and deeds, who spoke his mind and was honest with himself. Brian too is such a man, a man of "no guile."

You will read the passion in Brian's word in this book. He wants everyone to have the opportunity to be in a relationship with God, Jesus, and the Holy Spirit. That desire is the impetus behind this book.

Brian knows from personal experience the pain of needing to hide one's sexual orientation in order to be accepted within many Christian environments. Even as a closeted gay man while married and father of three, he claimed he was "delivered from homosexuality" so that he might be acceptable to not only fellow Christians but to God as well.

Brian understands why so many LGBTQ people leave churches or never feel welcome in some congregations and denominations. It is with this understanding and empathy that Pastor Brian calls them back with the truth of the Gospel. In this book, he tackles the verses that have been misused and mistranslated to show they are not weapons of exclusion but words of inclusion.

Brian will share with his readers some modern-day moves of the Holy Spirit. Even in the Old Testament, we see God's sensitivity to those who are willing to hear Him when others may not. God looks to the edges, to the oppressed who are often uniquely positioned to listen more acutely than those in the middle of the traffic. Pastor Brian senses we are in and about to enter another move of the Spirit, a move anticipated by several prophets, in which the LGBTQ community will be those at the forefront. Brian warns, "If we dismiss it, we'll miss it."

I can testify to what I have witnessed in my decade and a half amongst LGBTQ Christians. Many have had to strain and struggle to gain access to the mercy and compassionate love of God. They've worked to break down the barriers erected against them. We straight Christians rarely need to wrestle as hard. We say "yes, Lord," and into the Kingdom we stride. We are cheered on. This is not so for our LGBTQ siblings in Christ. The grappling, however, frequently produces people of strong faith, people who know more deeply Who God is and who they are in Him.

It should be no surprise that God would look again to the margins, to the discarded, and to the unlikely to show those who have contaminated their faith just how far they have strayed. Many Christian leaders resist LGBTQ people, yet they defile themselves while chasing political power.

In the final pages of the book, Brian shares the stories of several people who diligently work to end discrimination against LGBTQ people in Christian churches. These people are amongst millions of Christians who love and affirm fellow LGBTQ Christians. We each need to be educated and get louder.

We need to listen to the Spirit and return to the purity of the Gospel message, the message of inclusion.

While Brian was writing this book, our friend Devin took his own life. Devin came out as gay at eighteen years old and ended his life at age fifty-seven. Devin was a man of God. He prayed, he served, he gave, and he sacrificed for others. There was deep sorrow underpinning his life—sorrow birthed in the constant rejection of who he was by the greater Christian church and his conservative Christian family that accepted lies as truth.

For the sake of the Kingdom, we need to pay attention to the work of the Spirit in the LGBTQ Christian community. Again, as Pastor Brian warns us, "If we dismiss it, we'll miss it."

Be alert and work for justice,

> Kathy Baldock
> Executive Director of Canyonwalker Connections, Reno, Nevada
> Author of *Walking the Bridgeless Canyon: Repairing the Breach between the Church and the LGBTQ Community* and *Forging a Sacred Weapon: How the Bible Became Anti-Gay.*

Introduction

DOES GOD HAVE A GAY AGENDA? is a book for our time: it is a sociopolitical-religious treatise intended to shed light on exactly why the Evangelical church in America, caught up in Christian Nationalism, is in the ineffective spiritual condition she finds herself in today; and it's a prophetic revelation to not only the church but to the LGBTQ community. This book is intended primarily for Christians who believe in Jesus as the Son of God and who trust God's Word as revealed to us in Holy Scripture, and secondarily to the non-believers in the LGBTQ community who have never been told that salvation was for them too. I pray that anyone who reads, regardless of their beliefs, will find value and inspiration and a call to action to further the Kingdom. As we explore with open hearts and minds, let us pray and ask God to reveal the truth of His Word, of His plan, and to join us as we embark on this incredible journey together.

The acronym LGBTQ will be used throughout this book; it stands for lesbian, gay, bisexual, transgender, queer. The last word can be controversial, because queer has been used as a derogatory slur; however, those who identify as queer have taken back the word that was once used to hurt them, and they now proudly identify themselves as queer. The people in the LGBTQ community are in a minority in terms of their sexual orientation (their attraction) and/or their gender identity (the gender they most identify with). As we'll discover, people do not choose to be a part of this community; their minority status is part of the beautiful diversity of God's creation.

There are a couple of spiritual principles found in scripture that are pertinent to understanding the premise of this book. Without scripture to back them up, the assertions found in these pages would be conjecture at best, and a complete waste of the reader's time. Everything presented here has a scriptural reference, cited in the body of this work.

Scripture tells us that the people knew God's *deeds* (the original Hebrew says His *acts*), but that God made His *ways* known to Moses (Psalms 103:7). There's a huge difference between knowing someone's deeds and knowing their ways. The first comes from a place of observation; the second comes from a place of intimacy.

In this book we're going to delve into what happens when an entire group of people know God's deeds but are oblivious to His ways. In this case, the group of people is the modern-day Church of Jesus Christ: the Christian Church, not to be confused with the Church of Jesus Christ of Latter Day Saints. I'm taking about the Church Universal, the Body of Christ. All references to the Church hereafter are referencing this Body and are simply referred to as the "Church."

The second principle to keep in mind is that God loves to do things His people don't see coming. He states in Isaiah 43:19a (KJV), "Behold, I am doing a new thing; now it springs forth, do you not perceive it?" If it were not possible for God's people to miss the "new thing" He's doing, He wouldn't have asked that question.

Pastor Steven Furtick put it so eloquently when he asked, "What would keep me from perceiving what God is doing now? Maybe it's expecting it to look like what He's done in the past."

The final principle I want to bring to your attention is the repeated comparison in scripture between the nation of Israel, "natural Israel," and the Church. It's imperative that we understand how these two are *both* the apple of God's eye and how He desperately loves them and desires the complete restoration of both through Jesus Christ, Yeshua Messiah. You'll understand how and why this is imperative as you read through these pages, and may Holy Spirit reveal His plan to and through you.

Be blessed!

About the Author

IT WILL HELP most readers to know where I'm coming from as an author. I am not a liberal, or what many would call a progressive, Christian. I am, in the truest sense of the word, Evangelical. I am Pentecostal in my beliefs and style of worship.

I come from a family made up of immigrants—some were from the British Isles, others were European, while still others were German Jews. I am very much in touch with my Jewish heritage. On my father's side, I have true American roots in the Cherokee Indian tribe.

I self-identify as a born-again, Spirit-filled Christian, who is madly, passionately in love with Jesus Christ, Yeshua Messiah, and who also happens to be gay. I've been sexually abstinent for over ten years now—not because I believe that scripture condemns sex between two people of the same gender who are in a loving, monogamous, covenant/married relationship, but because sexual immorality is denounced in about twenty-five passages in the New Testament: the word translated as sexual immorality or fornication is the Greek word *porneia*, meaning illicit sexual intercourse. Sex before marriage has been included in that definition, and I am unmarried.

I believe scripture, as it was originally written, is definitely the inspired Word of God. I also believe, however, as it has been proven numerous times, that people have misinterpreted some scripture from its original writing—sometimes accidentally and other times for ideological or political gain, as we will discover in this book.

In keeping with original biblical content and context, I purposely use the traditional pronouns of "He," "His," and "Him" in reference to God and Jesus, and "she" in reference to the Church—a nod to the Church being referred to as the Bride of Christ. When I refer to the third person of God, Holy Spirit, I do not use the definite article "the," as is commonly done, because I want to reflect the intimate nature of my relationship with Him.

I am Senior and Founding Pastor of Reignite Palm Springs, and Bishop over the Reignite Ministries International, Inc. (RMI) network of churches. RMI is a small network of Spirit-filled, affirming churches and ministries, currently with churches in Palm Springs, Houston, Venezuela, India, and the Philippines.

I am a father to two beautiful daughters, one very handsome son, and two "fur babies" named Kayde and Brodie, as well as grandfather to eight amazing grandchildren who are the loves of my life.

SECTION I– WHERE WE ARE NOW

CHAPTER 1
A Spirit of Stupor

THERE'S A WAR raging all around us. It's a war for the souls of men and women—for the souls of not only a generation, but of an entire people group—an entire nation, if you will. That nation is the LGBTQ community, and their adversary, sad to say, is the mainstream Evangelical Church in America.

Make no mistake, this war was not birthed in the courts of Heaven, but rather in the very pit of Hell itself. It's a war conceived by the enemy of humanity, being fought by people totally unaware that, in truth, they're fighting *against* the very one they claim to be fighting for. The incredibly sad thing is that so many embattled in this war are truly good people who honestly believe they're fighting for God and His plan. But please remember, the Pharisees of Jesus' day thought they too were doing God's will when they crucified the King of Glory.

You may ask, "How could this possibly be?" And if this is true, "Why? Why would a loving God allow this?" Well, let's take our first dive into scripture to see if Holy Spirit can shed some light on this for us.

As mentioned in the Introduction, there is a distinct correlation between the nation of Israel and the Church. The Church is in the exact same state in 2021 that Israel was in during Jesus' ministry on earth.

In Romans 11:7–8 (NIV), we read this about the people of Israel: "What the people of Israel sought so earnestly they did not obtain. The elect among them did, but the others were hardened, as it is written: 'God gave them a spirit of stupor, eyes that could not see and ears that could not hear, to this very day.'"

An anonymous Wordpress.com writer defines the spirit of stupor as follows:

> A state of near-unconsciousness or insensibility, mental numbness, a condition of greatly dulled or completely suspended sense or sensibility; a person in a stupor is considered barely conscious or stunned; or dazed and confused.

This would explain what so many theologians have pondered for nearly two millennia: "How could the people of Jesus' time not see and know who He was?" He had fulfilled over three hundred Old Testament prophecies, including the place of the Messiah's birth, His exile to and return from Egypt, His physical appearance, His ride into Jerusalem on a donkey, His betrayal, the method of His death, and hundreds of others. And yet Israel missed it!

In his classic book, *Science Speaks,* Professor Peter Stoner calculates that the odds of a single person fulfilling even forty-eight of the over three hundred prophecies about the Messiah would be an astronomical one in ten to the 157th power! And the mathematical odds of a single man fulfilling all three hundred-plus prophecies were incalculable.

I present to you that the Evangelical Church, especially in the United States of America, is under the influence of a "spirit of stupor," the same spirit of stupor that fell on the people of Israel two thousand years ago. They have eyes that cannot see what the Spirit of God is doing on the earth, and ears that cannot hear what He's speaking. Not only do they not see what He's doing or hear what He's speaking, but they do not want to see or hear anything that doesn't agree with their preconceived notion of what He's "supposed to be" doing and saying.

Now, you may ask yourself, what is God doing? This is what I hope to demonstrate in this book. It is my conviction that God is about to pour out His Holy Spirit upon the earth in an unprecedented way, resulting in the largest harvest of human souls coming into the Kingdom of God that the church has ever seen … and it's going to begin with the LGBTQ *community*. My goal is to show, through scripture, why Father God has chosen this most unlikely group of people to accomplish His purpose in this end time, and I believe that you'll become as excited about it as He is, and as I am.

In Mark 7:13, Jesus told the Pharisees of His day that they made the Word of God of no effect by the traditions they handed down to the people. There's a great danger in taking something for truth just because you've heard a preacher tell you for the past forty years that this is what scripture says. As the Church, we have not only not been diligent in studying the Word of God for ourselves, but we've regurgitated what we've heard from generation to generation, making doctrine of things the Word of God never speaks about—or at least, doesn't reference in the way we've interpreted.

To illustrate, we'll look at three examples: the first is an example of complete mistranslation, the second an example of misquoting, and the third accredits something to scripture that is from an entirely different religion.

First, let's look at a passage from the book of Job, chapter 2 in the NIV. Most Christians are familiar with the story of Job and how God allowed everything He had blessed Job with to be stripped away from him. Job's health, wealth, children, and reputation were all gone, but still he held to his faith in God. In verse 9 we read what may well be the most famous passage in the entire book: "Then his wife said to him, 'Do you still hold fast to your integrity? Curse God and die!'" Harsh words, but not at all what she actually said. The Hebrew word for "curse" is *qalal*. The word in the original Hebrew that the King James translation team got wrong is *barak* (Strong's H1288). According to Strong's Concordance, the Hebrew word *barak*" appears 330 times, and 302 of those times the word means "bless." Wow! Talk about a huge translation error. The actual meaning of the word is literally as far as one could get from the meaning the translators ascribed to it. It completely changes not only the meaning of the verse, but it implores us to dive deeper into the conversation: What exactly was Job's wife saying? Was she using sarcasm, as some would suggest, or was she making a statement as to the immovability of her husband's faith? The answer to these questions is not the focus of this book, but the fact that a translation error of this magnitude has been overlooked for thousands of years should give us pause to consider the credibility of what has been taught. I've heard dozens of sermons on this passage over the years, and apparently not a single one of those preachers, most of them devout men of God, ever bothered to ensure that what they were preaching was based on an accurate translation of the Bible.

The next example of folks getting scripture wrong and preaching something that was not said or intended is found in 1 Timothy 6:10 (NIV): "For the love of money is the root of all kinds of evil". How many times have we heard lay ministers as well as pastors misquote this and tell their congregations that money is the root of all evil? Yet scripture never says that money is evil; it says the *love of* money is the root of all evil. The Greek term that applies to the love of money is the word *philarguria,* which translates as "avarice." Merriam Webster defines avarice as an "excessive or insatiable desire for wealth or gain." Scripture never even suggests that money, in and of itself, is evil. In fact, it implies just the opposite when God Himself declares in Haggai 2:8 (KJV), "The silver is mine, and the gold is mine, sayeth the Lord of Host." Last I looked, God doesn't possess anything evil. It's not in His nature to abide evil. In First John 1:5 we read that God Himself is light, and in Him there is no darkness at all. Some preachers get this passage wrong due to lack of study; others misquote it in their attempts to discredit the prosperity doctrine many of the megachurches in America are preaching today (that's a discussion for another time, and maybe even another book). The purpose of these examples is to show that not everything being preached from our pulpits is accurate.

The last example is one that really hits home for me because not only is it completely absent from scripture, but it's used regularly by Christians to defend their stance against the LGBTQ community. The quote I'm talking about is, "Love the sinner, hate the sin." I've actually heard pastors say that scripture tells us this is the way we're to live, when in fact it's a quote taken from Mahatma Gandhi, a Hindu, and even then they get it wrong! The saying is from Gandhi's 1929 autobiography, *The Story of My Experiments with Truth,* wherein he states, "Hate the sin and not the sinner is a precept which, though easy enough to understand, is rarely practiced, and that is why the poison of hatred spreads in the world."

In his article of January 4, 2017, titled, "Our Problem with Kim Burrell's 'Hate the Sin, Love the Sinner' Argument," Jonathan Merritt of *Religion News Service* beautifully expounds on the quandary Gandhi brought to light, writing, "Gandhi rightly observed that it is difficult—perhaps impossible—to see someone else firstly as a 'sinner' and to focus on 'hating their sin' without developing some level of disdain for the person. Perhaps this is why Jesus did not ask us to love 'sinners' but to love 'neighbors' and 'enemies.'"

Take a moment and ask yourself this question: "How much more effective would the Church of Jesus Christ be if we focused on loving the people of the LGBTQ community as 'neighbors' instead of focusing on hating their supposed 'sin?'" You cannot effectively do both.

Later we'll go into specific detail on how not studying scripture for ourselves has affected the LGBTQ community, but here I'll say that in his second letter to Timothy, chapter 2, verse 15, the Apostle Paul warns his spiritual son, Timothy, about the dangers of not studying for himself. He says that the consequence for not studying is that we are unable to rightly divide the Word of Truth, and consequently bring shame upon not only ourselves but ultimately the name of Jesus Christ.

In his "Open Letter to Christians," the author John Pavlovitz, a Christian pastor and activist, writes, "Thinking sustained over time doesn't always equal Truth. Sometimes it just equals tradition. Just because many religious people get something wrong over and over and over again doesn't eventually one day make it right."

In her book *Will They Laugh If I Call You Daddy?*, my good friend, Jenny Rain, recounts:

> The church believed that the Earth was the center of the universe, and used scripture to justify their belief; the church believed that black men and women were less valuable than their white counterparts, and used scripture to justify their belief; the church believed that Jews were morally inferior, and used scripture to justify their belief; some churches still believe that women are less valuable than men, and they use scripture to justify their belief, and, I'm beginning to see a frightening rash of anti-Muslim sentiment brewing in Southern Evangelical churches that follows the exact same pattern. Each of the traditions above (except for the last two) have been debunked and removed from regular church practice, yet we are following the same pattern with the LGBTQ discussion.

To recap, so far we've discovered that there is such a thing in scripture as a "spirit of stupor," and the Evangelical Church in America appears to have all the signs that she has fallen victim to it. We've seen that God loves doing new things that His people aren't expecting, and that a combination of mistranslations, misquotes, and the incorporation of non-scriptural rhetoric into our preaching has led to opinion being taught from America's pulpits as truth—the very thing that the Apostle Paul warned his young protégé, Timothy, would bring him shame.

You may think that I'm being way too hard on the Church right now, but I'm here to tell you that if you think the folks who are blindly accepting the things that are happening in this country are sober and of a sound mind, consider this: bigotry, racism, marginalizing, and demeaning people—these things are not of God. After two hundred years of trying to make amends to the African American community, how could anyone think that bringing back the hatred and persecution they faced as slaves could ever make America great again?

Why, after the atrocities the US government perpetrated on Native Americans, would we ever think that treating them the way we are treating them today is going to make America great again?

What we should have done, what a truly godly people would have done, is repent before God on our knees and faces for what we did to these people and vow to never let it happen again. Yet from 1851, when Alexander H. H. Stuart, the Secretary of the Interior, said that the only alternatives left were "to civilize or exterminate them," until 2019, when Covington High School students tormented and bullied a tribal elder who was opposing construction on sacred land, we haven't made much progress in undoing the injustices done to native peoples in America. The Church is not only turning a blind eye to this abhorrent behavior by our politicians, but her leaders are embracing it in total defiance of all that Jesus Christ and His gospel dictate.

And what about the "crisis" on our southern border? People in detention centers, children stripped from their parents and locked in cages? In 2020 I saw a picture of our then-vice president, a man who is *very* vocal about his Christian faith, standing solemnly and staring at a group of South American migrants being held in a makeshift detention center. The photo was shown next to an eerily similar picture of Hitler's number-two man, Heinrich Himmler, overseeing a group of Jews being detained in Nazi Germany. As the grandson of a German Jew who lost part of his family in the Holocaust, I was raised to believe that "never again" meant "*never again!*" Yet here I see this abhorrent behavior not only being tolerated by our government officials but celebrated by those who profess to be Christians. Remember, the Christian Church in Germany stood by and did absolutely nothing to stop the atrocities they saw happening all around them—and it's happening right here, today, in our beloved United States.

"Do not mistreat foreigners who are living in your land. Treat them as you would an Israelite, and love them as you love yourselves. Remember that you were once foreigners in the land of Egypt. I am the LORD your God" (Leviticus 19:33–34). This is just one of many scriptures that flies in the face of what we're seeing pass as Christian theology in America today.

In a study released by Pew Research in May of 2018 (https://pewrsr.ch/2s5lyAj), we see that white Evangelicals feel no need to follow the instructions of the scripture: "By more than two-to-one (68% to 25%), white evangelical Protestants say the U.S. does not have a responsibility to accept refugees. Other religious groups are more likely to say the U.S. does have this responsibility. And opinions among religiously unaffiliated adults are nearly the reverse of those of white evangelical Protestants: 65% say the U.S. has a responsibility to accept refugees into the country, while just 31% say it does not."

Although my focus is on the spiritual condition of our country, not politics, when the party of choice for the overwhelming majority of evangelical Christians is complicit in undermining the Gospel of Jesus Christ, I have to call it for what it is: heresy and an embarrassment to the Church and our nation.

I'm not saying, "Open the borders and let anyone and everyone flood in." I understand there is more to it than that, but where's the compassion? Where's the heart of the Father? Where's the Church being Jesus to "the least of these?"

There's a popular saying that's been around for a decade or two, and you're sure to have heard its acronym, WWJD: What would Jesus do? I'd like to pose a different question: "What would we, the Church, do if Jesus came to the United States today in the original state in which He came to Israel two thousand years ago?" His teachings would be the same, but the doctrine and practices of the majority of our Church leaders today would be antithetical to His words and lifestyle. He lavishly poured out His love on the least of the people of His day, yet our top Church leaders today pander to politicians and the wealthy. Immigrants aren't shown hospitality; the downtrodden and broken aren't comforted; they're turned away, imprisoned, shunned, marginalized, and cast out. What would we do? Would we repent and take up our cross and follow Him? I honestly don't think so. Why? We're spiritually deaf, dumb, and blind, lulled to sleep by a spirit of stupor that's left the church drunk in tradition and comfort and unable to recognize what God is doing on the earth in this hour.

Yes, just as Israel missed it and crucified the darling of Heaven, we too are missing it and condemning an entire "nation" of people to hell. I've searched the scriptures to find even the slightest reference that condones what the Church in America is doing to the LGBTQ community, but for the life of me I can't find a single one. The entire biblical narrative from Genesis to Revelation reveals the radical, inclusive love Father God has for His creation. Nowhere do we see Jesus condemning *anyone,* but rather, in the Gospel of John, chapter 3, verse 17, we read some of the most beautiful, powerful words ever penned: "For God sent not his Son into the world to condemn the world, but that the world through him might be saved" (KJV).

SECTION II– HERE'S WHAT YOU NEED TO KNOW

CHAPTER 2
Laying a Scriptural Foundation

"JUST SPEAK YOUR TRUTH."

How often have you heard someone say that recently? How many times a day do you read it as an encouragement on a social media blog or post? We're in a place in our society and culture today where there are no longer absolutes; everything is relative. The problem with this is that without absolutes there's chaos and confusion. If one person's truth is diametrically opposed to another person's truth, how can they both hold on to their position of being right? Truth, by its very nature, is not subjective.

Merriam Webster defines truth as: "a transcendent fundamental or spiritual reality."

Truth cannot be subjective. It is based on verifiable facts—something that can be proven. Truth doesn't change from one set of circumstances to another. Truth must always be based on reality, not one's perception of reality as seen through a particular filter or lens. Let me give you an example.

World famous Australian soccer player, Israel Folau, recently came under fire for his homophobic views when he issued a rant on Instagram, stating: "Hell awaits" people who are "drunks, homosexuals, adulterers." This was not the first of such outbursts; earlier, Folau had posted a similar social media blurb, saying, "God's plan for gay people was HELL" (https://www.dw.com/en/australian-rugby-star-israel-folau-faces-sack-over-anti-gay-outburst/a-48286386).

Now let's set aside the controversy over whether this should have been condemned as hate speech, and let's overlook the fact that he's presumptuous enough to believe he knows the Father's heart on such a delicate matter as where a group of people will spend eternity, and look at it strictly as one man "speaking his truth." Without being based on a transcendent spiritual reality, this man's "truth" is diminished to nothing more than his opinion. Your truth and my truth, unless it's based on something transcendent, like the Word of God, is only our opinion. And as passionate as he may be about his beliefs, Folau's statement was not based on the Word of God. It was based on his own beliefs, which were most likely the result of bad theology he was taught over the years.

For my fundamentalist, evangelical friends reading this, you may be stunned that I would have the audacity to make such a statement. But the truth, the actual, transcendent truth, is that scripture does not support Folau's beliefs. As we'll discuss in the next chapter, not only does the word "homosexual" not appear in any of the original translations of scripture, but it didn't appear in any language until 1892! Bottom line: telling people the Bible says something it doesn't say doesn't make it the truth.

A lie can never be used to support the truth, whether it's told intentionally or out of ignorance.

As noted, Folau's beliefs and resulting statements are most likely the result of bad teaching that he accepted as truth without researching it. Does that make him a bad person? No, not necessarily, unless he said what he said knowing it wasn't true, but we're not here to determine the motive of his heart; that's way above both my paygrade and yours. What it does make him, however, is the kind of person the Apostle Paul warned Timothy not to become. You see, Folau's lack of study caused him to improperly "divide the word of truth." Paul says doing this will bring shame on a person. Folau accepted what was taught to him as truth and repeated it in a very public forum, bringing massive condemnation and shame upon himself and others. This condemnation is worn by him as a badge of honor, and he claims he was the victim of "religious persecution" for his "Christian" beliefs. Nothing could be further from the truth. You can't claim Christian persecution for a statement that was erroneously ascribed to the Bible.

As we discussed in chapter 1, telling people the Bible says something that it doesn't say doesn't make it true. What was heaped upon Folau and those who rallied to his side wasn't persecution—it was condemnation for using his public platform to espouse hateful, damaging rhetoric. He wasn't being persecuted for standing up for biblical truth; he was being called out for being a bully and for using the Word of God as a weapon against a group of people. He was speaking *his* truth, which wasn't truth at all.

So in keeping with the truth, defined by Webster as "a transcendent fundamental or spiritual reality," we're going to use scripture as the basis for everything we discuss in this book.

If it doesn't line up with scripture as it was originally written, not as you may have heard it interpreted, we're not going to receive it as truth. Taking things out of context, or claiming that scripture says something it doesn't say, is not truth, and it's not acceptable in Father God's eyes.

CHAPTER 3
The Word "Homosexual" and the Lesson of Sodom

IN CHAPTER 2 we determined that in order for something to be considered as truth, it has to be based on something fundamental or spiritual, and it is transcendent. Inasmuch as this book is written primarily to Christians, we're going to accept scripture, as it was originally written, as the basis for spiritual truth. In chapter 1 we saw that words are not always translated correctly and that this can have a dramatic effect on the way a verse is read and interpreted. This is why the study of scripture is so incredibly important: a mistranslation can change the intent ("truth") of a statement or passage of scripture and all subsequent doctrines and practices based on that "truth."

As we learned in chapter 2, "homosexual" was not even a word in any language until 1892. In 1946, the word appeared for the first time in scripture in the then newly released Revised Standard Version (RSV), and again later in 1958 and 1966 in the Amplified Bible and Revised Standard Version—Catholic Edition, respectively. The big problem here is that the translation of the scripture verses wasn't accurate. There were two words from the Greek, *malakoi* and *arsenokoitai*, that the RSV translation team translated into one word: "homosexual."

Before we define the meanings of these two Greek words, or explore the passages that use these words, let's look at the definition of homosexual from Merriam Webster:

> homosexual
> <u>adjective</u>
> ho·mo·sex·u·al | \ ˌhō-mə-ˈsek-sh(ə-)wəl , -ˈsek-shəl \
> 1. now sometimes disparaging + offensive: of, relating to, or characterized by sexual or romantic attraction to people of one's same sex: gay
> 2. now sometimes disparaging + offensive: of, relating to, or involving sexual activity between people of the same sex
>
> homosexual
> <u>noun</u>
> plural homosexuals
> 1. now often disparaging + offensive: a person who is sexually or romantically attracted to people of their same sex

There are six passages in scripture that reference same-sex sexual behavior—three in the Old Testament and three in the New. In LGBTQ circles, these six are known as the "clobber passages." They're called that because non-affirming Christians use these scriptures to beat the LGBTQ community into submission: into "admitting" that God clearly wants no part of them or that they are inherently defective or of less worth than their heterosexual counterparts. There are 31,102 total verses in the Bible, and Christians have found six passages to use as ammunition to sentence an entire people group, an entire "nation," if you will, to hell.

The clobber passages we are going to talk about are Genesis 19:1–13, Leviticus 18:22, Leviticus 20:13, Romans 1:26–32, 1 Corinthians 6:9–10, and 1 Timothy 1:9–10.

Of these six passages, only two contain the words *malakoi* and *arsenokoitai,* which the *RSV* translates as "homosexual": 1 Corinthians and 1 Timothy. We'll dive into the meaning of the two original Greek words when we get to those passages, but for the sake of diligence, let's examine each passage in the order it appears in scripture. Although the first four passages don't contain the word "homosexual," they do appear to refer to same-sex behavior. In order to keep on point with the purpose of this book, which is to show you Father God's intentions and heart towards the LGBTQ community, I will briefly address these verses, because they form a part of the Evangelical Christian argument against LGBTQ people. For a more in-depth study of biblical references to same-sex behavior, including the six clobber passages, I highly recommend the following books: *Walking the Bridgeless Canyon* and *Forging a Sacred Weapon: How the Bible Became Anti-Gay*, both by Kathy V. Baldock; *God and the Gay Christian*, by Matthew Vines; and *Torn: Rescuing the Gospel from the Gays-vs-Christians Debate*, by Justin Lee. All four of these books are written by Christians who have studied and researched this topic for thousands of hours, validating their findings through multiple sources.

In order to streamline the examination of the Bible verses in question, I am printing the references along with the discussion below. I use different translations in my study and writing, not only for readability, but in an attempt to convey what I believe was the closest to the Father's heart when Holy Spirit spoke the scriptures. I reference which translation I'm quoting from for your convenience and edification.

The first passage is Genesis 19:1–13, the story of Sodom and Gomorrah, which has undergone an anti-LGBTQ narrative overlay for the past few decades when it's preached from American church pulpits.

In the NIV, the passage reads:

> The two angels arrived at Sodom in the evening, and Lot was sitting in the gateway of the city. When he saw them, he got up to meet them and bowed down with his face to the ground. 2 "My lords," he said, "please turn aside to your servant's house. You can wash your feet and spend the night and then go on your way early in the morning."
>
> "No," they answered, "we will spend the night in the square." 3 But he insisted so strongly that they did go with him and entered his house. He prepared a meal for them, baking bread without yeast, and they ate. 4 Before they had gone to bed, *all the men* from every part of the city of Sodom—both young and old—surrounded the house. 5 They called to Lot, "Where are the men who came to you tonight? Bring them out to us so that we can have sex with them."
>
> 6 Lot went outside to meet them and shut the door behind him 7 and said, "No, my friends. Don't do this wicked thing. 8 Look,

> I have two daughters who have never slept with a man. Let me bring them out to you, and you can do what you like with them. But don't do anything to these men, for they have come under the protection of my roof."
>
> ⁹ "Get out of our way," they replied. "This fellow came here as a foreigner, and now he wants to play the judge! We'll treat you worse than them." They kept bringing pressure on Lot and moved forward to break down the door.
>
> ¹⁰ But the men inside reached out and pulled Lot back into the house and shut the door. ¹¹ Then they struck the men who were at the door of the house, young and old, with blindness so that they could not find the door.
>
> ¹² The two men said to Lot, "Do you have anyone else here— sons-in-law, sons or daughters, or anyone else in the city who belongs to you? Get them out of here, ¹³ because we are going to destroy this place. The outcry to the Lord against its people is so great that he has sent us to destroy it."

The narrative that has been taught from pulpits for decades says that God destroyed Sodom and her sister city, Gomorrah, because of homosexuality. Some preachers go so far as to contend that God destroyed the cities because of what the men of the city tried to do to the angels. But scripture tells us that the whole purpose of the angels being in the city was to remove Lot before it was destroyed, making the claim that God destroyed the city because of homosexuality not only invalid but ludicrous.

Let's take a look at a couple of key components of this passage and try to determine exactly what was happening here.

The first section I want us to look at is in verse 4, where it says, "all the men from every part of the city of Sodom—both young and old" demanded that Lot turn the visitors over to them so that they could "have sex with them" (vs. 5).

In looking at the Bible's use of the word "all," we will explore two ideas: that the men of Sodom were not homosexual, and that their intent was nothing other than rape.

Remember the definition of the word homosexual—"a person who is sexually or romantically attracted to people of their same sex." Not men who are prone to violence towards other men, but men whose sexual desires are directed towards other men. Nothing in this passage indicates that all the men in the city were sexually attracted to the visitors in Lot's home. The wording of the passage shows malicious intent in the men of the city threatening Lot by saying, "We'll treat you worse than them" if he didn't send the angels out to them. As evangelicals, we've been taught for a hundred years that "scripture interprets scripture." Well, here it is: the men of the city wanted to perpetrate a heinous crime on the heavenly visitors. They didn't want to be sexually intimate with them; they wanted to rape them. And rape isn't about sex; it's about power and intimidation.

In their *Psychology Today* article of November 14, 2017, titled, "Sexual Assault Is About Power," the American Psychoanalytic Association states: "Despite its name, sexual abuse is more about power than it is about sex." They go on to say, "In heterosexual and same-sex encounters, sex is the tool used to gain power over another person."

Rape has nothing to do with sexual attraction, only power.

Or, as one anonymous Reddit user commenting on this passage put it:

> Rape shows dominance and humiliation. It wasn't sexual *per se* it was more like prison rape. This story comes from a cultural context in which hospitality to travelers was seen as very important because lives literally depended on it. Towns and cities were judged on how they treated strangers. Rape, as a story device, shows the most shocking and evil way that a "guest" in a town could be treated.

Jesus of Nazareth gave credibility to this position when he told His disciples in Matthew 10:15 (ESV), "Truly I tell you, it will be more bearable for Sodom and Gomorrah on the Day of Judgment than for that town." Who was He referring to when He said "that town?" In the preceding verses we see that Jesus is talking about *any* town that did not welcome the disciples, who did not show hospitality to them and the message of the Gospel they were there to preach. He is relating that town's lack of hospitality to the lack of hospitable behavior of the cities of Sodom and Gomorrah.

A second indicator that the men of Sodom were not homosexual—not attracted to the visitors—comes from the use of the word "all." It's important when you take into account the size and population of the cities involved. In my research on this topic, I learned that estimates of the population of these two cities ranged from 600 to 500,000 people: a very wide range! The truth is, no one actually knows for sure, but there are some historical, as well as biblical, clues that lead us to believe they were quite large cities. Before we look at the size of those cities, though, it's important for you to realize that even if the cities were only 600 in population each, having *all* the men of a city of that size be homosexual and wanting to have sex with the two strangers because they were sexually attracted to them is simply ridiculous. Again, their threat was not sexual.

Genesis 14:1–12 tells the story of the "kings of Sodom" going to war against their oppressor, Chedorlaomer, King of Elam and his allies. Moses, the writer of Genesis, doesn't give us any indication as to the size of the armies involved in this battle, which would be an indication of the size of the cities, but we do get a glimpse from another source, the Book of Jasher. While Jasher is not recognized as scripture, it is mentioned as a reference in two different places in the Bible. Joshua references it as a historical text in chapter 10, verse 13 of the The Complete Jewish Bible when he states, concerning his battle with Adonizedek, King of Jerusalem:

> So the sun stood still and the moon stayed put, till Isra'el took vengeance on their enemies. This is written in the book of Yashar (Jasher). The sun stood still in the sky and was in no rush to set for nearly a whole day.

We see a second reference giving credibility to the historical accuracy of the Book of Jasher in 2 Samuel 18:1:

> And he said it should be taught to the people of Judah; behold, it is written in the Book of Jasher.

If both Joshua and Samuel considered the Book of Jasher accurate enough to quote from it, it makes sense to use this reference for the purpose of determining how large Sodom and Gomorrah were in terms of population. The Book of Jasher gives an account of the same battle referenced in Genesis 14:1–12. In chapter 16, the writer of the Book of Jasher states that the size of the armies of Chedorlaomer, King of Elam, who was going into battle with the kings of Sodom, was 800,000 men. If this is anywhere close, Sodom and Gomorrah were extremely large cities, and the estimates I found of individual populations of 500,000 were probably the most accurate. It would be ridiculous to think that all the men of any city could be homosexual, but it's bordering on lunacy to believe that in two cities containing hundreds of thousands of people, all the men, young and old, were gay men. The definition of homosexual cited above refers to gay men. Do preachers seriously want us to believe that this was a reality nearly four thousand years ago? Roughly half the population would have been women, but no men interested in marrying them and certainly no one to procreate with them to keep the city alive. The cities could never have gotten to that size if none of the men were interested in having sex with women.

I live in Palm Springs, California, which the LGBTQ community proudly touts as "the Gayest City in the World." City officials estimate that out of a population of a little over 46,000 people, 50 to 54 percent of them are gay or lesbian. There are much larger total numbers of LGBTQ folks in some of the major metro areas, but even San Francisco only has a "homosexual" population of 6.2 percent, according to research done by Scott Van Voorhis for the online magazine *The Street,* published on June 5, 2018 (www.TheStreet.com). Nowhere in the world do we ever find a city of 600, let alone 50,000 to 500,000, where the male population is 100 percent LGBTQ, let alone all gay men!

Kevin DeYoung (PhD, University of Leicester) is senior pastor of Christ Covenant Church in Matthews, North Carolina, board chairman of The Gospel Coalition, and assistant professor of systematic theology at Reformed Theological Seminary (Charlotte). Kevin is married to a woman named Trisha, has eight children, and is not an ally to the LGBTQ community; however, he had this to say about the Genesis 19 "clobber" passage:

> Among those who agree that the Bible prohibits homosexual practice, there is a disagreement about whether the story of Sodom and Gomorrah should be used in support of this conclusion. Traditionally, the sin of Sodom has been considered, among other things, the sin of pursuing same-sex intercourse. Hence,

> the act of male-with-male sex has been termed sodomy. More recently, others have maintained that attempted homosexual gang rape is hardly germane to the question of committed, monogamous gay unions today. Sodom had many sins–violence, injustice, oppression, inhospitable brutality—but same-sex intercourse per se is nowhere condemned in the Genesis account. Some conservative scholars, while still holding conservative conclusions about marriage and homosexuality, have concurred with this line of reasoning, arguing that when it comes to deciding the rightness or wrongness of homosexual behavior, Genesis 19 is irrelevant.

For decades, preachers have been preaching that God destroyed Sodom because of homosexuality, but that's not the case. So what does scripture actually say about the sin that brought about total annihilation to these cities?

In her book, *Good News for Modern Gays*, the late Pentecostal Holiness preacher, Rev. Sylvia Pennington, a heterosexual, goes into tremendous detail as to the sins of Sodom as espoused by the prophets Isaiah, Jeremiah, and Ezekiel. While Rev. Pennington's book is currently out of print, I recommend it for anyone who is serious about getting to the bottom of what scripture actually says on the subject of same-sex attraction and sexual behavior.

In Isaiah, chapters 1–3 deal with the sins of Judah and Jerusalem, likening them to Sodom. In chapter 13, Isaiah addresses the sins of the Babylonians, once again comparing them to Sodom. Nowhere do we see same-sex or "homosexual" behavior referenced: not even rape.

In Jeremiah 23, we see God calling out the sins of Chaldeans and Samaritans and likening their sins to the sins of Sodom. In chapter 49, Jeremiah addresses the people of Moab and Edom and the sins that are going to bring them the same destruction as Sodom. Once again, there's no mention of anything remotely sounding like "homosexuality." In chapter 4 of the book of Lamentations, the prophet Jeremiah names the sins that brought about the destruction of Jerusalem and laments what he calls "a punishment worse than the punishment of Sodom," yet again, there's no mention of homosexual behavior of any kind.

So what does scripture say Sodom's sin was? We find the answer in Ezekiel 16:48–50, NIV:

> As surely as I live, declares the Sovereign Lord, your sister Sodom and her daughters never did what you and your daughters have done.
>
> ⁴⁹ Now this was the sin of your sister Sodom: She and her daughters were arrogant, overfed and unconcerned; they did not help the poor and needy. ⁵⁰ They were haughty and did detestable things before me. Therefore I did away with them as you have seen.

So what were Sodom's sins? Arrogance (pride), gluttony, apathy, refusal to help the poor and needy, and they did "detestable things!" Now before we jump to conclusions and decide that "detestable things" must refer to homosexual acts, let's take a look at what scripture says about the way Israel was to treat strangers who came to visit them. We'll start in the Old Testament, since this passage is found in the Old Testament.

> **Leviticus 19:33-34 (ESV)**
> When a stranger sojourns with you in your land, you shall not do him wrong. You shall treat the stranger who sojourns with you as the native among you, and you shall love him as yourself, for you were strangers in the land of Egypt: I am the Lord your God.
>
> **Deuteronomy 10:18-19 (ESV)**
> He executes justice for the fatherless and the widow, and loves the sojourner, giving him food and clothing. Love the sojourner, therefore, for you were sojourners in the land of Egypt.
>
> **Hebrews 13:2 (ESV)**
> Do not neglect to show hospitality to strangers, for thereby some have entertained angels unawares.

And finally:

> **Matthew 25:35 English Standard Version (ESV)**
> For I was hungry and you gave me food, I was thirsty and you gave me drink, I was a stranger and you welcomed me.

One of the recurring themes of both the Old and New Testament was the way Israel, and then the Church, were to treat strangers. I think that when we look at Father God's heart towards the strangers we encounter, as it's expressed all through scripture, we can see that it's really no stretch at all to believe that the "detestable things" Holy Spirit prompted Ezekiel to write about was the way all the men of Sodom presented their intention to rape the two angelic visitors.

Let's look at why this is such a big deal. When a preacher who hasn't done a proper exegesis of the original text stands up in front of his congregation and tells them that God destroyed Sodom and Gomorrah because of homosexuality, he's actually lying to them. That is his interpretation, and a severely flawed one at that, because it is not what the Bible says. Do you realize that when that sixteen-year-old boy sitting in the congregation who is struggling with coming to terms with his sexual desires, with his true sexual identity, hears that God destroyed thousands of people, possibly up to a million, because of men having sex with each other, he becomes hopeless and often contemplates taking his own life? Because once again, the Church has told him he deserves to die. Folks, the church is playing fast and loose with the gospel, and people are literally dying because of it.

Here are some statistics for you:

1. 40% of homeless youth are LGBTQ—https://truecolorsunited.org/our-issue/?gclid=Cj0KCQjw4s7qBRCzARIsAImcAxZlRyJIgnx80rVgjsVlPaKsS4ZF6wETnpQaOMKF8xfyVXgBBL6NYr0aAlEOEALw_wcB.

2. Suicide is the second leading cause of death among young people ages ten to twenty-four—CDC, NCIPC. Web-based Injury Statistics Query and Reporting System (WISQARS) [online]. (2010) {2013 Aug. 1}. Available from www.cdc.gov/ncipc/wisqars.

3. LGBTQ youth seriously contemplate suicide at almost three times the rate of heterosexual youth, and LGBTQ youth are almost five times as likely to have attempted suicide compared to heterosexual youth. CDC. (2016). Sexual Identity, Sex of Sexual Contacts, and Health-Risk Behaviors Among Students in Grades 9-12: Youth Risk

Behavior Surveillance. Atlanta, GA: U.S. Department of Health and Human Services.

4. LGBTQ youth who come from highly rejecting families are 8.4 times as likely to have attempted suicide as LGBTQ peers who reported no or low levels of family rejection. Family Acceptance Project™ (2009). Family rejection is a predictor of negative health outcomes in white and Latino lesbian, gay, and bisexual young adults. Pediatrics. 123(1), 346–52.

Look closely at #4. LGBTQ kids who come from families that reject them: those "good Christian" families who kick their kids out onto the streets when the kids finally get the nerve to confide in one of their parents or a sibling about who they really are—or when someone "outs" them, or they accidentally get "found out" by a parent. Those kids are 8.4 times more likely to attempt suicide than other LGBTQ kids, who are already five times more likely to attempt suicide than straight kids. And suicide is the second leading cause of death among *all* young people ages ten to twenty-four. That means that an LGBTQ son or daughter of a staunch evangelical family who refuses to accept their child's sexual orientation and rejects him or her is 42 times more likely to attempt taking their own life than a straight kid. Forty-two times: that's 4200 percent!

I wept the first half-dozen times I read those statistics! This both breaks my heart and makes me feel like vomiting at the same time. For the love of God and all Jesus Christ told us and showed us He stands for, consider the impact of rejecting a child because of his or her sexual orientation. Getting scripture wrong isn't just an "Oops!" It has real life-and-death implications.

> Since I originally wrote the section above, I lost one of my dearest friends, and a founding member of my church, by suicide. At the age of fifty-seven, he took his own life because he could no longer deal with the rejection his evangelical family had placed upon him since his coming out to them thirty-nine years prior. For thirty-nine years he bore the unbearable pain of their very conditional love and their constant attempts to "fix" him. Realizing that he would never have what he wanted most in this life, their acceptance of him as a child of God, he ended his life on my

birthday, May 7, 2020. This book is subsequently dedicated to him. I love you, Devin Buckner. Rest well in Papa's arms, little brother. I'll see you when my work here is done.

The incredibly destructive narrative overlay surrounding the story of Sodom and Gomorrah has become too prevalent in so many of our churches today. We must understand and act on the intended point: that welcoming the stranger is not just a cultural nicety but a command from God, and threatening to attack the strangers in Lot's hometown was worthy of the Lord's wrath and destruction.

CHAPTER 4
Clobber Passages in Leviticus

THE NEXT TWO clobber passages we're going to take a look at are both found in Leviticus. For these two I'm going to use the King James Version of scripture. Here they are:

> **Leviticus 18:22**
> Thou shalt not lie with mankind, as with womankind: it is abomination.
>
> **Leviticus 20:13**
> If a man also lie with mankind, as he lieth with a woman, both of them have committed an abomination: they shall surely be put to death; their blood shall be upon them.

The word that's been translated as "abomination" does not mean what you and I would think of today as something that is an abomination. There are two Hebrew words that are translated as "abomination" in the Old Testament, and both words can be found in different manuscripts of these two verses. They are *toevah* and *shiqquts*. According to Wikipedia, the word *shiqquts* is almost always used in reference to dietary violations, something that is "unclean," while in an archive article by *Religion Dispatches* dated July 29, 2010 (http://religiondispatches.org/does-the-bible-really-call-homosexuality-an-abomination/), we read "The term *toevah* (and its plural, *toevot*) occurs 103 times in the Hebrew Bible, and almost always has the connotation of a non-Israelite cultic practice."

This same word is used in Leviticus 11:10, referring to anyone eating shellfish, a dietary prohibition. Proverbs 6 (KJV) lists seven things that are an "abomination" to the Lord:

> [17] A proud look, a lying tongue, and hands that shed innocent blood,
>
> [18] An heart that deviseth wicked imaginations, feet that be swift in running to mischief,
>
> [19] A false witness that speaketh lies, and he that soweth discord among brethren.

We won't spend a lot of time or energy on the fact that Leviticus 20:13 says that both the men who were caught "lying" together should be put to death, because Deuteronomy 22:23–24 also says that a woman who is engaged to a man and is raped should be put to death along with her rapists, and Deuteronomy 20 demands that parents with rebellious sons have them stoned to death outside the city gate. Clearly, we do not follow the Old Testament laws requiring people to be put to death!

I do want to point out, however, the phrases "as with a woman" (Leviticus 20:13) and "as with womankind" (Leviticus 18:22). We've all been taught that every word of the original text was spoken to the prophets intentionally, right? If that is correct, and it *is* a widely respected belief among theologians, then we need to know what is actually meant by "as with a woman" or "as with womankind."

If God's condemnation was against any and all sexual contact between two men, He could have simply said, "Men shall not lie with men," but He didn't; He added the caveat "as with woman" or "as with womankind." To me, as a gay man, this point is significant, as it's indicating that a specific aspect of male-on-male sexual activity is the thing God has a problem with. In male/female intercourse, the typical practice is penetration, with the male penetrating the female vaginally. When a man lies with another man as with a woman, the phrase indicates there is penetration involved, and that would be anal penetration.

Inasmuch as one meaning of the word "abomination" has to do with dietary restriction of things that are "unclean" (remember, eating shellfish was an "abomination"), and the other is associated with non-Israelite cultic practices, the church may have been expanding on what Father God was saying by espousing a blanket condemnation of any sexual act between two men. There have been dozens of articles and books written about the cultic practices of not only the people who possessed the land Yehovah God gave to the descendants of Abraham, but also of all of their surrounding neighbors. One of those practices involved male temple-prostitutes. Without going into graphic detail about what acts transpired between a male temple prostitute and his client, I can report that they almost always culminated in anal penetration, with the worshiper depositing his "seed" as an offering to the god in question. The act had little to do with the sexual orientation of the two men involved, as sexual behavior at that time was relegated to the role of dominant and submissive: the penetrator and the one being penetrated. The concept of sexual orientation did not yet exist, nor did the word homosexuality.

The bottom line here is that anal sex during biblical times was designated as "unclean" and was also practiced ritually by the pagan nations that surrounded Israel as an act of worship to their gods. Even my most vehement critics would have to agree that the God of Abraham, Isaac, and Jacob was very specific in His instructions as to how His people would worship Him, and He was adamant that they not worship Him in any of the manners in which the pagan peoples around Israel worshiped their gods.

Although all of the points I've made about the Old Testament passages used to condemn sexual behavior between two men are salient, the entire debate over all three passages can be put to rest in three words—they're Old Testament! Some will say that we can't "throw out" the Old Testament, so let me remind you that I am Messianic in my core beliefs. I come from a Jewish family and am very much in touch with the Hebrew roots of my faith, so I definitely don't believe in simply dismissing or deleting something just because of where it's located in scripture. That being said, let's look at what scripture says about the "Law" portion of the Old Testament, because that's what Leviticus is—the law.

In Matthew 5:17 (ESV), Jesus says, "Do not think that I have come to abolish the Law or the Prophets; I have not come to abolish them but to fulfill them."

The law that once commanded death for two men who engaged in (anal) sex with each other was fulfilled on Calvary, as were the laws forbidding working on the Sabbath. These laws also required stoning a person caught breaking the laws forbidding eating shellfish and pork, having tattoos, wearing clothes of different fabrics, harvesting the corners of one's fields, trimming the corners of one's beard, and touching the skin of a dead pig! Thanks to the finished work of Jesus Christ on Calvary, I can enjoy Monday Night Football with no condemnation or worries that my favorite quarterback is going to go to hell for playing the game.

Every single law was fulfilled in the death, burial, and resurrection of Jesus Christ, yet the one law the Church insists on requiring people to observe is the law involving two men not lying together "as with a woman." Seriously? The only one, out of 613 Mosaic laws in the Old Testament? Hipster preachers will stand in their pulpits covered in tattoos (an abomination), wearing mixed-fabric shirts (forbidden), with their skinny jeans (there was a very strict dress code for anyone ministering to Yehovah), and then go to Red Lobster (shellfish, yikes!) for lunch after the service, all while telling that married gay couple in the church that they can't be on the worship team because of their sinful lifestyle.

Truly, Jesus either fulfilled all the law or He didn't fulfill any of it! Which is it? We can't have it both ways.

CHAPTER 5
Clobber Passages in the New Testament

THE OLD TESTAMENT is not the only source of clobber passages; the next passage we'll explore is in the New Testament. It will shed some light on Abba Father's heart towards not just His LGBTQ kids but all of His children. The verse is Romans 8, verses 1–2 (ESV), which states:

> Therefore, there is now no condemnation for those who are in Christ Jesus, ² because through Christ Jesus the law of the Spirit who gives life has set you free from the law of sin and death.

Thus, if you're a born-again Christian, there is no more condemnation for you, period. Are we expected to live a godly life as a result of being "in Christ Jesus?" Absolutely! We don't get to live the way the rest of the world does, chasing after every lustful desire. I know it's old-fashioned and not popular these days to say, but God ordained sex between two people who are in love with each other and willing to make a life-long covenant between themselves and Him.

Nowhere in scripture do we ever see God blessing a sexual union outside of a covenant relationship. Unbeknownst to the church at large, LGBTQ men and women who are devout Christians have been making covenant unions with each other for decades. The problem they've encountered is that there are very few places of worship that would both accept them and stay true to the Word of God. We'll delve into this situation later on in this book, but for now, let's get back to the subject at hand—examining the six clobber passages that non-affirming Christians use to either exclude LGBTQ people from the church altogether, or to try to convince them that they are broken and in need of repair before they can truly have a relationship with Jesus Christ. Truly, if there is now no condemnation for those who are in Christ Jesus, the church needs to stop condemning other Christians. And yes—you can be both LGBTQ and Christian.

So let me say this clearly: the passages in Leviticus do not condemn a loving, monogamous, covenant relationship between two people of the same sex. They condemn ritualistic sex and sex that was considered "unclean." (Just a little side note here: that same sexual act—anal penetration—is practiced by millions of heterosexual couples and would have been considered "unclean" for the same reason.)

The first clobber passage to appear in the New Testament is found in the book of Romans, in the first chapter, verses 26–32. The quote below is from the New International Version (NIV).

> Because of this, God gave them over to shameful lusts. Even their women exchanged natural sexual relations for unnatural ones. [27] In the same way the men also abandoned natural relations with women and were inflamed with lust for one another. Men committed shameful acts with other men, and received in themselves the due penalty for their error. [28] Furthermore, just as they did not think it worthwhile to retain the knowledge of God, so God gave them over to a depraved mind, so that they do what ought not to be done. [29] They have become filled with every kind of wickedness, evil, greed and depravity. They are full of envy, murder, strife, deceit and malice. They are gossips, [30] slanderers, God-haters, insolent, arrogant and boastful; they invent ways of doing evil; they disobey their parents; [31] they have no understanding, no fidelity, no love, no mercy. [32] Although they know God's righteous decree that those who do such things deserve death, they not only continue to do these very things but also approve of those who practice them.

I can't even begin to tell you how many messages I've heard on this passage, or how many articles I've read where the expositor declared that this one passage alone should be all the "proof" one needs to determine that God's final destination for each and every member of the LGBTQ community is eternal damnation. As a young Christian, I had to come to terms with the fact that even though I had accepted Jesus Christ as my Lord and Savior, and I was filled with His Holy Spirit, I still had the same desires I had always had towards other men. And this verse terrified me! But you don't have to be a theology major to know that when a verse—or in this case, a passage—begins with "therefore" or "because of this," you have to go back to see what precedes that verse/passage. Looking at the preceding passage is one of the first rules of hermeneutics:

> Biblical hermeneutics is the study of the principles of interpretation concerning the books of the Bible. It is part of the broader field of hermeneutics which involves the study of principles of interpretation for all forms of communication, nonverbal and verbal. (Wikipedia)

If you're going to correctly interpret a verse or passage, you have to take into consideration not only the entire section of scripture in which the verse/passage in question is contained, but also the context; to whom it was written; and what situation, problem, or question the author is addressing.

In order to rightly divide the word of truth, as the Apostle Paul admonished his young protégé, Timothy, we're going to have to do some due diligence in reading and understanding this passage. Let's start by seeing what lies before Romans 1:26–32, the passage that so many Christians are ready to beat gay folks over the head with. Let's start with Romans 1, verse 16, once again from the NIV, and read the whole passage from the larger perspective to see what Paul is actually addressing:

> I am not ashamed of the gospel, because it is the power of God that brings salvation to everyone who believes: first to the Jew, then to the Gentile. [17] For in the gospel the righteousness of God is revealed—a righteousness that is by faith from first to last, just as it is written: "The righteous will live by faith."
>
> [18] The wrath of God is being revealed from heaven against all the Godlessness and wickedness of people, who suppress the truth by

their wickedness, ¹⁹ since what may be known about God is plain to them, because God has made it plain to them. ²⁰ For since the creation of the world God's invisible qualities—his eternal power and divine nature—have been clearly seen, being understood from what has been made, so that people are without excuse.

²¹ For although they knew God, they neither glorified him as God nor gave thanks to him, but their thinking became futile and their foolish hearts were darkened. ²² Although they claimed to be wise, they became fools ²³ and exchanged the glory of the immortal God for images made to look like a mortal human being and birds and animals and reptiles.

²⁴ Therefore God gave them over in the sinful desires of their hearts to sexual impurity for the degrading of their bodies with one another. ²⁵ They exchanged the truth about God for a lie, and worshiped and served created things [idolatry] rather than the Creator—who is forever praised. Amen.

²⁶ Because of this, God gave them over to shameful lusts. Even their women exchanged natural sexual relations for unnatural ones. ²⁷ In the same way the men also abandoned natural relations with women and were inflamed with lust for one another. Men committed shameful acts with other men, and received in themselves the due penalty for their error.

²⁸ Furthermore, just as they did not think it worthwhile to retain the knowledge of God, so God gave them over to a depraved mind, so that they do what ought not to be done. ²⁹ They have become filled with every kind of wickedness, evil, greed and depravity. They are full of envy, murder, strife, deceit and malice. They are gossips, ³⁰ slanderers, God-haters, insolent, arrogant and boastful; they invent ways of doing evil; they disobey their parents; ³¹ they have no understanding, no fidelity, no love, no mercy. ³² Although they know God's righteous decree that those who do such things deserve death, they not only continue to do these very things but also approve of those who practice them.

We'll take this point-by-point to help us see that two folks of the same gender who are in love with each other and in a monogamous relationship that has been committed to God are not who the Apostle Paul is addressing here.

Let's start with the glaring statement in verse 16 that sets the tone for the rest of the passage, or at least it should. It really depends on the filter or lens through which you read scripture. Do you read it through the filter that God is angry, awaiting the right moment to exact vengeance on all of mankind, or do you read it through the filter of God being a loving Father who requires obedience from His children but whose heart is always one of restoration and redemption?

The statement I'm talking about is found at the beginning of the passage we're presently looking at, Romans 1:16, where Paul says, "The gospel ... is the power of God that brings salvation to everyone who believes." Before the apostle ever indicts a single person or act of sin in the following verses, he states that the Gospel is for everyone who believes. You see, nowhere in scripture do we ever see any kind of caveat that says, "except if you're lesbian, gay, bisexual, transgender, or queer." In fact, scripture repeatedly references salvation as Jesus' provision on Calvary and is explicit that it is for everyone.

> **John 3:16-17 (NIV)**
> For God so loved the world [all humanity] that he gave his one and only Son, that whoever believes in him shall not perish but have eternal life. ¹⁷ For God did not send his Son into the world [all humanity] to condemn the world, but to save the world [all humanity] through him.
>
> **Revelation 22:17 (KJV)**
> And the Spirit and the bride say, Come. And let him that hears say, Come. And let him that is athirst come. And whosoever will, let him take the water of life freely.

God has no prerequisite as to who can be saved. So why does the Church have one?

Getting back to our Romans 1 clobber passage, let's focus on the end of verse 17, where Paul states, "The righteous will live by faith." I was raised

Baptist turned Assemblies of God, so I know the majority of evangelical Christians believe that a gay man or woman cannot be righteous in God's eyes, but that couldn't be further from the truth. I have encountered many, many LGBTQ Christians who are incredible men and women of faith and live a life that is 100 percent devoted to Yehovah God and His Word. The only difference between them and most other Christians is that they interpret six passages of scripture differently, and it's my prayer that my readers will come to the same understanding and interpretation of these six passages.

In verse 18, Paul begins his diatribe about God's wrath being revealed due to the wickedness and godlessness of the people of Earth. He continues through verse 20, where he tells us that the people had no excuse because God had made Himself known to them through all of creation. Then in verses 21 through 23, we get down to the crux of God's anger: the people, even though they could see His Glory all around them, neither glorified Him as God nor gave thanks to Him, and they exchanged the glory of the immortal God for images made to look like a mortal human being and birds and animals and reptiles. Verse 21 says that they "knew God," meaning they were believers who had turned away from the faith and became idol worshippers.

Verse 23 says they worshiped idols. Remember that idol worship was the highest sin Israel could commit against God! All through the Old Testament we see God releasing His wrath upon Israel and wiping them out, all but a "remnant," because they worshiped the idols of the pagans around them instead of worshiping the One true God.

So let's look at verses 24 and 25, knowing that what directly preceded it was an indictment against worshiping idols.

> Therefore God gave them over in the sinful desires of their hearts to sexual impurity for the degrading of their bodies with one another. [25] They exchanged the truth about God for a lie, and worshiped and served created things rather than the Creator—who is forever praised. Amen.

Because of idol worship, Father God gave those who once worshiped Him over to sexual impurity. Remember, Romans was written to former pagans, not Jewish believers. These were believers who had returned to idol worship in much the same way as Israel had repeatedly turned to idols. Please keep in mind, though, that Father's heart is always towards restoration. Every single time Israel repented of chasing after foreign Gods, Yehovah received them back as His own and restored them. Why would we believe He would do any less for these people, or anyone else, if they were to repent, as vile as they were?

Romans 1:26–32 was preceded by an entire polemic against practicing idolatry: idol worship. *That* is the group of people being addressed in verses 26 through 32: those who were worshiping idols.

Now we come into the portion of this passage of scripture that the church has pulled out of context and isolated as an across-the-board indictment of all sexual behavior between people of the same gender, turning it into the fourth "clobber" passage.

> Because of this, God gave them over to shameful lusts. Even their women exchanged natural sexual relations for unnatural ones. [27] In the same way the men also abandoned natural relations with women and were inflamed with lust for one another. Men committed shameful acts with other men, and received in themselves the due penalty for their error.
>
> [28] Furthermore, just as they did not think it worthwhile to retain the knowledge of God, so God gave them over to a depraved mind, so that they do what ought not to be done. [29] They have become filled with every kind of wickedness, evil, greed and depravity. They are full of envy, murder, strife, deceit and malice. They are gossips, [30] slanderers, God-haters, insolent, arrogant and boastful; they invent ways of doing evil; they disobey their parents; [31] they have no understanding, no fidelity, no love, no mercy. [32] Although they know God's righteous decree that those who do such things deserve death, they not only continue to do these very things but also approve of those who practice them.

Now we know what the "because of this" is all about. The people had turned from their faith, and they were neither acknowledging nor worshiping the Creator of the Universe but instead were worshiping that which He created. Because of "this" (e.g. idolatry), God gave them over to "shameful lust."

The second part of verse 26 and verse 27 says that the women "exchanged" natural relations for "unnatural" ones, and the men "abandoned" natural relations with women and were inflamed with lust for each other. I researched several translations and found the same thing in all of them—the concept that the people Paul was talking about had once engaged in heterosexual relationships or intercourse and had "changed" and were now consumed with lust. These were men who were once what we would have called "straight" having sex with other men, and women with other women. This is a seriously different scenario than what we've been taught. This passage is addressing a specific situation in the ancient Roman church where former pagans had returned to their idol worship and because of it had become so consumed with lust that they went against their very natures as heterosexuals and indulged in wanton sex with each other. This is not addressing men and women who have always been attracted to and loved other people of the same sex. This isn't about love or even desire; it's about lust.

Is there rampant lust in the gay community today? Absolutely! But there's rampant lust in the Church of Jesus Christ as well among heterosexuals! As a pastor, I minister to people of all sexual orientations, and believe me when I tell you that the LGBTQ community does not have a corner on the lust market. Generally, the LGBTQ Christians I minister to are less sexually active, less sexually permissive, than the majority of "straight" Christians I minister to. Lust is a major problem in America, and the Church is in no way immune to it.

Once again, the verses we're looking at have nothing to do with LGBTQ folks who are sexually attracted to others of their own sex and looking to settle down with a mate for life. Everything we've looked at has referenced lust and perversion, not basic human sexual attraction.

But let's keep digging deeper into this passage. Verses 28 through 32 give us the additional characteristics of the people Paul was speaking about that go well beyond "burning with lust." Let's read that part again:

> [28] Furthermore, just as they did not think it worthwhile to retain the knowledge of God, so God gave them over to a depraved

mind, so that they do what ought not to be done. ²⁹ They have become filled with every kind of wickedness, evil, greed and depravity. They are full of envy, murder, strife, deceit and malice. They are gossips, ³⁰ slanderers, God-haters, insolent, arrogant and boastful; they invent ways of doing evil; they disobey their parents; ³¹ they have no understanding, no fidelity, no love, and no mercy. ³² Although they know God's righteous decree that those who do such things deserve death, they not only continue to do these very things but also approve of those who practice them.

The narrative the church has been preaching for well over a hundred years is that verses 28 through 32 are the result of homosexual sex between the people of Rome in the Roman church. In reality, when you study the entire passage and break it all down, verses 28 through 32 are additional symptoms of the people in the Roman church turning away from their worship of the God of Heaven and turning back to their pagan idol worship. As a result of turning away, and because of idol worship, they became enraged with lust and filled with every kind of wickedness, evil, greed, and depravity. They become full of envy, murder, strife, deceit, and malice. They became gossips, slanderers, God-haters, insolent, arrogant, and boastful; inventing ways of doing evil; disobedient to their parents; having no understanding, no fidelity, no love, no mercy. Knowing God's righteous decree that those who do such things deserve death, they not only continued to do those very things but also approved of those who practice them.

It would take a really warped mind and a heart so full of bitterness and hatred that only Jesus Christ Himself could redeem it to believe that all men and women who are sexually attracted to, love, and are intimate with members of their own sex are the vile people Paul describes in the discourse above. It grieves my heart to think that someone claiming to know the one true God of love and grace would actually believe that all LGBTQ folks are "enraged with lust, filled with every kind of wickedness, evil, greed and depravity. Full of envy, murder, strife, deceit and malice. Gossips, slanderers, God-haters, insolent, arrogant and boastful; inventing ways of doing evil; disobedient to their parents; having no understanding, no fidelity, no love, no mercy."

If you have fallen into this trap of false belief, I would encourage you to do two things: First, repent and pray for your heart to be opened. Seriously examine it to see if there's tangible evidence of a personal encounter with the risen savior; because God is love, God is grace, and God's heart is always towards redemption and restoration. Second, go meet and get to know some LGBTQ Christians. Make friends, spend time talking with them about their experiences. If they are truly born again and in love with Jesus Christ, you will discern the love of God in their hearts and see the fruit of this love in their lives.

I think you'll be quite surprised to find that their love for Jesus Christ is just as deep, just as genuine, just as caring and self-sacrificing as any truly committed Christian's love. There are so many men and women of great faith who identify as LGBTQ, and the only way many of them survived all those decades of the mainstream church telling them that Father God wanted nothing to do with them, rejecting them, cursing them, reviling them, speaking death over them, was to press in as close to Him as they could possibly get. Their faith, love, and devotion to their savior has been tried in the fire, and they've come through it not to the resounding praise of the church, but to the lone applause of two nail-scarred hands.

As Christian pastor, author, and activist John Pavolitz says, "When you have to fight for your faith it becomes real!" And hasn't church history proven this to be true? The times of greatest growth in the church throughout history have always been times of persecution.

CHAPTER 6
Combining Two Greek Words

THE LAST TWO clobber passages are in 1 Corinthians and 1 Timothy, and both contain the word "homosexual" in some translations, based on the mistake made in 1946 by the RSV translation team. They translated two Greek words, *malakoi* and *arsenokoitai,* into one word: homosexual. As we examine these two Greek words, keep in mind the definition of the word homosexual:

> ho·mo·sex·u·al
> /ˌhōməˈsekSH(oō)əl/
> adjective
>
> adjective: homosexual
> 1. (of a person) sexually attracted to people of one's own sex.
> • involving or characterized by sexual attraction between people of the same sex.
> "homosexual desire"
>
> Noun
> noun: homosexual; plural noun: homosexuals
> 1. a person who is sexually attracted to people of their own sex.

It's important to keep this definition in mind because people are being told they are unacceptable to God because of an incorrect translation, faulty theology, and downright dogma that have risen from that mistranslation.

The word homosexual means that someone is sexually attracted to others of the same sex. The definition says nothing about lust, fornication, sodomy, or any of the other characteristics most Christians associate with the word. You do not have to be having sex with someone to be homosexual. I've been sexually abstinent for over ten years now, but that doesn't mean I'm not still gay. Before I finally accepted my sexual orientation and "came out," I had given up everything I had and moved to a new city in another state to join an ex-gay conversion therapy group. What I discovered was that not even the facilitator, who had been leading that particular group for over eight years, had actually "changed" his orientation. His only sexual attraction was still towards other men. He had just "been given the strength" not to "give in" to his desires. When I confronted him on this, he broke down in tears and admitted to the group that he cried himself to sleep every single night because he longed to fall asleep in the arms of another man. For eight years he had been lying to those men, telling them that God had changed him, but he had not changed. His attraction was still towards other men. That's all it takes to be homosexual—an attraction. The facilitator's lies, loneliness, and pain were all based on his belief that as a gay man, he was damned. What a heartbreaking situation, not just for him individually, but for all those who believed he had changed his orientation and were poisoned by false hope.

With this understanding of the word homosexuality, let's turn to the two Greek words that were used as the basis for the mistranslation. The word *malakoi* appears in both of the last two clobber passages, and the mysterious word *arsenokoitai in one of them*. We'll look at the passages together, but we'll take the two words separately, starting with *malakoi* as it appears in both passages.

For comparison's sake, let's first look at both passages, starting with the King James version:

> **1 Corinthians 6:9-10 (KJV)**
> Know ye not that the unrighteous shall not inherit the kingdom of God? Be not deceived: neither fornicators, nor idolaters, nor adulterers, nor effeminate, nor abusers of themselves with mankind, [10] Nor thieves, nor covetous, nor drunkards, nor revilers, nor extortioners, shall inherit the kingdom of God.

And:

> **1 Timothy 1:9-10 (KJV)**
> Knowing this, that the law is not made for a righteous man, but for the lawless and disobedient, for the ungodly and for sinners, for unholy and profane, for murderers of fathers and murderers of mothers, for manslayers, [10] for whoremongers, for them that defile themselves with mankind, for menstealers, for liars, for perjured persons, and if there be any other thing that is contrary to sound doctrine.

My understanding of the two Greek words in question is built on a foundation of research and study, as well as prayer for understanding. I am not presenting an original revelation regarding the meaning of the words; the revelation God did give to me is the overall subject of this book. I am laying the foundation for others to see the evidence and come to their own conclusions as they seek the truth.

One of the sources for this chapter is my dear friend Kathy Baldock, a literary genius who has done thousands of hours of research on the mistranslation of these two Greek words. Her findings are available in her new book, *Forging a Sacred Weapon: How the Bible Became Anti-Gay*. The first time the word homosexual appeared in any language in the Bible was in the Revised Standard Version, published in 1946. The RSV team made the decision to combine *malakoi* and *arsenokoitai* and then translate them into one word: "homosexual." They were simply trying to apply the verse to what they understood homosexuals to be in the 1940s. Their decision was not malicious, but it did cause a ripple effect in subsequent Bible translations, as translators of other versions followed the RSV mistranslation. In 1959, the RSV translation team received a letter from a young Canadian seminary student who challenged their use of the word homosexual as inaccurate. Their correspondence shows that the team came to understand and agree with the objections to the use of the word homosexual; they admitted their mistake and corrected the original translation from "homosexuals" to "sexual perverts" (which includes bad behaviors by heterosexuals).

Unfortunately, by agreement with the publisher, the team was not to make any changes or updates for ten years, and the 1959 revisions had already gone to press when the letter arrived. Finally, the correction was made in 1971, without major fanfare. Today, it's tough to imagine that correcting such a significant mistake would not be widely announced, but at the time, it was not on anyone's radar because homosexuality was not yet politicized. The translation team could never have imagined the horrific impact of their error.

Now let's take a look at those same verses from the New Living Translation, one of the popular current translations that contains the word "homosexual."

> **1 Corinthians 6:9-10**
> Don't you realize that those who do wrong will not inherit the Kingdom of God? Don't fool yourselves. Those who indulge in sexual sin, or who worship idols, or commit adultery, or are male prostitutes, or practice homosexuality, [10] or are thieves, or greedy people, or drunkards, or are abusive, or cheat people—none of these will inherit the Kingdom of God.
>
> **1 Timothy 1:9-10**
> For the law was not intended for people who do what is right. It is for people who are lawless and rebellious, who are ungodly and sinful, who consider nothing sacred and defile what is holy, who kill their father or mother or commit other murders. [10] The law is for people who are sexually immoral, or who practice homosexuality, or are slave traders, liars, promise breakers, or who do anything else that contradicts the wholesome teaching.

In 1 Corinthians 6:9, we see the word *malakoi* appear for the first time in scripture. The King James translated this word as "effeminate," which is the actual meaning of the word. In fact, out of the over forty major translations of scripture I checked, eight others use some form of the word effeminate. They are: Valera Spanish (1602); Douay-Rheims (1609); Portuguese (1690); Daniel Mace New Testament (1729); Darby French (1885); Young's Literal (1898); ASV (1901); Louis Segund French (1910); and NASB (1963).

The other thirty-plus translations mentioned above contained no fewer than twenty-one different translations of the same Greek word, *malakoi*, running the gamut, from "weaklings" Tyndale (1526), to "catamites" (boys who have sex with men), Moffat (1913), to "any who are guilty of unnatural crime" Weymouth (1903). In doing my research on this, I can report that the most accurate translations stuck with the actual meaning at the time the verses were penned, the meaning in the original Greek: "effeminate." Ultra-conservative Christian pastor and author, Dr. John MacArthur, states that he believes the word *malakoi*, as used in 1 Corinthians 6:9, was referring to male temple-prostitutes, who were notorious for their "softness" or "effeminacy." Describing Corinthian Christians in the first century AD, he writes in *The MacArthur New Testament Commentary*, 1 Corinthians, Moody Press, Chicago, 1984, p. 146, (used with permission):

> They also lived in a society that was notoriously immoral, a society that, in the temple prostitution and other ways, actually glorified promiscuous sex. To have sexual relations with a prostitute was so common in Corinth that the practice came to be called "Corinthianizing." Many believers had formerly been involved in such immorality, and it was hard for them to break with the old ways and easy to fall back into them … it was also hard for them to give up their sexual immorality.

A protégé of Dr. MacArthur's had this to say in a January 11, 2011, blog (paraphrased):

> Corinth was a city filled with both temples and brothels. Fornication was literally deemed a religious rite in this city and that was the heart of the church in Corinth's problem. . The church was made up of mostly Gentiles after the vast majority of the Jewish community in Corinth rejected the gospel (Acts 18:6). The gentiles, of course, came from a culture that did not see sexual sin as unspiritual. In fact, it was just the opposite with most of the "religion" in the city involving temple prostitution and debauched sexual behavior.

Please keep in mind that both of these men are highly respected, conservative, and non-affirming to the LGBTQ community, yet even they don't buy the "homosexual" narrative the Church as a whole has assigned to this verse.

So if the word *malakoi* really means effeminate, it would only make sense that we look at the historical meaning of that word and how it was used at the time the Apostle Paul used it.

I've purposely limited the use of LGBTQ-affirming resources that are written or provided by openly gay or lesbian individuals to avoid the appearance of bias. Understandably, it's very difficult to find any quantity of research on this topic that has been done by straight, heterosexual individuals; after all, why would they spend their valuable time researching something that doesn't apply to them? And therein lies the problem. Christian preachers have been apathetic in researching the subject of homosexuality and the Christian faith because it doesn't concern them. It's much easier to just glibly regurgitate what they've heard for decades. LGBTQ folks, on the other hand, have had to dig into what scripture has to say on the subject as though their very lives depend on it—because they do.

That being said, I found some great insight into the meaning of the word *malakoi* during ancient times on a blog site called Gay Christian 101 (gaychristian101.com). The following excerpt from that site, used with permission, sheds light on the original meaning of the word *malakoi* and what it referred to in the Apostle Paul's time:

> The remarkable semantic shift in the meaning of *malakoi*, which by 1958 came to equate *malakoi* with homosexuality instead of softness, moral weakness or the effeminacy of temple prostitutes, was not prompted by new linguistic evidence. Instead, cultural factors influenced modern translators to inject anti-gay bias into their translation. In ancient times, the *malakoi* stem never referred exclusively to gays and lesbians. In fact, the *malakoi* stem rarely, if ever, referred to gays or gay behavior. In ancient times, it was used to refer to heterosexual men who followed the Greek custom of shaving the face daily.
>
> Until Scipio Aemilianus (185–129 BC) made it fashionable, daily shaving was considered an affectation of the effeminate Greeks.
> —*The Immense Majesty, A History of Rome and the Roman Empire,*

Thomas W. Africa, 1991, Harlan Davidson, Inc, p. 148 (used with permission)

Many preachers believe that "effeminate" in 1 Corinthians 6:9 condemns gay men. Yet in cultural and historical context, men who shaved daily were the effeminate ones. Isn't it odd that preachers who shave their faces every day love to make fun of and attack gay men as effeminate?

"Do not trim off the hair on your temples or trim your beards" (Leviticus 19:27, NLT).

"But for one who is a man to comb himself and shave himself with a razor, for the sake of fine effect, to arrange his hair at the looking-glass, to shave his cheeks, pluck hairs out of them, and smooth them, how womanly!" Clement of Alexandria, AD 195, *Ante-Nicene Fathers*, Volume 2, p. 275

"It is therefore impious to desecrate the symbol of manhood, hairiness. But the embellishment of smoothing (for I am warned by the Word), if it is to attract men, is the act of an effeminate person, if to attract women, is the act of an adulterer, and both must be driven as far as possible from our society." Clement of Alexandria, AD 195, *Ante-Nicene Fathers*, Volume 2, p. 276.

Scripture cannot mean now what it did not mean then.

Translating *malakoi* as homosexual imposes a twenty-first-century cultural meaning on the text that *malakoi* did not mean in the first century. In 1 Corinthians 6:9–10 in the Greek text, Paul uses nine masculine nouns to describe people who will not inherit the kingdom, yet the masculine nouns he uses in this case can apply to both genders. The issue is grammatical gender vs. biological gender. In the Greek language, masculine nouns (grammatical gender) include males (biological gender) but are not limited to or restricted to males. Masculine nouns sometimes include females. If translators focus on grammatical gender and specify male for each of the nine masculine nouns Paul uses here, by implication that would have Paul telling us that adulterous, thieving females (biological gender) *can* inherit the kingdom. Do you see the theological problem we create if we specify male in this case?

When translating *malakoi*, we must be careful not to give the word a meaning in the twenty-first century that it did not have in the first century. One of the meanings of *malakoi* in the first century AD was: a man who pretties himself with daily shaving of the face in the Greek manner, using makeup, hair coloring and fancy clothing "to attract females with whom to have sex."

If *malakoi* was not understood as a reference to gays and lesbians in the first century when Paul used it, but instead, often described heterosexual men who followed Greek customs like daily shaving of facial hair, then *malakoi* does not mean homosexual today. The word did not morph into a new meaning over the last two thousand years.

In reading the circa AD195 observation from Clement of Alexandria above, we get a look at why the Apostle Paul might have had a problem with "effeminate" men. Men who daily shaved their faces were deemed to be doing so to attract multiple sexual partners: "if it is to attract men, is the act of an effeminate person, if to attract women, is the act of an adulterer."

There are dozens of books and articles that go into different veins of reasoning as to what *malakoi* means, and why it doesn't have anything to do with what we know as gay men today, and I invite the reader to explore further if desired.

Let's turn to the second Greek word, *arsenokoitai*, which is made up of two parts: *arsen* means man, and *koitai* means beds. Many conservative Christians argue that the meaning the Apostle Paul was trying to convey here is simple and straightforward. They assume that Paul is pulling from the Old Testament law in his use of the term "man beds" and is condemning men who go to bed with other men. Unfortunately, that's not the case. Remember Paul's admonition to young Timothy in his second letter to him, chapter 2, and verse 15: "Study to shew thyself approved unto God, a workman that needeth not to be ashamed, rightly dividing the word of truth." (KJV). Study is imperative to discovery and discernment.

You see, just as the word homosexual wasn't a word in any language until 1892, *arsenokoitai* wasn't a word in the Greek language until the Apostle Paul used it in his letter to Timothy. There are no other uses of it in scripture other than this one verse, and less than a hundred uses of it in all Greek literature in the six hundred years following Paul's coining of the word. What plunges us even deeper into the quandary of trying to discern Paul's reasoning in using this word is the fact that there was already a word in Greek culture that meant sex between two men, the word *paiderasste*.

Paul was a brilliant man, inspired by the Holy Spirit of the living God; he was not one to play games with words. If he had meant two men who had sex with each other, he would have used the word his Greek-literate audience would have easily recognized: *paiderasste*. But he didn't, so logic tells us there was a different meaning he was trying to convey to the readers of his letter to the Church of Rome.

As to the question about why the apostle felt it necessary to coin a new word to convey his message to the ancient Roman Church, I found this explanation from Futurechurchnow.org (used with permission) http://www.futurechurchnow.com/2015/08/24/the-bible-and-same-sex-relationships-part-8-male-bedders-the-meaning-of-arsenokoitai/.

> ### Why Did Paul Make Up a Word—and What Does It Mean?
>
> In both of these passages, the author, Paul, uses a particular word to describe people who engaged in activities he considers to be sinful. The Greek word is *arsenokoitēs* and scholars agree that Paul actually made this word up. Consider this carefully. In a cultural context where homosexuality was considered acceptable and was commonplace, Paul had a number of options for the words he could have used to describe whatever was in his mind. These included, for example, *paiderastēs, pallakos, kinaidos, arrenomanēs,* and *paidophthoros*. There are also technical terms, such as the lover (*erastēs*), the beloved (*erōmenos, paidika*), to give the body for purposes of intercourse (*charis, charidzesthai*), as well as slang terms that could have been used to indicate various forms of culturally accepted homosexuality, or even homosexuality in general. Paul doesn't use any of these.

Justin Cannon, a brilliant young scholar, has done some incredible research into this matter and the apostle's use of a heretofore unknown word. Justin is an ordained clergyman in the Episcopal Church and holds a Master of Divinity from Church Divinity School of the Pacific.

The following is an excerpt from an article entitled "Homosexuality in the New Testament: Conservative and Liberal Views." It can be found on the website Religious Tolerance at http://www.religioustolerance.org/homarsen.htm (used with permission):

> Justin Cannon has provided an interesting analysis of 1 Corinthians. He noticed a pattern in verse 9 and 10. They are composed up of pairs or triads of related groups of people:
>
> - The lawless & disobedient: two near synonyms
> - The ungodly & sinners: also two near synonyms
> - The unholy & profane: two synonyms
> - The murderers of fathers & murderers of mothers & man-slayers: three kinds of murderers
> - Whoremongers & *arsenokoitai* & menstealers (traffickers)
> - Liars & perjurers, etc.: again, two near synonyms.
>   From the repeated pairs or triads made up of synonyms or near synonyms, one might expect that whoremongers, *malakoi arsenokoitai*, and menstealers are interconnected with a common theme—just like the other pairs and triads in the list.
> - In the original Greek, the first of the three words is *pornov*. An online Greek lexicon notes that this is Strong's Number 4205 and was derived from the Greek word *pernemi*, which means to sell. Its meanings are:
>   - A man who prostitutes his body to another's lust for hire.
>   - A male prostitute.
>   - A man who indulges in unlawful sexual intercourse, a fornicator.
> - The second term is *arsenokoitai*, which has not been given a Strong Number because it is a made-up word that is almost

never found in the Greek language other than in 1 Timothy and 1 Corinthians.

- The last of the three words is *andrapodistes,* the stem of the word *andrapodistai.* It is Strong's Number 405, which means:

  - A slave-dealer, kidnapper, man-stealer—one who unjustly reduces free men to slavery or who steals the slaves of others and sells them.

  If we assume that the three words refer to a common theme, as the other five groups are, then we have to look for some sense which the words have in common. Cannon suggests:

    › *pornoi* refers to an enslaved male prostitute.

    › *arsenokoitai* refers to a man who forces sex on an enslaved male prostitute

    › *andrapodistes* refers to a person who kidnaps and enslaves people.

The common theme is slavery. Cannon suggests a translation: "It is as if Paul were saying, 'male prostitutes, men who sleep with them, and slave dealers who procure them'." That is, all three words deal with slavery. They are unrelated to homosexual behavior in the modern sense of the term, i.e., consensual sex between persons of the same sex.

So, in essence, what Justin Cannon is saying is that the reason the Apostle Paul uses the heretofore unknown word, *arsenokoitai,* instead of the word *paiderasste* is because he wasn't talking about the extremely common Greek and Roman practice of two men having sex together. He coined a new phrase to complete his dissertation about men who use and abuse other men for sexual purposes against their wills.

Whether or not one accepts Cannon's analysis of 1 Corinthians, it's clear there is good reason to question the traditional narrative of these two passages. The case for the indictment in these two passages being against lust and exploitation is far more convincing than the traditional narrative that Paul was comparing two men who were sexually intimate with each other, as a part of a loving relationship, to people who were lawless, ungodly murderers of their parents.

So far, we've seen that not a single one of the clobber passages used by the mainstream church against the LGBTQ community actually says what we've been taught from the pulpit that it says. Not one! Sodom's "sin" wasn't homosexuality. The Levitical condemnation of two men lying together has deeper implications than originally taught, dealing with anal penetration as a practice of pagan worship. The Apostle Paul's rant in Romans chapter 1 isn't geared towards people attracted to the same sex but rather an incitement that turning away from worship of the God of Heaven to the worship of idols caused heterosexuals to burn so hot with lust that they were consumed with it for one another, against their own natural heterosexual orientation. We've learned that some words have been mistranslated and that we need to actually study to determine what the author of scriptural passages is saying. And failure to actually study, understand, and properly apply the Word of God can send people to hell.

As we bring this chapter to a close and press in to see what Father has planned for this group of marginalized members of society that the church has so rejected, I'd like you to take one last thought into consideration. In chapter 2 we determined that all of our truth had to have a biblical foundation to be considered truth for the purposes of this book. Now let's see what Jesus had to say about what He, as God incarnate, deemed to defile a man. We read His perspective in Matthew 15:18–20:

> **Matthew 15:18-20 (KJV)**
> But those things which proceed out of the mouth come forth from the heart, and they defile the man.
>
> [19] For out of the heart proceed evil thoughts, murders, adulteries, fornications, thefts, false witness, blasphemies:
>
> [20] These are the things which defile a man: but to eat with unwashen hands defileth not a man.

The bottom line is this: Jesus said adultery and fornication defile a man; He did not distinguish between fornication between a man and a woman, and fornication between two men or two women. As I've stated before, I don't believe being LGBTQ is a pass to have sex with anyone and everyone a person desires. Nor do I believe that it carries any different penalty for doing so than indulging in the same behavior carries for heterosexual individuals, and there is absolutely nothing in scripture to indicate any differently.

The Church has made this into an issue our Savior never intended it to be. We've used mistranslated words and our own sociopolitical agendas to oppress an entire people group and damn them to hell. There's blood on our hands, dear Church, and we are "Guilty, as charged!" As the psalmist penned long ago, "Lord have mercy, Christ have mercy."

CHAPTER 7
God Is Not Done with Israel

NOW THAT WE have examined the clobber passages and seen that they do not apply to loving, covenant relationships between equals, you may be wondering, "Does God have a gay agenda, and if so, what is it?" If you're anything like me, you're probably eager to get to the point of this book and learn what I believe Holy Spirit has revealed to me about Father God's plan, His "agenda," if you will, for the LGBTQ community. And I'm eager to share it with you and let you meditate on it. Scripture tells us in Isaiah 22:10 that God establishes things "line upon line and precept upon precept." That's what we're doing here: following the pattern outlined in scripture to establish what I believe is the truth of what Holy Spirit wants to reveal to His church in this hour.

As we discussed in chapter 2, if what I'm telling you is from the Spirit of the Living God, it has to line up with scripture. If anything goes against scripture as it was originally written, it cannot be accepted as truth and must, at the very least, be set aside and disregarded, if not condemned and branded as heresy.

That being said, we've got more foundation to lay before addressing the "agenda." Part of that is examining the correlations between first-century Israel and the twenty-first-century church, and correlations between the first-century church and the twenty-first century LGBTQ community.

In the next few chapters, we're going to dispel some false teachings that have plagued the Church for literally centuries. We're going to discuss where they came from and why they've got to be dispelled for the Church to enter into the fullness of what Father God has for her in this hour.

Replacement Theology—A Doctrine of Devils

The very first thing you're going to need to know if you're ever going to be able to accept what Holy Spirit is speaking in this hour is that God is not done with Israel. In 1 Timothy 4:1 (KJV), we read Paul's warning to young Timothy concerning false doctrines in the latter days:

> Now the Spirit speaketh expressly, that in the latter times some shall depart from the faith, giving heed to seducing spirits, and doctrines of devils.

There are many false doctrines plaguing the Church today: practices of the New Age, paganism, and even witchcraft and divination are infiltrating the Church; there are many "doctrines of devils" being taught from our pulpits. Having been raised in an ultra-conservative home and church, I know that many people from my same background will harden their hearts after reading this book and declare that the very words I'm writing are, in themselves, a doctrine of devils. To those I can only respond—pray. Ask Holy Spirit what *He* has to say about what I'm presenting to you.

> Scripture tells us in **1 John 4:1 (NIV):**
>
> Dear friends, do not believe every spirit, but test the spirits to see whether they are from God, because many false prophets have gone out into the world.

So I encourage you, test what you read, not only in this book but in others you may read on this and every other spiritual subject. And remember, the admonition is that you test the "spirit" behind the words. It's not about whether or not you like me, or my choice of words, or my writing style. It's about the message: Is what I'm saying from the Holy Spirit of God, or not? Does it line up with the heart of the Father as revealed throughout scripture?

The demonic doctrine at hand is what theologians call "replacement theology," or to be more technical, "supersessionism." These two terms are interchangeable, and there are many Christian sources that go into extensive detail on this doctrine. For brevity's sake, I am quoting from the more succinct Wikipedia definition:

> Supersessionism, also called replacement theology or fulfillment theology, is a Christian doctrine which asserts that the New Covenant through Jesus Christ supersedes the Old Covenant, which was made exclusively with the Jewish people.
>
> In Christianity, supersessionism is a theological view on the current status of the church in relation to the Jewish people and Judaism. It holds that the Christian Church has succeeded the Israelites as the definitive people of God or that the New Covenant has replaced or superseded the Mosaic covenant. From a supersessionist's point of view, just by continuing to exist [outside the Church], the Jews dissent. This view directly contrasts with dual-covenant theology, which holds that the Mosaic covenant remains valid for Jews.

I have a problem with calling this detestable, demonic doctrine "Christian;" however, in defense of Wikipedia, the majority of the Church has embraced this doctrine for the last two millennia. It was only after, and because of, the holocaust and the subsequent return of the Jewish people to their homeland in Israel that some of the mainstream churches and denominations began to reject supersessionism.

So that's the technical definition. The bottom line is that replacement theology, or supersessionism, teaches that the Church has replaced Israel in God's plan. People who adhere to replacement theology believe the Jews are no longer God's chosen people, and God no longer has any specific future plans for the nation of Israel. Anyone who has bought into this lie should read their Bibles. Again. There are no fewer than twenty-one verses stating that the covenant God made with Israel through her patriarchs was an "everlasting" covenant. Here are just a few of them:

> **Genesis 17:19 (ESV)**
> But God said, "No, but Sarah your wife will bear you a son, and you shall call his name Isaac, and I will establish My covenant with him for an everlasting covenant for his descendants after him."

> **1 Chronicles 16:17 (NIV)**
> He also confirmed it to Jacob for a decree, To Israel as an everlasting covenant.
>
> **Psalm 105:8 (KJV)**
> He has remembered His covenant forever, the word which He commanded to a thousand generations.

In Jeremiah 33:19, we read that only if man can break God's covenant with the day and with the night, then could God break His covenant with man. Clearly, that just can't happen. We can break covenant with God all day long, and as human beings we do. But as surely as day follows night, God can never go back on His word to His people, and His word to Israel is that they would be His people for all time.

> **Jeremiah 33:19-22 (ESV)**
> The word of the Lord came to Jeremiah: [20] Thus says the Lord: If you can break my covenant with the day and my covenant with the night, so that day and night will not come at their appointed time, [21] then also my covenant with David my servant may be broken, so that he shall not have a son to reign on his throne, and my covenant with the Levitical priests my ministers. [22] As the host of heaven cannot be numbered and the sands of the sea cannot be measured, so I will multiply the offspring of David my servant, and the Levitical priests who minister to me.

So replacement theology is definitely not scripture-based; it is rather a doctrine birthed out of a hatred for the Jewish people that has existed as long as they have been a race. A doctrine taught by man but inspired by hell itself: a doctrine of devils. It lies at the base of much of the antisemitism in the Church and in the world today. And yes, antisemitism is rampant in the Church. The majority of our mainstream denominations are antisemitic at their core. You may not hear anyone "Jew-bashing" from the pulpit, but you'll see it in their support of boycotts against the nation of Israel and hear it in their sociopolitical rhetoric (though half of the evangelical population is more supportive of the state of Israel, possibly because of its role in end-times prophecy).

According to JewishVoice.org, in an undated article on their website, (https://www.jewishvoice.org/learn/replacement-theology), the roots of replacement theology and the antisemitism that came with it can be traced back to the fourth century and the First Council of Nicaea. Here is an excerpt from that article used with permission:

> In the first century, the Messianic/Christian debt to Hebrew Scripture, Jewish exegesis, and divine revelation were evident to all followers of The Way. In fact, Jewish-Christian relations, in spite of second and third century Christian elitist assaults upon all things Jewish, continued with good rhythm and solid relationship until the mid-fourth century with the advent of the First Council of Nicaea. At the Council of Nicaea, under Constantine's oversight, the Church formally disconnected from the Jewish roots of Christian theology and practice by separating the celebration of Easter from the Celebration of Passover.

Replacement theology and its accompanying antisemitism set their roots deep into the mainstream denominations in the centuries that followed the First Council. In fact, they ran so deep in some denominations as to actually drive families apart, including my own.

My maternal great-grandmother was Dutch, from an upstanding Lutheran family. Martin Luther's doctrine, as well as the doctrine of the Lutheran church, was steeped in antisemitism as a result of Luther's supersessionism beliefs. For my great-grandmother to fall in love with a young Jewish boy was unconscionable to her family, but that's exactly what happened.

Enraged at the thought that his daughter would allow herself to feel anything but contempt for a "filthy Jew," her father forbade them to ever see each other again. So, like so many star-crossed lovers, my great-grandmother eloped with her young Jewish love. When her father caught up with the two newlyweds, he seized my great-grandmother and locked her away in his house, refusing to allow her to see her new husband, the love of her life. He immediately had the marriage annulled. Fortunately for me, it was too late. My great-grandmother was already pregnant with my grandmother.

When my half-Jewish grandmother was born, she was immediately taken away from her "rebellious" mother to be raised by her grandparents, who named her LaVerne. My great-grandmother was disowned, cast out from the family, and kicked out of the house, never to be heard from again.

As my family relates the story, my grandmother LaVerne never saw her mother from the day she was born until she was an old woman. Not many years before her own death, my great-grandmother tracked down my grandmother to tell her how much she had always loved her. But the story isn't over yet.

Raised in the Lutheran church and instructed to hate all things Jewish, young LaVerne did the unthinkable. You see, what my great-great grandparents didn't realize was that their granddaughter resented them for taking her mother away from her. She knew she was being raised by her grandparents, and that her grandparents hated her mother for "betraying" them, and she resented them for the hatred they had tried so desperately to instill in her. So in revenge, at the age of thirteen and following in her mother's footsteps, my grandmother LaVerne married a Jewish boy. Although they were only teenagers, (he had attained the ripe old age of fifteen), they knew they would have to run away to a new city and start a new life if they were going to break away from the antisemitism of my grandmother's Lutheran family. So they did just that and were married and had ten kids; their fifth child was my mother. Even though my grandfather became an atheist after WWII, my mother's family followed the Jewish customs when she and her brothers and sisters were young. Imagine the joy LaVerne felt when her elderly mother was able to track her down and express her love! The corrosive hatred espoused by her grandparents was not able to stop the love both had for their Jewish husbands.

This type of divisive, vehement antisemitism ran rampant and completely unchecked in so-called Christian churches from the fourth century on, but really became mainstream with the birth of the Protestant Reformation.

That being said, let's revisit my first statement in this section of the book: God is not done with Israel. Israel may have been temporarily "put on a shelf," but He is by no means done with her. The Apostle Paul makes this extremely clear in his letter to the Church in Rome. In Romans chapter 11, verses 1 through 8, we read God's disposition towards Israel.

> **Romans 11:1-8 (NIV)**
>
> I ask then: Did God reject his people? By no means! I am an Israelite myself, a descendant of Abraham, from the tribe of Benjamin. ² God did not reject his people, whom he foreknew. Don't you know what Scripture says in the passage about Elijah—how he appealed to God against Israel: ³ "Lord, they have killed your prophets and torn down your altars; I am the only one left, and they are trying to kill me." ⁴ And what was God's answer to him? "I have reserved for myself seven thousand who have not bowed the knee to Baal." ⁵ So too, at the present time there is a remnant chosen by grace. ⁶ And if by grace, then it cannot be based on works; if it were, grace would no longer be grace.
>
> ⁷ What then? What the people of Israel sought so earnestly they did not obtain. The elect among them did, but the others were hardened, ⁸ as it is written:
>
> "God gave them a spirit of stupor, eyes that could not see and ears that could not hear, to this very day."

Ah, yes, that spirit of stupor we began the book with. Now you know how it came about for the Jews. We'll dive deeper into it as it relates to the Church in America, because not only has the Church missed it with the Jews—they missed it with the LGBTQ community.

In-Grafted Branches

God not being done with Israel is the greatest news we as Christians could ever receive, after the news of the Gospel itself, because it shows that no matter how badly we blow it, no matter how many times we miss God's will for our lives, He will never give up on us. As with Israel, God's promises to us in Christ Jesus, as stated in scripture, are: "Yes, and amen."

> **2 Corinthians 1:20 (CJB)**
>
> For however many promises God has made, they all find their "Yes" in connection with him; that is why it is through him that we say the "Amen" when we give glory to God.

So if God isn't done with Israel, then exactly where does that put Christians, the Church, in God's overall plan? Scripture gives us the answer to that question in the form of a beautiful metaphor in which Israel is a well-groomed olive tree and we, the Christian Church, are branches from a wild olive tree that have been engrafted. We read about it in the Book of Romans.

> **Romans 11:17-24 (ESV)**
> But if some of the branches were broken off, and you, although a wild olive shoot, were grafted in among the others and now share in the nourishing root of the olive tree, [18] do not be arrogant toward the branches. If you are, remember it is not you who support the root, but the root that supports you. [19] Then you will say, "Branches were broken off so that I might be grafted in." [20] That is true. They were broken off because of their unbelief, but you stand fast through faith. So do not become proud, but fear. [21] For if God did not spare the natural branches, neither will he spare you. [22] Note then the kindness and the severity of God: severity toward those who have fallen, but God's kindness to you, provided you continue in his kindness. Otherwise you too will be cut off. [23] And even they, if they do not continue in their unbelief, will be grafted in, for God has the power to graft them in again. [24] For if you were cut from what is by nature a wild olive tree, and grafted, contrary to nature, into a cultivated olive tree, how much more will these, the natural branches, be grafted back into their own olive tree.

Scripture teaches us in 1 Corinthians 13:1 that a thing is established "in the mouth of two or more witnesses." We can never pull a single verse or passage out of scripture and build doctrine or theology from it; there has to be more than one scriptural reference for us to consider something to be absolute truth. In keeping with that principle, the Apostle Paul gives us several more references to Gentiles, the Church, being permanently tied to Israel. Here are three of them:

> **Ephesians 2:11-13 (ESV)**
> Therefore remember that at one time you Gentiles in the flesh, called "the uncircumcision" by what is called the circumcision, which is made in the flesh by hands— [12] remember that you were at that time separated from Christ, alienated from the commonwealth of Israel and strangers to the covenants of promise, having no hope and without God in the world. [13] But now in Christ Jesus you who once were far off have been brought near by the blood of Christ.
>
> **Ephesians 2:19 (ESV)**
> So then you are no longer strangers and aliens, but you are fellow citizens with the saints and members of the household of God.
>
> **Ephesians 3:6 (ESV)**
> This mystery is that the Gentiles are fellow heirs, members of the same body, and partakers of the promise in Christ Jesus through the gospel.

As in-grafted branches, we don't take the place of Israel in God's promises or in the fulfillment of scripture concerning Israel, but we get to partake of it right along with her. There's room enough for all of us at the table! Many, many scriptures that talk about Israel in the later days now have a double meaning and a double fulfillment in not only the Jewish people and the nation of Israel, but also for God's people, the Christian Church.

So God is not done with Israel, even after close to two thousand years without a homeland to call their own, and He's not done with the church. We're both branches of the same glorious tree that Father God so lovingly prunes.

* * *

Brothers and sisters, I would like to present you with one last thought before we move into the next chapter, and that is this: God doesn't care who or what you are; if you love Him, you are His. A lot of folks can't get beyond the fact that they or someone they know doesn't seem to fit the world's standards of who can be a Christian. Just as the first Jewish converts were resentful that God would offer salvation to the Gentiles, thinking them unworthy, so many Christians today still struggle with the idea of "whosoever" being able to become a child of God.

But as the scripture declares when the Roman centurion, Cornelius, receives salvation and the baptism of the Holy Spirit:

> **Acts 10:34–35 (KJV)**
> Then Peter opened his mouth, and said, "Of a truth I perceive that God is no respecter of persons": ³⁵ But in every nation he that feareth him, and worketh righteousness, is accepted with him.

So there we have it: God, unlike His Church, is no respecter of persons. He's not impressed by who or what we are, and therefore doesn't care who or what we are. It's His extension of grace to us as sinners that levels the playing field. In fact, not only isn't God impressed by those of us who have it all together in the world's eyes and by their standards, but He tends to go the opposite direction in choosing whom to use to accomplish His will.

In 1 Corinthians 1:27, we read that God makes choices we would never think of making to accomplish Kingdom purposes, which shows us how much different His ways are than ours:

> But God chose the foolish things of the world to shame the wise; God chose the weak things of the world to shame the strong.

One may wonder why this matters today. and what in the world any of this could possibly have to do with God Almighty having any sort of "plan" for the LGBTQ community. Just as the religious leaders of Jesus' day missed it with Jesus being the Messiah, the Church has consistently been on the wrong side of history when it comes to many doctrines and beliefs. Supersessionism was actually considered a "Christian" doctrine and was taught in churches around the world for over 1,500 years. The Christian thinking that God was done with the Jewish people allowed Adolph Hitler to dehumanize the Jews to the point that God-fearing people turned their heads and looked the other way while six million people were slaughtered.

Dr. Erwin Lutzer relates this story from an eyewitness in Germany during the Holocaust:

> I lived in Germany during the Nazi Holocaust. I considered myself a Christian. We heard stories of what was happening to Jews, but we tried to distance ourselves from it because what could we do to stop it? A railroad track ran behind our small church and each Sunday morning we could hear the whistle in the distance, and then the wheels coming over the tracks. We became disturbed when we heard the cries coming from the train as it passed by. We realized that it was carrying Jews like cattle in the cars. Week after week the whistle would blow. We dreaded to hear the sound of those wheels because we knew that we would hear the cries of the Jews *en route* to a death camp. Their screams tormented us. We knew the time the train was coming, and when we heard the whistle blow, we began singing hymns. By the time the train came past our church, we were singing at the top of our voices. If we heard the screams, we sang more loudly and soon we heard them no more." And then the eyewitness shared with Pastor Lutzer, "Although years have passed, I still hear the train whistle in my sleep. God forgive me, forgive all of us who called ourselves Christians and yet did nothing to intervene."

Tragically, the church missed it then, and they're missing it now. God is not done with the Jews, nor has He excluded any people group from His plan of redemption for humanity.

The enemy of mankind's soul is hauling off trainload after trainload of LGBTQ folks, and they're headed to certain death and destruction. But it's because the Church, not God, has condemned them. The Church has shut them out and told them they're not welcome in the kingdom and refused to share the Good News with them. So I ask you, you personally, the one reading these words: How much longer will you continue to sing? How much longer will you ignore the cries of a people who so desperately need salvation? Who so desperately long to be told that God's provision on Calvary was for them too?

When the Apostle John penned what is now the most famous verse in scripture, John 3:16, he actually meant what he wrote. Whosoever. No one is excluded from God's plan.

> For God so loved the world that he gave his only begotten Son, that whosoever believeth in him should not perish, but have everlasting life.

SECTION III– A LOOK AT TWENTIETH-CENTURY CHURCH HISTORY

CHAPTER 8
The Start of Something New: Azusa Street

> **Isaiah 43:19 (ESV)** says:
> Behold, I am doing a new thing;
> now it springs forth, do you not perceive it?
> I will make a way in the wilderness
> and rivers in the desert.

THE HEBREW WORD translated as "new" in the text above is the word *chadash* (Strong's Concordance #2319), meaning "pertaining to something not previously known, something never before seen."

In this chapter, we're going to take a look at the rather checkered past of the Church when it comes to perceiving any new move of God as it begins manifesting on the earth. I thoroughly believe the reason Holy Spirit inspired the prophet Isaiah to pen the scripture above is that Father God knows that it is human nature to dismiss anything we don't understand.

We erroneously believe that anything new, anything different than the way God did it before, couldn't possibly be from Him. Or could it?

From the day of Pentecost, where in Acts 2:5 the Apostle Luke describes the crowd gathered in Jerusalem for the festival as "devout Jews from every nation," who thought the Spirit-filled disciples were "drunk," all the way up to present day, righteous, godly men and women have been blind-sided by the new ways in which God chooses to move ...

Every. Single. Time.

Let's look at the way the Christian Church in America has handled three of the last five major moves of Holy Spirit. For brevity's sake, we'll examine just three, but the response from the Church has been consistent through all five moves. It's important that we look at these past moves because there's a new move on the horizon, and if we dismiss this new move as not being of God, as our fathers and forefathers did, we will miss it. As I tell the folks in my church, it's coming whether we like it or not, and we can either be prepared for it and be swept up in it, or try to dismiss it and be swept away by it!

In order to see how these three movements appeared in our history, we'll go back to 1906, to Azusa Street in Los Angeles, California—the birthplace of modern-day Pentecost and the place it all began for this, our generation. For those who are not of a Pentecostal/Charismatic background, let's begin with the basics, as this is foundational to where we're going with this book. The following answer to "What Was the Azusa Street Revival?" is from GotQuestions.org:

> **"Question: 'What was the Azusa Street Revival?'**
>
> **Answer:** The Azusa Street Revival was a Pentecostal gathering that occurred in Los Angeles, California, in April 1906. Most of today's Pentecostal denominations point to the Azusa Street Revival as the catalyst of the worldwide growth of the Charismatic movement, as they believe the Holy Spirit was once again poured out in a "new Pentecost."

The Azusa Street Revival had its roots in Kansas, where a preacher named Charles Parham was one of the early proponents of the Pentecostal movement in the United States. Parham was the first to suggest that speaking in tongues was the inevitable evidence of being baptized in the Holy Spirit. He started a Bible school in Topeka, Kansas, and one of his students was an African American preacher named William Joseph Seymour.

In 1906, Seymour was invited to preach at a church in Los Angeles. There he preached Parham's doctrine that speaking in tongues was evidence of the Holy Spirit. After a couple of sermons, the elders of the church barred him from preaching anymore because they disagreed with his message. However, Seymour began to hold Bible studies in the home of one of the members of the congregation. Shortly after, Seymour's group relocated to another home. Within a few weeks, various members of the group began to speak in tongues for the first time. As word spread about what was happening, larger and larger crowds began to form—not only of African Americans, but also Latinos and whites—this in a time when segregated church services were the norm. In need of a facility, the group rented a run-down building at 312 Azusa Street in downtown Los Angeles. The building was used to house the main meeting room, offices, a prayer room, and lodging for Seymour and his wife. Seymour also started a rescue mission there. Less than four months after arriving in Los Angeles, Seymour was preaching to crowds in Azusa Street that numbered anywhere from three hundred to fifteen hundred. The meetings were loud and boisterous. There were reports of healings and, of course, speaking in tongues along with shouting and spontaneous preaching by those who felt led of the Spirit to speak. The leaders were sure that this was evidence of revival and even a new Pentecost.

Seymour published various testimonies in his newsletter, *The Apostolic Faith*. Those who participated in the Azusa Street Revival had this to say: "The audience was carried into ecstasy of 'amens' and 'hallelujahs.' Emotion mounted higher and higher, and the glory of God settled on Azusa Street" (A. G. Garr). "The fire fell and God sanctified me. The power of God went through me like thousands of needles" (Florence Crawford). "The power of God descended upon me, and I went down under it. I have no language to describe what took place, but it was wonderful. It seemed to me that my body had suddenly become porous, and that a current of electricity was being turned on me from all sides, and for two hours I lay under His mighty power" (William H. Durham). "Someone might be speaking. Suddenly the Spirit would fall upon the congregation. God himself would give the altar call. Men would fall all over the house, like the slain in battle, or rush for the altar en mass [*sic.*], to seek God. The scene often resembled a forest of fallen trees" (Frank Bartleman).

These meetings continued with intensity for about seven years, with hundreds of thousands having attended, and missionaries being sent out. Many Pentecostal denominations today trace their roots back to the Azusa Street Revival, and many individual Pentecostals trace their spiritual roots back to the same.

Although the revival started in Los Angeles, it's important to note that William Seymour began his preaching career in Houston, Texas, preaching alongside his teacher and mentor, Charles Parham. The only records I could find of Seymour preaching in Houston said that he preached the message of the infilling of Holy Spirit as evidenced by speaking in tongues. The message was not received by the churches he and Parham preached to. The churches dismissed the biggest new move of God in over a millennium because it came in a way they didn't recognize, and it went against everything they had been taught.

When William Seymour first moved to Los Angeles, it was to help a young pastor by the name of Julia Hutchins, who pastored a small Holiness Church in LA. Seymour preached his new Pentecostal doctrine there using Acts 2:4 as his text, but that didn't sit well with Pastor Hutchins. She rejected his teaching on the gift of tongues and literally had the church door padlocked, keeping him and his message out. Once again, the new thing God wanted to do on the earth wasn't perceived by those it was sent to.

After Pastor Seymour was kicked out of the church he'd moved across the country to help build, he was invited to stay at the home of Richard Asberry, one of the members of his now-former church. That home was located at 214 Bonnie Brae Street. From this point, as they say, it's history. Seymour started having meetings in the small house, and on April 9, 1906, after a month of intense prayer and fasting, Holy Spirit fell during one of those meetings and William Seymour and several others spoke in tongues for the first time. You see, even though he was preaching about speaking in tongues, Seymour himself had not experienced the gift of tongues. He just had the faith, combined with an unction from Holy Spirit that what he was preaching was from God, and he didn't care who accepted it or who rejected it. He knew in his spirit that he had heard from God and that God wanted to pour His Spirit out on the earth and move in a way that hadn't been seen in almost two thousand years. So in obedience to God, even without the gift himself, he preached the message he had been given, and people received the infilling of Holy Spirit and the gift of tongues.

Parham, Seymour, Hutchins, and the other folks in Houston—none of them could have possibly imagined what the results of this new move of God would be, yet here we are 112 years later:

> According to the Pew Research Center, Pentecostals and Charismatic Christians numbered over 584 million or a quarter of the world's two billion Christians in 2011. (Pew Forum on Religion and Public Life (December 19, 2011), *Global Christianity: A Report on the Size and Distribution of the World's Christian Population* Archived 2013-07-23 at the Wayback Machine, p. 67. See also *The New International Dictionary*, "Part II Global Statistics: A Massive Worldwide Phenomenon".)

A quarter of the world's Christian population has been caught up in this move of God's Holy Spirit, and that's phenomenal! Yet that means that three-quarters of the Church still hasn't accepted a move that started over a century ago. And that's because they've fallen victim to another demonic doctrine called cessationism, not to be confused with supercessionism, which we discussed earlier.

So then, what is cessationism? Well, let's take a look at that from the website referenced earlier, gotquestions.org, which happens to be a "pro-cessation" website (quotes used with permission). https://www.gotquestions.org/cessationism.html:

> Cessationism is the view that the "miracle gifts" of tongues and healing have ceased—that the end of the apostolic age brought about a cessation of the miracles associated with that age. Most cessationists believe that, while God can and still does perform miracles today, the Holy Spirit no longer uses individuals to perform miraculous signs.

The article then goes on to give some "biblical" exhortation as to why tongues and healings were present in the first century and "only" for the early church:

> The biblical record shows that miracles occurred during particular periods for the specific purpose of authenticating a new message from God. Moses was enabled to perform miracles to authenticate his ministry before Pharaoh (Exodus 4:1–8). Elijah was given miracles to authenticate his ministry before Ahab (1 Kings 17:1, 18:24). The apostles were given miracles to authenticate their ministry before Israel (Acts 4:10, 16).
>
> Jesus' ministry was also marked by miracles, which the Apostle John calls "signs" (John 2:11). John's point is that the miracles were proofs of the authenticity of Jesus' message.
>
> After Jesus' resurrection, as the Church was being established and the New Testament was being written, the apostles demonstrated "signs" such as tongues and the power to heal. "Tongues are for a sign, not to them that believe, but to them that believe not" (1 Corinthians 14:22, a verse that plainly says the gift was never intended to edify the church).

Before we go any further, I want us to take a look at the very first sentence in that statement above:

> The biblical record shows that miracles occurred during particular periods for the specific purpose of authenticating a new message from God.

It seems cessationists shot themselves in the foot with that statement. Without even realizing it, they completely validate the outpouring at Azusa Street as being from God using their own litmus test—*miracles,* to authenticate a "new message" from God. You see, it doesn't take a lot of research into the events of Azusa Street to discover that one of the things that fueled this incredible move of God was the miracles, the "signs and wonders," which were commonplace.

I'm not talking about people being healed of a headache or a rash. I'm talking creative miracles: an arm that had been ripped from the socket growing back in full sight of all in attendance—bones, muscles, ligaments, fingernails, the whole thing. Attendees of a particular meeting recounted hearing bones crack as God rearranged the face of a man who had been born with a hideously deformed jaw. A woman whose ear had been brutally ripped off was the recipient of a new ear—much to the amazement of all who watched. And the stories go on and on. There are so many, in fact, that an entire book of first-hand accounts was written about them, *True Stories of the Miracles of Azusa Street and Beyond,* by Tommy Welchel and Michele Griffith.

In addition to these creative miracles being commonplace, so were the "signs and wonders." Remember those tongues of fire that appeared over the disciples' heads in the book of Acts? In Acts 2:1–4 we read of the supernatural events, the "signs" that accompanied the first outpouring of Holy Spirit on the day of Pentecost. Even by the admission of cessationists, these signs were sent to "authenticate" this new move of God.

> When the day of Pentecost came, they were all together in one place. ² Suddenly a sound like the blowing of a violent wind came from heaven and filled the whole house where they were sitting. ³ They saw what seemed to be tongues of fire that separated and came to rest on each of them. ⁴ All of them were filled with the Holy Spirit and began to speak in other tongues as the Spirit enabled them.

Eyewitnesses of the Azusa Street outpouring recount seeing the roof of the church where they met "on fire." Here is one account found on the site https://www.newhoperevivalchurch.com/azusa-street-revival-william-seymour:

> When they prayed in the Spirit a literal fire would come out of the roof of the building. And then there was a fire about 50 feet away from it that would come down and mingle with it.

Other reports said that the Los Angeles Fire Department was called on numerous occasions for the roof of the house being on fire. The fire department responded multiple times to find a fire they couldn't explain—one that was perfectly visible but was not consuming the structure. This happened so many times that the fire department just quit responding to the calls and eventually ignored them altogether.

Surely this was a genuine move of God, even by cessationists' own standards.

Turning back to the gotquestions.com article that describes cessationist beliefs, it goes on to list all the reasons tongues and healings aren't for the Church today. In their argument, they quote 1 Corinthians 13:8, where Paul states that tongues will cease. This passage forms the only basis for the cessationist doctrine:

> **1 Corinthians 13:8 (ESV)**
> Love never ends. As for prophecies, they will pass away; as for tongues, they will cease; as for knowledge, it will pass away.

Using this one passage of scripture for the basis of the cessationist doctrine requires using the entire passage. The end of the verse tells us that when prophecy and tongues cease, so will knowledge! I know there are some pretty ignorant people out there in our churches, but even the most ardent proponent of cessationism could not claim that knowledge has ceased. After all, don't we refer to new believers as having a "saving knowledge" of Jesus Christ?

All nine of the gifts, including tongues, will cease, but it won't be anytime soon. So why do cessationists believe that the time has already come for the cessation of the gifts? Because of the mistranslation of another single verse of scripture, 1 Corinthians 13:10. So let's read the whole passage in context:

> **1 Corinthians 13:8-10 (ESV)**
> Love never ends. As for prophecies, they will pass away; as for tongues, they will cease; as for knowledge, it will pass away. [9] For we know in part and we prophesy in part, [10] but when the perfect comes, the partial will pass away.

Cessationists believe that word in verse 10, "perfect," refers to the Holy Bible. They believe that Paul is telling us that with the canonization of scripture, Holy Spirit stopped moving on the earth through the "Gifts of the Spirit" as established by the Apostle Paul earlier in 1 Corinthians 12:7–11.

> **1 Corinthians 12:7-11 (KJV)**
> But the manifestation of the Spirit is given to every man to profit withal. ⁸ For to one is given by the Spirit the word of wisdom; to another the word of knowledge by the same Spirit; ⁹ To another faith by the same Spirit; to another the gifts of healing by the same Spirit; ¹⁰ To another the working of miracles; to another prophecy; to another discerning of spirits; to another divers kinds of tongues; to another the interpretation of tongues: ¹¹ But all these worketh that one and the selfsame Spirit, dividing to every man severally as he will.

There you have all nine gifts, but let's take a closer look at the original Greek word translated as "perfect" to understand what Paul may have been trying to tell us.

The Greek word used in verse 10 above is τέλειον, from the root word, *telos* (Strong's Concordance 5046). The translation of that word is, "having reached its end, i.e. complete, by ext. (extension) perfect."

Although we do find the word "perfect" included in the definition, it's "by extension," in other words, not the main meaning.

The following is a closer, more accurate translation of what Paul, the author of over half the New Testament, is saying:

> Love never ends. As for prophecies, they will pass away; as for tongues, they will cease; as for knowledge, it will pass away. ⁹ For we know in part and we prophesy in part, ¹⁰ but having reached its end, the partial will pass away.

Here he's not talking about the end of the age of biblical Apostles and gifts. He's not talking about the canonization of scripture but about the return of Jesus Christ. How can I be so sure? Because the very words of Jesus Christ Himself, found in the book of Mark, defy the cessationist interpretation and teaching.

> **Mark 16:17-18 (KJV)**
> And these signs shall follow them that believe; in my name shall they cast out devils; they shall speak with new tongues; ¹⁸ They shall take up serpents, and if they drink any deadly thing, it shall not hurt them; they shall lay hands on the sick, and they shall recover.

These signs shall follow them that believe … for the first one hundred years or so? No! We must stop interpreting scripture to suit our own agendas and get back to studying for ourselves, with an open mind, to see where Father God stands on a subject. It took me over a decade of reading everything I could get my hands on about the subject of being both saved and gay, and countless hours looking into the original Greek and Hebrew text to come to the conclusion that not only did God love me just the way I am, but He actually made me this way. This is not my "agenda;" this is the truth, as laid out in Holy Scripture.

As glorious as the Azusa Street Revival and outpouring was, not only did the majority of the church miss it, they still haven't accepted it as being of God in spite of **millions** of people receiving the gifts of tongues and countless reports of miracles and healings from around the world.

Literally three times as many Christians have dismissed the biggest thing God has done on the earth since the Day of Pentecost as have accepted it. And to this day, the majority of those folks will argue until they're blue in the face that it's still not a legitimate move of God.

The most important aspect of this move of God was how it showed the heart of the Father to be one of restoration and unity. You see, William Seymour was African American. Up until the Azusa Street Revival, the Black community and the white community didn't worship together. But when Holy Spirit fell on Seymour's congregation meeting in that little house on Bonnie Brae Street, they quickly outgrew that space and had to find a new location to meet in. That location was an old African Methodist Episcopal Church on Azusa Street that had most recently been used as a warehouse and then as a stable. One LA newspaper described it as a "tumble down shack," but the presence of God was there, and soon it was filled with folks of all ethnicities. Black, white, and Latino believers all worshiped together for the first time in history, and it was glorious.

Father's heart is never about building walls; it's always about tearing them down. This is unity in the Spirit, and as we'll see, unity accompanies every genuine move of Holy Spirit for those who are willing to accept what He's doing on the earth.

Many people denied and rejected the outpouring at Azusa Street, but many accepted it and were blessed beyond belief by what Holy Spirit did in their lives. There's a new move of Holy Spirit on the horizon—will you accept it or reject it? Which side of history will you be on?

CHAPTER 9
The Great Charismatic Renewal

THE GREAT HEALING Revival that took place in the 1930s, 1940s, and early 1950s, stewarded by healing Evangelists like A.A. Allen, William Branham, Jack Coe, Kathryn Kuhlman, and Oral Roberts, helped establish Pentecostalism as a part of the Christian Church in the United States, although up to that point it was still considered a "fringe" movement, or sect, by many. It was this revival that set the stage for the next great movement of God's Holy Spirit—the Great Charismatic Renewal. This movement is distinctly different from the Jesus People Movement that followed closely behind, which we'll examine in the next chapter.

First, some background to set the stage: In 1936, a very quirky, internationally-known healing evangelist by the name of Smith Wigglesworth gave a young South African preacher of French Huguenot descent a prophecy that would change not only his life, but the face of Christianity. That young pastor was David Johannes du Plessis. Born in Cape Town, South Africa on February 7, 1905, du Plessis' life's journey is a fascinating story and deserves a lot more time and space than we have here; our focus is not on the move of God that David was used to usher in, but rather on the way the church reacted to it.

I highly recommend reading *The Smith Wigglesworth Prophecy and the Greatest Revival of All Time* by Dr. Roberts Liardon for in-depth detail about this fascinating man and his part in one of the greatest spiritual movements of all time. All references concerning Rev. du Plessis contained in this chapter are found in the aforementioned book by Dr. Liardon and are used with his permission.

The prophecy Smith Wigglesworth gave Rev. du Plessis was that God was going to use him to steward one of the greatest moves of His Holy Spirit the world had ever seen. This prophecy was of great weight in light of the Azusa Street Revival, which had begun roughly thirty years earlier, but the actual fulfillment of the prophecy spoken by Wigglesworth didn't begin until about fifteen years after the time it was first delivered.

Rather than going into all the details of the prophecy, we'll touch on the main highlight, and that was that Father God was going to pour out His Spirit on the mainstream denominations. By this point in history, the folks who had received the infilling of Holy Spirit during the Azusa Street outpouring had formed not only Pentecostal churches but their own Pentecostal denominations. The mainstream churches had completely rejected the outpouring at Azusa Street and had become extremely leery of, and in some cases downright hostile toward, their new Pentecostal brothers and sisters, and the Pentecostals had grown to resent it deeply. To say there was disunity between the two parts of the Church would be a gross understatement.

The story of Rev. du Plessis is lengthy, as is his entrance and rise to prominence within the ecumenical churches. But the fulfillment of the prophecy he had received, and the manifestation of what Holy Spirit was doing on the earth, began to come into full view in 1956 when Rev. du Plessis was invited to attend a conference of ecumenical leaders in Connecticut. By 1961, Rev. du Plessis was speaking to the third assembly of the World Council of Churches, where his message was overall received quite positively. While Holy Spirit was still laying groundwork among the Catholics, where He wouldn't manifest completely until 1967, the new move God had promised exploded onto the scene in the Episcopal Church. I prefer to use secular sites such as Wikipedia to confirm some historical spiritual matters, as they tend to be biased towards the negative, if any bias exists, and can be at times more reliable. The following is an excerpt from Wikipedia's "History" section on their page describing the charismatic movement:

> https://en.wikipedia.org/wiki/Charismatic_movement
>
> The high church wing of the American Episcopal Church became the first traditional ecclesiastical organization to feel the

impact of the new movement internally. The beginning of the charismatic movement is usually dated to Sunday, April 3, 1960, when Dennis J. Bennett, rector of St. Mark's Episcopal Church in Van Nuys, California recounted his Pentecostal experience to his parish, doing it again on the next two Sundays, including Easter (April 17), during which many of his congregation shared his experience, causing him to be forced to resign. The resulting controversy and press coverage spread an awareness of the emerging charismatic movement. The movement grew to embrace other mainline churches, where clergy began receiving and publicly announcing their Pentecostal experiences. These clergy began holding meetings for seekers and healing services which included praying over and anointing of the sick. The Catholic Charismatic Renewal began in 1967 at Duquesne University in Pittsburgh, Pennsylvania.

Despite the fact that Pentecostals currently tend to share more in common with evangelicals than with either Roman Catholics or mainline Protestants, the charismatic movement was not initially influential among evangelical churches.

You may be thinking, "What does any of this have to do with God having some sort of Gay Agenda?" As we examine the doings of Rev. du Plessis and how the different denominations responded, you may start to see parallels with today's responses of various Christian factions when it comes to the rights and affirmation of LGBTQ Christians. Just as "the charismatic movement was not initially influential among evangelical churches," the modern inclusion of members of the LGBTQ community has initially been rejected by evangelical churches. Neither the charismatic movement nor the inclusion and affirmation of LGBTQ people were initially seen as being genuinely from God.

In his aforementioned book, Dr. Roberts Liardon recounts that Rev. du Plessis began to receive backlash from the Pentecostal Churches and ministries he was involved with.

In 1955, that backlash came in the form of being "uninvited" to speak at events at which he had previously been the featured speaker. Then in 1962, not long after Rev. du Plessis' work came to fruition in the Episcopal

Church, the Assemblies of God revoked his ordination with them *sans* explanation; apparently, they feared he had given in to heretical teaching. To understand the severity of this move, consider that up until his open involvement with the ecumenical churches, Rev. du Plessis was one of the most influential, well-respected men in the Pentecostal world.

So we have a new move of God on the earth—the outpouring of Father's Holy Spirit upon the mainstream and ecumenical churches—and the Pentecostals were having none of it. In fact, many of them were actually angry that God would do such a thing. This seems puzzling until we look at their theology: the Pentecostals thought the mainstream denominations, such as Presbyterian and Methodist, were too liberal, and doubted if they should even be called Christian. The mainstream denominations thought the Pentecostals were uneducated fanatics, and thereby socially unacceptable. And the one thing they both agreed on was that the ecumenical churches, such as Catholic, Episcopal, and Lutheran, weren't even Christian at all.

To gain some insight into the heart and mindset of the primary person involved in this amazing outpouring, let's review an excerpt from Rev. du Plessis' autobiography concerning a message he received from the Lord one day while in prayer. Notice the attitude of his heart towards those to whom he was being told to go, and how he responds to God's prompting:

> "The time for the fulfillment of the prophecy Smith Wigglesworth gave you has arrived. It's time to begin. I want you to go to the leaders of the churches."
>
> I argued back, "Lord, what can I say to those dead churches?"
>
> "I can raise the dead." As simple as that.
>
> "But Lord, they are enemies," I almost whined.
>
> "Yes, but I have told you to love your enemy."
>
> Ignoring the truth of scripture in my frustration, I continued to argue. "How can I love people like this? I can agree with neither their doctrines nor their practices."
>
> "Well," the Lord said firmly, deep inside of me, "you will have to forgive them."

"Dear Lord"—it was just a whine by then—"how can I forgive them if I can't justify them?"

"I never gave you authority to justify anybody. I only gave you authority to forgive. And if you forgive, you will love them. And if you love you will want to forgive. Now you choose."

Du Plessis goes on to recount that when the conversation was over, he had seen his error. He had expected God to send him in like a prophet of old to pound the people with the truth, but that wasn't what God was sending him to do. God was sending him to these church leaders in meekness and humility to simply share the message God had given him.

As Dr. Liardon then puts it, "This revival would come through forgiveness offered without its being asked for."

So let's recap Rev. du Plessis' attitude towards the mainstream churches as stated in his conversation with God:

1. He didn't want to take the new move of Holy Spirit to them.

2. He considered them dead.

3. He considered them enemies.

4. He found them unlovable.

5. He didn't agree with anything they did.

6. He did not want to forgive them.

7. He thought it was his place to justify them.

As noted, at the time Rev. du Plessis was sent to the mainstream and ecumenical churches, he was one of the most influential men in the Pentecostal world, and the leadership of that world all held his same beliefs and feelings about the churches God was sending him to: they wanted nothing to do with a move of God in "those" churches.

You see, the move of God the Pentecostals had envisioned, and this by Rev. du Plessis' own admission, was one where Holy Spirit would come upon folks in the mainstream and ecumenical churches and "get them saved" and make them act the way they thought proper Christians should act. Those folks would then leave their "dead" churches and join the Pentecostal churches, thereby validating them further in the eyes of the church world. But that's not what happened. At Rev. du Plessis' instruction, which he claimed he received from God, the folks stayed right where they were, in their "dead" churches, and Holy Spirit fire exploded in them!

In "The Wigglesworth Prophecy": A Sermon by David du Plessis, we find this admission:

> This is a total new level of revival. We've been praying for something like this, but we want it for ourselves to show everyone else how special we are—we don't really want it for everyone.

Rev. du Plessis was not immune to the prejudices of his denomination's beliefs. He resisted God's prompting to reach out to those who needed this move of His Holy Spirit. After a conversation with his wife, Rev. du Plessis made the following statement. Notice his humility and recognition of his prejudice against other Christians who believed differently. He was faithful, yet he enjoyed reading negative things about others, because it confirmed his prejudice. May we all strive to be aware of how our prejudice delights in putting down others, in refusing to deal with them, even though God is prompting us to reach out and love them.

> I might have to apologize—I might have to apologize. Oh, I was as faithful as you could find a man, but if I could, how I enjoyed reading stuff that makes these other groups and traditional denominations look bad, because I wanted them to be bad. We were the good guys; they were the bad guys. I only read the worst stuff about the Catholics, because I wanted to have an excuse to have nothing to do with them. It is easy to find an excuse to believe that the old crowd's too bad to associate with, that God is calling us to "come out from among them." Yet, if they were really as bad as we think, then we ought to go in and save them, not sit back and condemn them. Shouldn't we save bad people? Or, are we only looking for good people to save? If you are looking for good people, you're looking for the other fellow's sheep, and I guarantee you'll end up with his goats. We are not called to sheep stealing; we are called to seek and save the lost.

The Pentecostal Church of Rev. du Plessis' time wanted nothing to do with the traditional churches, yet God had a very definite agenda for them. The Evangelical Church today wants nothing to do with the LGBTQ community, yet, once again, Father God has a very definite agenda, and it's completely contrary to what the Church wants.

CHAPTER 10
Lonnie Frisbee and the Jesus People Movement

SOMETIMES THE CHURCH rejects the new move of God's Holy Spirit because it doesn't look like what they thought it should look like—as was the case with Azusa Street. Other times it's because the move focuses on a group of people the Church doesn't believe are "worthy" of a movement of God—as was the case in the Great Charismatic Renewal. And still other times, the church will push back against what God is doing, because not only does the Church dislike the people the movement is targeting and as Rev. du Plessis put it, they can't "justify" them, but they don't like the vessel God chooses to steward the movement. This was the case in the next great movement of Holy Spirit we're going to take a look at: The Jesus People Movement.

The Jesus People Movement began in 1967, when young people were fed up with the Vietnam War, which had been going on for over a decade. A counter-culture had arisen across our land: the Hippie movement, which Britannica describes as follows:

> A countercultural movement that rejected the mores of mainstream American life. The movement originated on college campuses in the United States, although it spread to other countries, including Canada and Britain.

The Hippie movement came to its climax during what would be dubbed "The Summer of Love:"

> The Summer of Love was a social phenomenon that occurred during the summer of 1967, when as many as 100,000 people, mostly young people, sporting hippie fashions of dress and behavior, converged in San Francisco's neighborhood of Haight-Ashbury. (Wikipedia)

At the heart of the Hippie movement was the desire to shake off the chains of traditional restraint and the bonds of war, and to reinvigorate the American people and eventually the world by rejecting materialism, resurrecting the word "love," and "opening the people's eyes to the hypocrisy of violence and prejudice in a nation dedicated to peace and accord" ("The Flowering of the Hippies," *The Atlantic Magazine*, September 1967). The movement was earmarked by an "anything goes" type of personal freedom, which carried over into every aspect of hippie life, from clothing, to drug experimentation, to a no-boundaries expression of sexuality, to a quest for a "new" spirituality, which included a combination of meditation, the occult, Native American spirituality, Zen Buddhism, and Krishna teachings. Mainstream America was not ready for the hippies, and neither was the Church. But God was!

The Jesus People Movement was born from the Summer of Love. By the end of the summer, many of the hippies were growing disillusioned with life in "The Haight," as it was called. The overcrowding, crime, sexually transmitted diseases, and bad drug trips precipitated by the thousands of penniless young people trying to find a place to "crash" for the night, or to simply sleep on the streets, proved to be the perfect conditions for a new group of hippies that appeared on the scene: the Jesus Freaks Evangelists. The Jesus Freaks were a group of hippies that had gotten saved, many of them during LSD trips. They urged the people to follow Jesus Christ and forsake the drugs and promiscuous sex that riddled the Hippie movement.

Enter Lonnie Ray Frisbee. At the age of eighteen, Lonnie, a self-described "nudist-vegetarian-hippie" (https://en.wikipedia.org/wiki/Lonnie_Frisbee) joined the tens of thousands of other hippies and flower children for the "Summer of Love" in Haight-Ashbury. Lonnie had gotten saved at the tender young age of eight and had been raised in a Pentecostal church until his early teens, when he started experimenting with all sorts of drugs and began questioning not only his faith but everything he had been taught (*Lonnie Frisbee—Not by Might, Nor by Power*, by Roger Sachs, used with the permission of Freedom Crusade). At this time, Lonnie had just come back to Jesus but hadn't gotten a hold of any sound teaching yet.

To say that Lonnie's return to Christ was unorthodox would be a laughable understatement. Earlier that year, Lonnie took his second trip to Taquitz Canyon Falls just outside of Palm Springs, CA. While high on LSD and reading the Gospel of John, Lonnie sought God, yelling, "Jesus, if you're really real, reveal yourself to me!" He recounted this in his autobiography, *Lonnie Frisbee—Not by Might, Nor by Power*, written from interviews with Lonnie before his death by his long-time friend, Roger Sachs. Lonnie stated that as a result, God came to him in a vision and told him of His plans for his life:

> Suddenly the whole atmosphere began to change around me. It began to tingle and shimmer and glow. I thought, Uhh–ohhhh! I don't even want to be here! I was scared and shocked, positive it was not an LSD flashback. I didn't hear an audible voice but I was sure I was in the presence of God Almighty. Then I saw a radiant vision, clear as crystal. I saw thousands and thousands of young people at the ocean lined up in huge crowds along the coast, going out into the water to be baptized. I could see it! I knew instantly that Jesus was real and that He was calling me to follow Him. As the Lord lifted up my eyes, I saw a harvest field of people. They were like a huge wheat field. I saw in the vision thousands of people in the valley of decision.
>
> The power of the Holy Spirit surrounded me from within and without. Then I saw a light from heaven come down and ordain me, and I could hear Him say, "Go in My name, for I have touched your lips with a coal of fire that burns ever before the presence of God. Proclaim to the people that I am coming soon."
>
> It was the most radical moment of my life. At eighteen years old I was being called by God to serve him. It blew my mind, but I definitely said, "Yes, Lord!"

This has been a problem for many a skeptic in the church over the years, but in fact, many people in that day came to Jesus while "dropping acid." As bizarre as it may seem to us in this day and age, it was actually a commonplace occurrence during the hippie days; so many of the former Jesus Freaks have openly admitted that their conversions were accompanied by LSD, also known as acid. It was truly one of the purest examples of God meeting people exactly where they are that has ever been displayed on the earth.

A lifelong friend and confidant of Lonnie's, and now a pastor, Neil Liebig recounts what Lonnie shared with him about his vision that day:

> He said he saw, like the Pacific Ocean, emptied out of water, filled with people with their hands raised, crying out to God to be saved. He said he saw a sea of humanity crying out to the Lord. He said the Lord told him that he would have a unique ministry, and that he was not to be afraid.

The 2005 documentary movie, *Frisbee: The Life and Death of a Hippie Preacher*, by David Di Sabatino, was a great resource and source of inspiration as I researched this chapter, and all quotes in this chapter are from the film unless otherwise noted. I highly recommend that everyone watch it at least once; however, be advised that not everything in the movie concerning Lonnie's personal life and ministry lines up with his autobiography, *Not by Might, Nor by Power*, which I referenced earlier. That three-volume book series was undoubtedly my most valuable resource, as it contained Lonnie's story as told by Lonnie himself.

In the documentary, there's a clip of Lonnie talking about some of what he experienced during that vision of the Pacific Ocean, as well as another former hippie friend of Lonnie's, David Sloane, recounting some of what Lonnie had shared with him about the experience. David fills in some addition detail, saying:

> All of a sudden the Spirit of God hit him hard and he went almost into a trance and saw himself standing up there with a Bible and he was preaching the gospel powerfully to young

people. And God told him he was going to use him to bring young people to Christ.

The movie then goes into an audio clip of Lonnie:

> And then the Lord showed me that there was a light on me that He was placing on my life and it was Jesus Christ, and that I was going to go bear the word of the Lord.

Despite this clarity and depth of detail about the vision Lonnie saw, too many Christians completely discount not only the vision, but Lonnie's entire conversion experience because of the drugs involved when it happened. One article goes so far as to say that Lonnie "being taken seriously as a convert and embraced by evangelical leaders … sounds too strange to be taken seriously, but one could argue that it is precisely at this point that American Evangelicalism goes awry" (http://www.breakpoint.org/2017/03/lonnie-frisbee-sad-story-hippie-preacher/).

There are so many not only negative but downright nasty, vicious comments about Lonnie anywhere the subject comes up and affords people a venue to voice their opinions. What grieved my spirit the most was that every single nasty comment was from someone quoting scripture or condemning Lonnie in Jesus' name. I came to realize that no one hates quite like Christians, and it broke my heart.

> And Jesus said unto them, **(John 13:34-35)**
> A new command I give you: Love one another. As I have loved you, so you must love one another. By this everyone will know that you are my disciples, if you love one another.

Well, so much for that.

When it comes to any vision or new revelation, scripture tells us that we're to "test the spirits" to see if something is really of God or not.

> **1 John 4:1-3 (ESV)**
> Beloved, do not believe every spirit, but test the spirits to see whether they are from God, for many false prophets have gone out into the world. ² By this you know the Spirit of God: every

> spirit that confesses that Jesus Christ has come in the flesh is from God, ³ and every spirit that does not confess Jesus is not from God.

Additionally, we read:

> **Matthew 7:15-16 (NIV)**
> Watch out for false prophets. They come to you in sheep's clothing, but inwardly they are ferocious wolves. ¹⁶ By their fruit you will recognize them. Do people pick grapes from thorn bushes, or figs from thistles?

In this case, Lonnie received a vision that told him to preach Jesus Christ to people, and he did just that. Satan doesn't inspire people to preach about Jesus! And Jesus is more than capable of intervening in our lives, regardless of the circumstances we're in, if we're sincerely seeking him with all our hearts. Lonnie was sincerely seeking in that canyon—seeking God in the only way he knew. And Lonnie's "fruit" speaks for itself: it's estimated that during his ministry, Lonnie Ray Frisbee personally led 100,000 to 300,000 people to a saving knowledge of Jesus Christ. Many of these Christians are now retired from full-time ministry.

Those who knew him closely witness that the experience Lonnie had with God in the canyon that day transformed him and changed his life forever. In the documentary, Lonnie recounts that after entering into the "born-again" experience, he told everyone he could that he had found the truth, and the truth wasn't drugs— it was Jesus Christ. Lonnie said he started telling everyone about Jesus, and that cost him everyone. His parents, brothers, and friends all wrote him off as a fanatic, thinking it was another one of his drug trips. But it wasn't. This was real, it lasted, and it changed Lonnie's life.

In those days, Lonnie hitch-hiked back and forth between his home in Laguna Beach and San Francisco a lot. Lonnie was at the Summer of Love because he had won a scholarship to the San Francisco Art Academy (https://en.wikipedia.org/wiki/Lonnie_Frisbee) and he had just moved to San Francisco to go to school in the fall. It was then that he met Ted Wise, another hippie and a Jesus Freak. Ted and his wife, Liz, ran a Jesus

Freaks coffee shop in The Haight, called The Living Room, and later opened a small commune in Novato, California, called The Big House. It was at The Big House that Lonnie poured himself into the Word of God under Ted's direction and became hungry for everything God had to offer. Lonnie developed a thirst for Holy Spirit and all that came with the Pentecostal experience.

About a year later, Lonnie reconnected with and married his former girlfriend, Connie Bremer, whom he had recently led to Jesus. They hitch-hiked back to the beaches of Southern California to tell the hippies there about Jesus. As fate, AKA Holy Spirit, would have it, *Christian Life Magazine* had done a feature article on The Big House a few months earlier in their January 1968 edition. The article was controversial, to say the least, but landed in the hands of a pastor named Chuck Smith, who was "wrestling with his feelings towards the hippies."

Chuck Smith had a small, struggling church in Costa Mesa, CA, and according to David Di Sabatino's documentary, was contemplating leaving the ministry when Lonnie walked into his life. Chuck's son, Chuck Smith, Jr., recounts in an interview with Robert Ricciaridelli on his show, *The Converging Zone,* that his mom and dad would drive down to the beaches in the evenings and watch the hippies. Chuck referred to these excursions as "driving down to the beach to watch the freaks." In an audio clip from the movie, Chuck admits he saw the hippies as "dirty," needing a bath and a haircut, but his wife, Kay, had a genuine compassion for these souls that fortunately influenced Chuck Sr., and he began asking God for a way to reach the hippies for Jesus Christ.

I feel led by Holy Spirit to go into detail about Lonnie Frisbee and his role in the Jesus People Movement and the resulting rise of the two megachurch denominations that he helped birth. I can't explain it, but Holy Spirit has come upon me and left me undone, just weeping, more times that I can count during the time I've been writing this. He has an agenda in this that I'm not fully aware of, but that's OK. It's His agenda, and I'm writing this book at His direction. So I go where He leads me.

By divine appointment, the straight-laced, Evangelical pastor and the young hippie preacher first met when Chuck Smith asked his daughter's boyfriend at the time to "go find him a hippie." The hippie God arranged for him to meet was, of course, Lonnie Frisbee. Flowers in his hair, barefoot, wearing bells on the bottoms of his jeans, with a Bible tucked under his arm, Lonnie arrived at Chuck's home, and within just a few weeks, the Jesus People Movement was in full swing.

In an audio clip taken from Lonnie's ordination, Chuck recalls what he experienced at that first meeting:

> And Lonnie extended his hand, and there was such a warmth and love manifested in his greeting that I was caught off guard. There was an instant bond. There was a power of God's Spirit upon his life that was very easily recognized.

Lonnie started attending Chuck's church, Calvary Chapel in Costa Mesa, that very week, and the people loved him. Chuck Smith, Jr. recounts that there were only about thirty to forty people attending his father's church for Sunday evening services when Lonnie joined them.

Lonnie was incredibly charismatic. People who knew him said he talked about scripture as if it had just happened. It was real and relevant to him, and people responded to him in great numbers whenever he preached.

It was at that very first service that Kay Smith, Chuck's wife, prophesied over Lonnie that God was giving him a ministry that would "bless the whole coast of California" and have a world-wide impact. In a combination of naivety and humility, Lonnie thought Kay was making up what she was saying. But when he began to receive the word as being from the Lord, the power of Holy Spirit fell on the small group of fifteen or so people gathered at the altar. In an audio clip from the documentary, Lonnie shares about how people began to weep aloud and how others saw visions of what Kay was prophesying.

On May 28, 1968, at just nineteen years old, Lonnie and his new bride were put in charge of the rehab house run by Calvary Chapel in Costa Mesa, called The House of Miracles. Wikipedia states that thirty-five new converts were added the first week and bunk beds had to be built in the garage to accommodate the new believers. After this, Chuck asked Lonnie to take over running the Wednesday night service, and the church exploded. Wednesday night soon became the central night for the church, and people from all around came by the thousands to hear the hippie preacher. Lonnie spent his days at the beach, preaching and baptizing his new converts, then he would bring them to Calvary Chapel in the evenings. In an interview in the Di Sabatino documentary, Chuck Girard, a Christian musician, says that the church grew to about two thousand people in the next six months. The growth was so rapid they had to move their services into a large revival tent until a new building could be constructed. Holy Spirit's anointing was so heavy on Lonnie that he really didn't have to do or say much to get people to come to Jesus. David Sloan, an early hippie Christian and friend of Lonnie's, who was around when he was preaching, recalls a particular day at the beach when Lonnie climbed up onto a bench and yelled out to the crowd, "Hey! Hey! God loves you! Come to God!" And that was all it took. David recalls that a crowd of people got up off their towels and came down to where Lonnie was, weeping as he led them to Jesus. David goes on to say:

> Lonnie was like two different people, silly and goofy, but when the anointing came upon him he spoke with absolute authority.

Chuck Smith, Jr. says:

> It was like walking with an apostle—someone tuned in to a divine frequency.

Not only was Lonnie charismatic and a gifted evangelist, but he walked under a heavy anointing of Holy Spirit with "signs and wonders" following his ministry. People couldn't get enough of the "hippie preacher" and the way Holy Spirit used him. Report after report can be found of people being healed when Lonnie prayed for them, and demons being cast out of people. Demons being cast out is another proof that it was God's Holy Spirit working in and through Lonnie and no other spirit. Jesus himself addressed this in scripture:

> **Matthew 12:24-26 (NIV)**
> But when the Pharisees heard this, they said, "It is only by Beelzebul, the prince of demons, that this fellow drives out demons." [25] Jesus knew their thoughts and said to them, "Every kingdom divided against itself will be ruined, and every city or household divided against itself will not stand. [26] If Satan

> drives out Satan, he is divided against himself. How then can his kingdom stand?

In his November 3, 2016 history of church leaders, *7 Broken Men: Lonnie Frisbee*, https://mikefrost.net/7-broken-men-lonnie-frisbee/, author Mike Frost summed up Lonnie's ministry style beautifully, saying:

> He would walk the beaches during the day, converting young people seemingly at will. Then he would bring them back to the nightly church services for lashings of groovy Christian folk-music and intense Bible teaching. Afterwards he would dispense the Holy Spirit, leaving the room looking like a battlefield as young people hit the floor, began to shake and speak in tongues.

The people who were closest to Lonnie, those who knew him intimately, like David Sloan, John Ruttkay, Ken Fish, Joe Martinez, Darrell Ballman, Roger Sachs, Kenn Gulliksen, and others, all agree on one thing: the miracles, like Lonnie, were the real deal. Lonnie had no pretense, no agenda, and he just didn't care what people thought. That, combined with Lonnie's absolute lack of concern for money, allowed God to use him beyond most people's wildest imagination.

Under Lonnie's direction, The House of Miracles expanded over the next three years to nineteen communal houses that later migrated to Oregon to form Shiloh Youth Revival Centers, the largest and one of the longest-lasting of the Jesus People communal groups, with 175 "houses" and over 100,000 converts across the western and northwestern United States (Wikipedia—Lonnie Frisbee). Additionally, attracted by the youthful energy the hippies displayed, and Chuck's acceptance of them, surfers and high school students alike flocked to Calvary Chapel. You would think that would be enough to garner job security for Lonnie, but alas, you'd be wrong. In addition to Lonnie not being paid for his work with Calvary Chapel at this time, his ministry style was beginning to become a problem for Chuck Smith.

Although Chuck was a brilliant Bible teacher and had relied on Lonnie's rather flamboyant Pentecostal ministry style to build Calvary Chapel, he had not fully embraced the dynamics of Pentecostal doctrine himself, the very doctrine that fueled Lonnie's and his ministries. Believing that love was the greatest "gift of the Spirit," Chuck gave Lonnie a stern warning that the manifestations of Holy Spirit that were trademark to Lonnie and his style of ministry, specifically people being "slain in the spirit" when prayed for, had to stop.

In the movie, Lonnie's former ministry partner at Calvary Chapel, Debbie Kerner-Rettino, recalls that Chuck Smith told Lonnie that if people continued to fall down when he prayed for them, that he would be removed from ministry. Lonnie was told, "We don't want this at Calvary Chapel." Kerner-Rettino then goes on to relate how she and the team would literally hold people up by their hair to keep them from falling down so that Lonnie wouldn't be forced to leave. Keep in mind that this was the very same ministry style that had grown Calvary Chapel to a congregation of multiple thousands by this point. This story is corroborated in Lonnie's autobiography, Volume 1.

As a result of feeling used, and now unwanted, Lonnie accepted a position with another ministry. Calvary Chapel leaders told the congregation that Lonnie had left to "work on his marriage," something Lonnie himself verifies in his autobiography, but in actuality, that was not the main reason for his departure. The Calvary Chapel leaders never allowed the people to know that they had literally forced Lonnie to leave by putting such tight restrictions on him that it was impossible for him to minister, and Lonnie refused to say anything negative about Chuck Smith, the man he considered to be his spiritual father. Chuck Smith, Jr. said that Calvary's refusal to tell the truth about why Lonnie had left caused a great feeling of betrayal among the people who had loved him so dearly, and a lot of very painful wounds resulted in negative feelings towards Lonnie.

As it turned out, life with the other ministry Lonnie had left to join wasn't all he had hoped it would be. His marriage to Connie crumbled, and after only four short years, Lonnie made a phone call to Chuck Smith, asking to come back to Calvary Chapel, where he was brought on as an associate pastor. By this time, all the hurt, disappointment, and what many consider spiritual abuse at the hands of Chuck Smith as well as the leader of the other ministry Lonnie was involved with, had begun to take its toll, and Lonnie had changed. His friend Joe Martinez recalls that he couldn't believe his eyes when he saw Lonnie for the first time after his return to

Calvary Chapel. Lonnie was in a three-piece suit with his hair cut and styled, sporting a manicured beard. Joe says that regardless of the new look, the reaction in his spirit was that Lonnie "had been incarcerated."

During the four years that Lonnie had been gone, Calvary Chapel had mushroomed into a full-fledged movement with satellite churches all over the southwestern United States, and tens of thousands of members. In his documentary film, David Di Sabatino says Chuck Smith had replaced the aggressive Pentecostal dynamic with a focus on Bible teaching. According to friends, it wasn't long before Lonnie realized that he was an uneasy fit, to say the least, in the new, reserved Calvary Chapel. He began asking God for a place to utilize the explosive gifts God had placed within him.

In 1977, John Wimber, a former professional musician and producer for The Righteous Brothers, now turned preacher and the pastor of Calvary Chapel in Yorba Linda, California, had grown weary of the powerless denomination he was a part of. With encouragement from his wife, Carol, John began teaching about spiritual gifts and healing, which began happening in his church (Wikipedia—Lonnie Frisbee). By 1980, Wimber had developed a real desire for the miracles he read about in the New Testament and had heard were manifest regularly when Lonnie was ministering in the early days of the Calvary Chapel movement. Hungry for that type of outpouring and demonstration of Holy Spirit in his church, John invited Lonnie to speak at the evening service on Mother's Day, Sunday, May 11, 1980. That service sealed the fate of what would become the Vineyard movement and catapulted John Wimber onto the world stage.

In Di Sabatino's documentary, John Fulton, a Vineyard church leader who was at that first service, shares what happened that night:

> He asked people 25 and under to come forward, so we had all these young people, probably 300 or so, go forward. He just says the words, "Holy Spirit come," and almost immediately everybody just fell on the floor. One of the kids, named Ricky, when he fell to the floor he pulled the microphone down. Well, a lot of them were speaking in tongues, others were crying, and the sound, well, it was shocking.

John Fulton goes on to say that he didn't know what to do, so he just stood there watching. He said John Wimber was shocked and trying to figure out what to do, and a lot of people got angry and got up and left. This might be a good place to interject that John Wimber and his church members had been praying to see God move in their presence. But, as with other previous moves of God, it wasn't what the people were expecting, and as David Di Sabatino reports, there was a "considerable uproar" the day after Lonnie preached that Mother's Day in 1980.

In the aftermath of the Holy Spirit bomb God dropped on his church that night, John Wimber decided to part ways with Calvary Chapel, citing "theological differences" and aligning himself with a fledgling work called "The Vineyard," which had been started by Kenn Gulliksen. In 1982, Wimber officially changed the name of his church to "Anaheim Vineyard Christian Fellowship." Gullikens turned over the other churches under his oversight to John Wimber, and Wimber began his leadership of the Vineyard movement. In doing so, Wimber enticed a number of other Calvary Chapel pastors to change their affiliations and take on a "more aggressive Pentecostal outlook."

People involved with the Vineyard movement in those early days said John Wimber and Lonnie worked together so well that they were dubbed the "Dynamic Duo." Steve Zarit, an early Vineyard member recalls:

> John would speak and Lonnie would minister; they were the Dynamic Duo. Lonnie got up there and he would wave his leather coat and the power of God would come and people would be falling all over these old pews in these old Baptist churches. And Lonnie would climb over the pews laying hands on people saying, "Speak in tongues, speak in tongues!" and he'd hit them on the forehead and they'd instantly begin to speak in tongues.

Another Vineyard member from that period, Ken Fish, who became friends with Lonnie, recounts how Lonnie cast a demonic spirit out of his mother:

> So I came to the Vineyard one night, and I had my mother with me that night. Something had happened in her mouth and she

> had broken out with black lesions on her tongue and the roof of her mouth and all on her gums. Lonnie walked up to us and said, "What do you guys need?" and all of a sudden Lonnie steps back and says, "You foul spirit, in the Name of Jesus I command you to come out of this woman!" And then my mom started coughing and hacking and retching and when she stopped her mouth was healed.

Reports say that even those people who were ambivalent towards Lonnie as a person would just shake their heads in wonder at the things they saw with their own eyes. Additionally, although no credit was ever given to him by the Vineyard, Wikipedia credits Lonnie with being the main influence in John Wimber's "Signs and Wonders" theology, a paradigm of teaching that suggests that all Christians could operate in the giftings of Holy Spirit in a similar way as Lonnie did.

As was the story with Calvary Chapel, Lonnie was only with the Vineyard a few short years. During that time, he traveled to South Africa with John Wimber, where revival broke out at their meetings and swept across the country. The same thing happened in Denmark, Sweden, Brazil, and the UK. Lonnie was an "evangelist extraordinaire," and Holy Spirit went with him everywhere he went.

At what many would argue was the height of Lonnie's ministry, and the apex of the Jesus People Movement, which by now was not only hippies but a full-fledged youth movement, Lonnie's world came crashing down on him one day with a call from John Wimber. John had had coffee with Chuck Smith, Jr., who casually asked him how he reconciled working with a "known homosexual." During the conversation, Chuck, Jr. told John that he had gotten a call from a distraught member of their Laguna congregation, claiming he had just ended a six-month sexual relationship with Lonnie.

When confronted, Lonnie readily admitted to the relationship and was fired on the spot. Many sources claim that Lonnie's sex life was an "open secret" in both Calvary Chapel and the Vineyard, but my research turned up no original source to verify that. It's also stated in numerous places that it was well known that Lonnie would "party on Saturday night and preach on Sunday morning." Again, no verification and no source is given in any of the articles I found. One person, identified in the Di Sabatino documentary only as an early hippie Christian, Steve Toth, says it was hard for him to understand how "he could party on Saturday night and preach on Sunday morning," but we don't know if Toth was speaking first-hand, or repeating something he had heard. The articles use quotation marks but never credit a source, so we don't know if the accusatory comments were made by someone who had actual, first-hand knowledge of the situation, or if it was conjecture. For the record, Steve Toth finished his statement by saying, "the Spirit of God moved, and there was no doubt about it."

During my research for this book, a delightful set of circumstances, ordained by Holy Spirit Himself, led a long-time, dear, personal friend of Lonnie's to reach out to me to ask if there was anything she could do to help me. That friend was Marsha Stevens-Pino—musician, singer, and songwriter. Marsha was a product of the Jesus People Movement and a part of the early Calvary Chapel, recording what would go on to become one of the anthems of not only the Jesus People Movement but the emerging church, "For Those Tears I Died," released in 1969. That song touched untold millions of lives, ending up in not only the Calvary Chapel hymnbook but in numerous other hymnals, including Baptist hymnals as well.

Marsha used to hang out with Lonnie during his days with Calvary Chapel and maintained a close friendship with him until his death in 1993. I asked Marsha about the rumors I had read about Lonnie's promiscuity, seeking a close, credible source to verify whether these rumors were true. Marsha's response was completely out of sync with the articles I had read: she told me that she did not believe those things to be true of Lonnie. She stated that in the early days she had spent way too many Saturday nights with Lonnie, Connie, and a group of their friends for that to have ever been possible.

Marsha told me that if Lonnie ever did engage in indiscriminate sex, it would have been out of a spirit of self-loathing and not duplicity. She said that she completely disagreed with the articles that stated that Lonnie would "party on Saturday night and preach on Sunday" because "to intentionally go out and party and get high and have sex and then go home and clean up for Sunday morning would be duplicitous, and there was absolutely nothing duplicitous about Lonnie Frisbee."

Many of Lonnie's friends interviewed in the Di Sabatino documentary said they knew of Lonnie's struggle with homosexuality. If you find the phrase "struggling with homosexuality" offensive or strange, know that at this point in history, this is exactly how Christians and non-Christians alike looked at it. In the past two decades or so, "struggling with same-sex attraction" has been used by Christians to put LGBTQ people in a box labeled "broken." Before 1973 (or in the early 1970s) the American Psychiatric Association still classified homosexuality as a "mental disorder," so his friends would have viewed his "struggle" to mean that he fought his desires and that he wasn't constantly looking for sex. They all believe he periodically had occasions where he "fell into sin," but that's because Lonnie was a gay man, and any sex he had was viewed as sin. We now know it wasn't just a struggle—it's who he was—and as he struggled against his own nature, he occasionally gave in to who he was.

As far as the affair Lonnie had with a member of the Laguna congregation, Lonnie admitted it—but it wasn't indiscriminate. Falling in love with someone and having a sexual relationship with them is not the same thing as going to a bar and looking for a casual hook-up for the evening. The young man was hurt by the end of the affair with Lonnie and went to his pastor about it, just as a straight congregant might seek pastoral counsel upon a painful breakup.

Many people, especially straight, devout, Bible-believing Christians, believe that same-sex desire is equivalent to lust. Lonnie's experience with his former lover is similar to experiences I've had: it's not just about lust or having sex. It's about that mind-numbingly, powerful need to be intimate with someone. To hold their hand, to caress their face, to taste their lips against yours and feel those lingering embraces that totally engulf you and momentarily make you forget that there's anything wrong in the world. Pursuing these precious moments has never been forbidden, never deemed illegal, never prompted excommunication, never sent any straight person to jail or a mental institution. Simply expressing one's attraction, desire, or need is a human endeavor, and growing up in a culture and working in a church environment that actively denied and forbade it caused Lonnie, myself, and countless other Christians to endure intense loneliness and longing for a partner. Is it any wonder that in the midst of such demanding work, Lonnie succumbed to the universal human need for intimacy and comfort?

Because evangelical Christians have been indoctrinated to look at sexual sin as being more grievous to God than other forms of sin, and scripture does state that sex outside of a covenant relationship is sin, Lonnie was branded as an outcast and treated with contempt by those he had helped establish in the ministry. Since then, Lonnie has been completely written out of the histories of both the Vineyard movement and Calvary Chapel. In John Wimber's book, *The Way It Was,* July 1, 1999, in referencing the message Lonnie brought on that Mother's Day evening in 1980 that caused both John and the Vineyard to skyrocket to fame, Lonnie is referred to not by name but simply as "the young man." How heinous and cowardly.

In addition to writing Lonnie Frisbee out of the history of the two denominations he helped found—Calvary Chapel, with over 1,800 churches in the United States alone, and Vineyard Christian Fellowships, with 2,400 churches worldwide—some modern-day mega-church pastors even go so far as to deny having ever had anything to do with Lonnie. Ever!

Greg Laurie, senior pastor of Harvest Christian Fellowship in Riverside, California, is one such person. Greg denies having ever known Lonnie, even though it's well documented that Lonnie Frisbee is the one who led Greg to Jesus and was his mentor for years. Here's the story in Lonnie's own words taken from volume 1 of his autobiography, *Not by Might, Nor by Power,* in speaking of his involvement with a group of kids at Newport Harbor High School in Newport Beach, California.

> There was a young student who was working on building a certain reputation at the school. Some said he was a small time pot dealer, but rumors are rumors. Our group was on the lawn area, and I was preaching the Gospel like Peter on the day of Pentecost. Believe me! It was like the day of Pentecost. The believers were standing all around, and I stood in the midst. I began to open my mouth, and the anointing of God was on me—I'm telling you!
>
> In the background I could hear someone saying things like, "So, you think you know it all, huh?" Little railing accusations from a brat came flying at me. He said rude things, and then he began

to mock openly. It was like when mosquitoes come around your head—swatting them away is not the same as getting them with a bug zapper. I started to lose my train of thought because he was spewing disrespectful, blasphemous things.

Then the Lord said, "Stretch forth thine hand, and with the authority I've placed on your life, bring him down."

So I did exactly what the Lord had said. I stretched forth my hand and used the authority God put in my words, and I turned everything that he was saying around on him in divine judgement. He fell on the ground, powerless. Before everyone, God struck him with His power and presence. The young student, Greg Laurie, was saved that day, and God also baptized him with the Holy Spirit. It was dramatic. Subsequently, God raised him up to be a pastor at the age of nineteen years old. He was seventeen when he was converted, and two years later, he was raised up to pastor Harvest Christian Fellowship in Riverside, CA, (from a group I started at All Saints Episcopal Church, which is right down the street from the present church location). Harvest has grown tremendously, and Greg Laurie still pastors one of the largest churches in America. Harvest Christian Fellowship, the first Calvary Chapel offspring, is an excellent evangelistic church and Bible-teaching center, which I highly recommend.

But I'm telling you that back on that hot day at Harbor High School, Greg Laurie got converted when he was struck by the power of God. He was struck down a mocker, but raised up a son of God. It was a very powerful Saul of Tarsus type of conversion with an experience literally from the sky. He became my little brother and spiritual son from that day forward. We were together almost every day while God had him in my school. Greg knew my schedule and followed me everywhere. He spent time with my family and came to my meetings.

Lonnie then goes on to relate how Chuck and Kay Smith "adopted" Greg as a future spiritual leader, and then finishes his section on Greg Laurie off with this statement:

> I'm recognizing Greg Laurie as a spiritual son who went on to have great success independently of my decisions in his life. It's really important that people find their individual priesthoods like Greg did and not be controlled by headquarters. Otherwise the anointing of God cannot have freedom. Many say that Greg is like a young Billy Graham, with thousands of people coming to a saving knowledge of our Lord through his ministry. Greg recently packed out Anaheim Stadium with over sixty thousand people in one of his huge Harvest Crusades. Greg Laurie was the son I never had, and it was "not by might, nor by power, but by my Spirit," saith the Lord!

Wow! Disowned by a man he had not only personally led to Jesus Christ but mentored for the first years of his spiritual life. One source I read stated that Greg refuses to talk about Lonnie and that even the mention of his name in Greg's presence was "verboten."

As a born-again, Spirit-filled Christian man who also happens to be gay, I get that mainstream, heterosexual pastors and preachers don't know what to do with the whole "gay and being used by God thing." It took me until I was thirty-eight to "come out" and then another 15 years to reconcile my faith with my sexuality. So, I get it. But there is a way to handle it; it's called honesty, and it's called transparency. You stand up before your congregations and you face it head-on and say something like this: "I don't get this. It doesn't line up with my theology, but God is in this and I'm just going to have to trust Him and that He knows what He's doing."

But in order to do so, you have to have completely banished pride from your life and be willing to admit that you don't have all the answers. How many church leaders have you ever heard say that?

In the movie, Lonnie's friend, Ken Fish, makes one of the saddest indictments I've ever read about a man of God. He says:

> Lonnie wasn't wise enough to understand that people constantly wanted to use him for his anointing, and then throw him away as a human being.

Mike Frost in *7 Broken Men: Lonnie Frisbee* calls Lonnie a "fragile flower, crushed by a church that couldn't make room for him," and folks, this is what's happening to the entire LGBTQ community. They're being told "there's no room for you at the table."

Chuck Smith, Jr. doesn't hold the same stance as his father did on how the church should deal with the LGBTQ community. In the documentary, he makes an observation that's extremely profound in evangelical circles, saying:

> My dad made an announcement saying "If we have to turn away one young person because they're barefooted and their bare feet are going to ruin our carpet then we'll pull out the carpet, remove the pews and sit on the concrete floor. These kids have nowhere else to go to connect with God. If we turn them away where else will they go?" Now we can say that about drug dealing, free sex rock-n-roll hippies, but not about homosexuals? If the church says to anyone "You cannot come here, you cannot engage in the life of the church." Then where are they supposed to find Jesus?

And that's exactly what's happened. The mainstream, Evangelical Church in America has told the LGBTQ community that not only are they not wanted, but they're downright not welcome and will not be tolerated. The overwhelming majority of the church I'm talking about doesn't even believe that you can be both saved and gay, let alone saved, filled with the Holy Spirit, and gay. I can't tell you how many times I've had trolls on Facebook send me private messages, telling me I'm not saved, that I can't possibly be saved, and that "whatever spirit it is I'm possessed by sure isn't the Holy Spirit." I've had strangers tell me that to my face when we start talking about me being a Christian.

The Rev. Dr. Mel White, who was the darling of the Evangelical Church in America and wrote for such notables as Jerry Falwell, Pat Robertson, and Billy Graham, was another man of God ostracized by the church when he came out as gay in 1994. He made a statement in the Di Sabatino documentary that clarifies the situation men who are both gay and Christian find themselves in:

> By the church closing its doors to this issue it drives us out into the darkness, and in the darkness we do things, because we're afraid, because we're alone and because we don't know how else to do it.

Back in the early days of his ministry, during one of Lonnie's appearances on Kathryn Kuhlman's TV show, *I Believe in Miracles,* Lonnie made a statement about what God was doing at the time, and as it turns out, it had a "double meaning" for him. He said, in that youthful exuberance of his:

> The church for so long has expected a certain "mold" of what a Christian should look like, what a Christian should be, or what a Christian should say, and God is blowing everybody's mind, because he's saving the hippies. And nobody thought a hippie could be saved.

Little did he know then that the church would eventually accept the hippies but would later reject him for something he had no control over. Yes, I know we have control over our actions, but he had no control over the desires he had fought with his entire life.

Alone and maligned by the church he so dearly loved, Lonnie died of AIDS in 1993 at the age of forty-three. Although the *LA Times* reported "Relatives said he died of a brain tumor," the official medical determination was that Lonnie died from "complications related to AIDS." Ultimately, Lonnie died from "complications related to a broken heart that manifested as AIDS." None of the great men of God to whom Holy Spirit had given world-wide ministries through Lonnie were at his side—only a few close friends and family. Chuck Smith gave the eulogy, and his words at Lonnie's funeral were perceived by Lonnie's friends as one last chance for Chuck to hurt him—one last "stab," despite the fact that Lonnie had repeatedly begged Chuck for his forgiveness and to be restored to ministry. Reports say that Lonnie's wife, Connie, was so outraged that she literally came out of her seat at Smith's comments and had to be restrained by her friends, a report that Marsha Stevens-Pino verified during my conversation with her.

When I first started writing this section on Lonnie Frisbee and the Jesus People, I couldn't figure out why I experienced crying jags that would go on for hours. The second day in, Holy Spirit prompted me to drop everything and take the day and go visit Lonnie's gravesite at the Crystal Cathedral. So I did. I called my ex-wife, Staci Weber, who is a dear friend, and told her she was going with me. When we arrived, all I could do was cry and say, "I'm sorry." I sat there on his grave and over and over again, all I could say was that I was sorry as the tears streamed down my face.

During my conversation/interview with Lonnie's friend, Marsha Stevens-Pino, I told her about my experience and the overwhelming emotions that hit me every time I started researching, writing, or talking about Lonnie, and I asked her something my friend Jenny Rain had put in my heart. I asked her if there was anything she thought Lonnie would want people to know. Anything that Father God would want me to say about Lonnie. Her response had me in tears once again. She said that she had read so many things about Lonnie that just didn't line up with who he was. Things that were written that he would have never spoken. That he never said anything defensive or self-justifying. Then she made the statement that went right to my heart; she said:

> Lonnie was not about Lonnie. He was only ever about Jesus. Lonnie never stopped looking, longing, seeking, agonizing over his place in Holy Spirit.

By the time I finished researching Lonnie, I realized why I was so "wrecked" in those early days of writing. You see, I didn't read all three of the series of Lonnie's autobiography until after I had finished this chapter, but I kept on reading and researching. I'm writing this now as part of the final edit, having been directed by Holy Spirit to do so. In Lonnie's autobiography, *Not by Might, Nor by Power*, which he dictated over the last three years of his life, Lonnie goes into great detail about his accomplishments in ministry. He acknowledges that he "fell into sin" on numerous occasions, describes his battle with drugs, and even recounts that he was raped as an adult on two different occasions, but the one thing he never does is admit that he was gay. Over seven hundred pages and he manages to sidestep his sexuality at every turn. I asked Holy Spirit "Why?" It was an open secret.

He had admitted to John Wimber that he'd had a six-month affair with a male congregant. His wife spoke openly in the documentary about him frequenting gay bars at the end of their marriage. Why would he spend his last breath trying to hide his sexuality? The answer I received in my spirit brought me back to those same tears I had shed while sitting on his grave. "Because he knew it was the one thing the Church would never forgive him for," was the answer I heard Holy Spirit whisper in my ear. Lonnie desperately wanted to be remembered as a man of God, and not a gay man who was dismissed from the ministry in abject shame. This shame fell on Lonnie, but in all honesty, the shame wasn't Lonnie's at all.

Truly, the Church's shame, more specifically, Calvary Chapel's shame, the Vineyard's shame, and most definitely Greg Laurie's shame, isn't that Lonnie Ray Frisbee was a gay man, and that a gay man was used by God to birth all three of their ministries, or even that he later died of AIDS. No, the Church's shame, their shame, is the way they treated a man of God. It doesn't matter how badly Lonnie may have failed in some areas, he was a man of God, and God's Holy Spirit rested mightily upon him, and to deny that is downright blasphemy.

The Church of Jesus Christ in America needs to repent for the way they've marginalized, terrorized, victimized, and ostracized the LGBTQ community, and there needs to be repentance from the leaders of both Calvary Chapel and the Vineyard movements, and from Greg Laurie himself, for the way they maligned Lonnie and completely wrote him out of their histories.

What was done to Lonnie Ray Frisbee was a sin—a plain, old-fashioned sin. And like any other sin, it can't be forgiven until it's acknowledged and forgiveness is asked for.

SECTION IV– WHERE THE CHURCH HAS MISSED THE MARK

CHAPTER 11
The Religious Right: A Study in Hypocrisy

IN THIS CHAPTER, we're going to take a look at a couple of places where the Church of Jesus Christ has missed the mark: places where her blatant hypocrisy is obvious to all but those guilty of it, as is usually the case.

As we get started, I know that my political statements will be upsetting, frustrating, or possibly enraging to some readers. Tickling people's ears is not what I'm here for; I'm here to speak the word of truth, in love, to bring about the maturing of the Body of Christ, Ephesians 4:15.

The acceptance of Donald Trump as not only a Christian but a "Man of God" juxtaposed against the erasure of Lonnie Frisbee from Church history is one of the most mind-boggling dualities I've ever witnessed. In the case of former President Trump, we have a man who never made a profession of faith in Jesus Christ until he decided to run for president of the United States. Up until that time, and every day since, he has spewed foul, vulgar, hateful rhetoric from every platform and venue. He doesn't attend church, can't quote a single Bible verse, and has said he doesn't need to ask for forgiveness of sin because he's never sinned! (Interview with CNN - https://

www.cnn.com/2015/07/18/politics/trump-has-never-sought-forgiveness/index.html)

Seriously? What happened to "All have sinned and fall short of the glory of God (Romans 3:23)?

Remember the article quoted in the last chapter:

> "http://www.breakpoint.org/2017/03/lonnie-frisbee-sad-story-hippie-preacher/ goes so far as to say that Lonnie "being taken seriously as a convert and embraced by evangelical leaders … sounds too strange to be taken seriously, but one could argue that it is precisely at this point that American Evangelicalism goes awry."

How can we reconcile this take on Lonnie Frisbee when we look at a man who still, after his "conversion," spews venom and vitriol about anyone and everyone who opposes him, a man who threatens to destroy his opponents and has never spoken a single godly word before or after his "acceptance of Jesus Christ as Savior" (a savior he claims he doesn't need, as he has stated that he's never sinned, and therefore never asked God for forgiveness, which is the primary tenet of salvation). This man is declared a Christian and a "Man of God" to be honored and lauded by the Evangelical Church in America? In January of 2016, Donald Trump told CNN's Jake Tapper in an interview that he doesn't regret never asking God for forgiveness and doesn't have much to apologize for (https://www.washingtonpost.com/news/acts-of-faith/wp/2016/06/08/trump-on-god-hopefully-i-wont-have-to-be-asking-for-much-forgiveness/).

This man couldn't hold a candle to Lonnie Frisbee, a spiritual leader who led over 100,000 people to Jesus Christ, was used to found two mega-denominations, healed the sick and cast out demons, and started revivals all across Europe. How is he an embarrassment to the Church? Do we really think he deserves to be completely deleted from Church history because he was gay? This is impossible to reconcile!

Before you shut your mind to my message, let me bring some balance here. As I said, I'm not here to tickle anyone's ears. I'm here to speak the word of truth in love to bring about the maturing of the Body of Christ. As much as I may personally dislike the man, I'm seriously "pro-Jesus," and I do, with everything in me, believe God put Donald Trump in office. I know many of you strongly disagree with me on this, but if you'll recall at the beginning of this book, we determined that scripture was going to be our basis for truth, and scripture tells us God places kings in power—translate that to "presidents" in modern times.

> **Daniel 2:21**
> He changes times and seasons; he removes kings and sets up kings; he gives wisdom to the wise and knowledge to those who have understanding.

As discussed earlier, if we can't find two scriptures that back each other up, we may be espousing a doctrine that God didn't establish, because scripture tells us:

> **2 Corinthians 13:1 (KJV)**
> This is the third time I am coming to you. In the mouth of two or three witnesses shall every word be established.

So for the second "witness," I give you:

> **Romans 13:1 (NIV)**
> Let everyone be subject to the governing authorities, for there is no authority except that which God has established. The authorities that exist have been established by God.

Now that conservative readers may be feeling more comfortable, knowing that I can be friends with someone whose opinions are diametrically opposed to mine as long as they're civil, let's remember an "inconvenient truth." If God put Donald Trump in office, and scripture definitely says He did, that means God also put Barack Obama in office for eight years, and He has now placed Joe Biden in the White House. You can't claim divine intervention for one and not the other. Scripture says God puts His choice in power: not yours, not mine, His.

So for those of you wondering why—why on earth would God put a man like Donald Trump in office—the answer is simple: because there were things that Donald Trump would do that no other politician would or could do. Mr. Trump has brought out our nation's hidden shadow side, with all the darkness and ugliness that accompanies it. God brought out our hatred, bigotry, racism, misogyny, and homophobia and put it on full display for the world to see so that He could do what only He can do—heal our land. A nation, like a person, can't be healed if they deny the cancer that's eating away at them from the inside out.

Personally, I believe that placing Donald Trump in the presidency of the country was the ultimate demonstration of God's love for the United States. He loved this nation so much that He was willing to enact some divine "tough love" to expose the things we needed to repent of in order to bring us to repentance so that He could heal our land. And I'm just optimistic enough to believe that as ugly as it has been, God will work it out for us in the end.

So that's what no other president could do. Let's take a look at what no other president would do.

Remember that God is not done with Israel; He has an agenda, and it always revolves around Israel, because in scripture, God refers to Israel as His land. Yes, scripture says He gave it to the Israelites, but He still refers to it as His land, and as we saw, He says His covenant with the Jewish people is eternal.

> **Joel 3:1-2 (NIV)**
> In those days and at that time, when I restore the fortunes of Judah and Jerusalem, ² I will gather all nations and bring them down to the Valley of Jehoshaphat. There I will put them on trial for what they did to my inheritance, my people Israel, because they scattered my people among the nations and divided up my land.

So if you're trying to figure out what Donald Trump did that no one else would do, I'd like to direct you to the Jerusalem Embassy Act of 1995:

> "The **Jerusalem Embassy Act of 1995** is a public law of the United States passed by the post-Republican Revolution 104th Congress on October 23, 1995. The proposed law was adopted

by the Senate (93–5), and the House (374–37). The Act became law without a presidential signature on November 8, 1995.

The Act recognized Jerusalem as the capital of the State of Israel and called for Jerusalem to remain an undivided city. Its purpose was to set aside funds for the relocation of the Embassy of the United States in Israel from its location in Tel Aviv to Jerusalem, by May 31, 1999. For this purpose it withheld 50% of the funds appropriated to the State Department specifically for "Acquisition and Maintenance of Buildings Abroad" as allocated in fiscal year 1999 until the United States Embassy in Jerusalem had officially opened. Israel's declared capital is Jerusalem, but this is not internationally recognized, pending final status talks in the Israeli–Palestinian conflict. Despite passage, the law allowed the President to invoke a six-month waiver of the application of the law, and reissue the waiver every six months on "national security" grounds. The waiver was repeatedly renewed by Presidents Clinton, Bush, and Obama. President Donald Trump signed a waiver in June 2017. On June 5, 2017, the U.S. Senate unanimously passed a resolution commemorating the 50th anniversary of reunification of Jerusalem by 90-0. The resolution reaffirmed the Jerusalem Embassy Act and called upon the President and all United States officials to abide by its provisions. On December 6, 2017, Trump recognized Jerusalem as Israel's capital, and ordered the planning of the relocation of the embassy. However, following the announcement, Trump signed an embassy waiver again, delaying the move, as mandated by the Act, by at least six months. Legally, however, the U.S. embassy can be moved at any time without reliance on the Act.

On February 23, 2018, President Trump announced that the US Embassy in Israel would reopen at the Arnona consular services site of the then US Consulate-General in Jerusalem. The United States Embassy officially relocated to Jerusalem on May 14, 2018, to coincide with the 70th anniversary of the Israeli Declaration of Independence. (https://en.wikipedia.org/wiki/Jerusalem_Embassy_Act)

The key to God's plan for Israel has little to do with the American Embassy, or any embassy, for that matter: it has to do with Jerusalem being recognized as Israel's capital and an "undivided city." Make no mistake, there will be a third Temple erected in Jerusalem, and Jerusalem being recognized as an undivided city is requisite for its construction.

I know most Evangelicals understand this, and many hopped on the pro-Trump bandwagon because of this, spouting the "Cyrus" theory. That theory suggests that, like Cyrus, ancient King of Persia, God chose Donald Trump for what he would do for Israel. I've reprinted an article from the *New York Times* below that beautifully sums up this belief. The article can be found at:

> https://www.nytimes.com/2018/12/31/opinion/trump-evangelicals-cyrus-king.html. (Reprinted under PARS Content License 000089000 dated 12/04/20)
>
> **Why Trump Reigns as King Cyrus**
>
> The Christian right doesn't like the president only for his judges. They like his style.
>
> The month before the 2018 midterms, a thousand theaters screened *The Trump Prophecy,* a film that tells the story of Mark Taylor, a former firefighter who claims that God told him in 2011 that Donald Trump would be elected president.
>
> At a critical moment in the film, just after the actor representing Mr. Taylor collapses in the flashing light of an epiphany, he picks up a Bible and turns to the 45th chapter of the book of Isaiah, which describes the anointment of King Cyrus by God. In the next scene, we hear Mr. Trump being interviewed on "The 700 Club," a popular Christian television show.
>
> As Lance Wallnau, an evangelical author and speaker who appears in the film, once said, "I believe the 45th president is meant to be an Isaiah 45 Cyrus," who will "restore the crumbling walls that separate us from cultural collapse."
>
> Cyrus, in case you've forgotten, was born in the sixth century B.C.E. and became the first emperor of Persia. Isaiah 45

> celebrates Cyrus for freeing a population of Jews who were held captive in Babylon. Cyrus is the model for a nonbeliever appointed by God as a vessel for the purposes of the faithful.

I honestly think they're on to something here, but read that last sentence again: "Cyrus is the model for a nonbeliever appointed by God as a vessel for the purposes of the faithful."

Nowhere in scripture or secular history do we ever read that Cyrus was a godly man, or ever bowed his knee to the God of Israel. Cyrus was not a godly man; he was not a man of God; he was a man used by God.

I would purport that Donald Trump did have a Cyrus anointing to benefit Israel, but like Cyrus, he was no man of God. Evangelicals swoon over him; some go so far as to make blasphemous statements, like Pat Robertson, who stated that he had a vision of Donald Trump sitting at the right hand of God. Folks, there's only one person seated at the right hand of God, and that's His only begotten son, Yeshua Messiah, Jesus Christ.

And let's not forget that giant, outrageous, barbaric billboard in Missouri sporting a picture of The Donald with the scriptural tag, "… and the Word became flesh."

The mainstream, Evangelical Church must wake up and recognize Donald Trump for what he is and quit making him out to be a pre-incarnate second coming. This is blasphemous and downright idolatry, and there will be a price to pay for it!

Let's acknowledge that the politician-businessman Donald Trump was placed in office to accomplish certain things: to place Israel one step closer for the prophecy concerning her end-time temple being rebuilt, and to expose the dirty underbelly of American politics and society.

In prayer several months ago, I asked God, "Why Trump? Why couldn't someone of decent moral fiber move on Israel's behalf?" The answer I heard in my spirit shocked me. The response I heard in my spirit wasn't an audible voice, but it was clear as a bell: "I chose Donald Trump to show My Church her shame, but she has none." This may sound harsh or shocking, but it has echoes of God's word in Jeremiah 8:12a: "Are they ashamed of their detestable conduct? No, they have no shame at all; they do not even know how to blush!"

In the time immediately following the election of Joe Biden, I read a post by a friend on Facebook relating how sad he was because he was going to have to leave the Evangelical Church he'd been raised in. This was a heterosexual man who did not drink the Kool-Aid of Trumpism and was deeply grieved by the reactions of his friends and his church to the election results. The Sunday after the election, he felt heartbroken as his pastor stood behind his pulpit literally screaming about the election results. He said this went on for close to twenty minutes and ended with the pastor, fits pounding the air, screaming, 'This is a Trump Church!' My eyes welled up with tears and cold chills ran up and down my spine as I remembered the words of Jesus to the Apostle John concerning the Church of Ephesus in Revelation 2:5: "Consider how far you have fallen! Repent and do the things you did at first. If you do not repent, I will come to you and remove your lampstand from its place."

The Evangelical Church has lost herself in politics, and itis in a dangerous place.

CHAPTER 12

Love Lost

IN LOOKING FOR hypocrisy in the mainstream church, one need look no further than who they love and who they hate. After all, scripture does tell us that God is love. What does scripture actually tell us to hate? Proverbs 6:17–19 (KJV) gives us this list:

> 17 A proud look, a lying tongue, and hands that shed innocent blood, 18 An heart that deviseth wicked imaginations, feet that be swift in running to mischief, 19 A false witness that speaketh lies, and he that soweth discord among brethren.

Other scriptures mention evil, dishonest gain, false ways, falsehood, bribes, wickedness, lawlessness, idols, and the deeds of the Nicolatians. These are all deeds, not people.

When confronted by one of the religious leaders of his day as to which of the commandments was the most important, we read in Mark 12:29–31 Jesus' rather surprising answer:

> "The most important one," answered Jesus, "is this: Hear, O Israel: The LORD our God, the LORD is one. [30] Love the LORD your God with all your heart and with all your soul and with all your mind and with all your strength.' [31] The second is this: Love your neighbor as yourself. There is no commandment greater than these."

What's so surprising about this is that neither of the commandments in Jesus' response were one of the Ten Commandments, as so many people have thought over the years. Here are the Ten Commandments in more modern vernacular:

1. You shall have no other gods before Me.
2. You shall make no idols.
3. Take not the name of the LORD your God in vain.
4. Keep the Sabbath day holy.
5. Honor your father and your mother.
6. You shall not murder.
7. You shall not commit adultery.
8. You shall not steal.
9. You shall not bear false witness against your neighbor.
10. You shall not covet.

Love isn't mentioned in any of the Ten Commandments. The first part of Jesus' response is from a more obscure commandment recorded in the book of Deuteronomy, chapter 6, verse 5:

> Love the LORD your God with all your heart and with all your soul and with all your mind and with all your strength.

And the second is original to this text, and the accounts of this story found in the books of Matthew and Luke as well:

> Love your neighbor as yourself.

Somehow, the command to love has gotten lost with the mainstream Evangelical Church. There's very little evidence of love going to anyone beyond their ranks. In fact, research shows that the majority of non-Christians now have a negative view of Christianity as a result of the way the mainstream Evangelical Church treats people.

According to the Barna Group, an independent organization that "conducts tens of thousands of interviews every year, attempting to make sense of public opinion, cultural trends and religious identity," and probably the most respected Christian-based research organization in the country, the majority of non-believers in the United States have a negative overall opinion of Christianity. In fact, even many younger Christians have a problem with it!

In 2007, David Kinnaman of Barna released his research in a study entitled "A New Generation Expresses Its Skepticism and Frustration with Christianity." Barna would not allow a reprint of the article in its entirety, which is unfortunate, as it contains extensive, enlightening statistics that are vital to this chapter; however, you can read the entire article at this link: https://www.barna.com/research/a-new-generation-expresses-its-skepticism-and-frustration-with-christianity/. The following is a summary of key points from Kinnaman's research:

> 16- to 29-year-olds exhibit a greater degree of criticism toward Christianity than previous generations at the same stage of life. In just a decade, many of the Barna measures of the Christian image have shifted substantially downward, fueled in part by a growing sense of disengagement and disillusionment among young people. A decade ago the vast majority of Americans outside the Christian faith, including young people, felt favorably toward Christianity's role in society. Currently, however, just 16% of non-Christians in their late teens and twenties said they have a "good impression" of Christianity.
>
> One of the groups hit hardest by the criticism is Evangelicals. The negative views are crystallizing and intensifying among young non-Christians. The new study shows that only 3% of 16- to 29-year-old non-Christians express favorable views of Evangelicals. This means that today's young non-Christians are eight times less likely to experience positive associations toward evangelicals than were non-Christians of the Boomer generation (25%).

The study explored twenty specific images related to Christianity, including ten favorable and ten unfavorable perceptions. Among young non-Christians, nine out of the top 12 perceptions were negative. Common negative perceptions include that present-day Christianity is judgmental (87%), hypocritical (85%), old-fashioned (78%), and too involved in politics (75%)—representing large proportions of young outsiders who attach these negative labels to Christians.

Even among young Christians, many of the negative images generated significant traction. Half of young churchgoers said they perceive Christianity to be judgmental, hypocritical, and too political. One-third said it was old-fashioned and out of touch with reality.

Interestingly, the study discovered a new image that has steadily grown in prominence over the last decade. Today, the most common perception is that present-day Christianity is "anti-homosexual." Overall, 91% of young non-Christians and 80% of young churchgoers say this phrase describes Christianity.

And this research is fourteen years old! The figures at the beginning of this article show a "favorable" perception of Christianity at a "vast majority" only ten years prior, while at the time of this study, only 16 percent of young "non-believers" share that view. And only 6 percent of young "non-believers" had a positive view of the Evangelical church in 2007. And the study shows that "Half of young churchgoers said they perceive Christianity to be judgmental, hypocritical, and too political." Good Lord! Can you imagine the perception the new generation must have of Christianity, with what goes on in Evangelical churches today?

People's negative perception of Christianity is based on what they hear and the attitudes they perceive Christians displaying towards people who are outside the body of Christ, or at least the Church's dogma as to who or what you have to do or be to be a part of that glorious, living, breathing organism.

Let's go back and take a look at the case of Australian soccer superstar Israel Folau, whom we discussed back in chapter 2; he's a perfect example of what I'm talking about. Folau's words reflected the attitude of his heart, what was hiding just below the surface. How do I know what's in his heart? Because "out of the abundance of the heart the mouth speaks" (Luke 6:45).

Now, we're not allowed to judge the motives of someone's heart—why they do something—but we are allowed to discern and judge the attitude of their hearts as betrayed by their words. Why is this so important? Because words reveal not only the attitude of the heart but the spirt behind those words.

> Jesus said, in **1 John 4:1**
> Beloved, believe not every spirit, but try the spirits whether they are of God.

How do we "try" a spirit? We listen carefully to see if it lines up with the Word of God. This is how we can determine what spirit is speaking through someone. It can either be Holy Spirit, the spirit of the world, or a demonic spirit, like fear or hate.

As Christians, Father God takes our words very seriously, as we read in scripture:

> **Matthew 12:36 (NIV)**
> But I tell you that everyone will have to give account on the Day of Judgment for every empty word they have spoken.

Folau's words were actually an extremely sad indictment against him as someone who claims Jesus Christ as his Lord and Savior, because what spewed from his mouth was venom and vitriol towards a group of people that Father has never told us to do anything to other than love. Father God has never commanded us to do anything to any people group other than to love them. As we've already seen, Jesus considered this the second most important commandment: "Love your neighbor as yourself."

In Romans 13:8 (NIV), Paul tells us that the only debt we're to owe any man is to love him. He then goes on to state that whoever loves others has fulfilled the law.

> Let no debt remain outstanding, except the continuing debt to love one another, for whoever loves others has fulfilled the law.

You can't trust your heart and you can't trust your conscience; the only thing you can trust is the true, living Word of God. Neil Anderson, a famous evangelical author, acknowledges this in his now famous quote, "Conscience is always true to itself, but not always true to God."

Hating anyone is not acceptable in God's eyes, even if your conscience is clear. Hating a group of people and blaming God for your hatred is heresy, and it's sin. It goes against everything scripture tells us to do and against the very character and nature of Jesus Christ himself, the one we claim we serve.

Those who seem determined to use scripture as justification for hating people who are immigrants, or of a different race, or Muslim, or poor, or a member of the LGBTQ community, need to remember Jesus and His greatest commandment: to love one another.

In Luke 10:25–37, we read the Parable of the Good Samaritan. If there's any one story or passage in scripture that tells us we are not allowed to hate anyone, it's this one. The Jews of Jesus' day absolutely despised the Samaritan people. They referred to them as "dogs" and would spit on them when they encountered them in public. When walking down the street, they would cross to the other side so as not to have any contact with them.

In the parable, Jesus tells an "expert in the law" that in order to inherit eternal life, he must love his neighbor as himself. Scripture says that "wanting to justify himself," the man asked Jesus whom he should consider his neighbor. Jesus answered with the story of the Jewish man who was ambushed by thieves, beaten, and left for dead. In His parable, we see two prominent members of the Jewish religious system of that day happen upon the man in his state of distress and have absolutely no pity on him. They don't want to be bothered to help this downcast brother, and they avert their eyes and cross to the other side of the road. However, a despised Samaritan, someone the beleaguered man would have spit on, cursed, and shunned, comes across the man and helps him at not only great inconvenience, but also great personal expense. Jesus asked the "expert in the law" who the stranger's neighbor was: the two esteemed religious leaders, or the much hated Samaritan? The man replies that it was "the one who had mercy on him." Jesus responded with "Go and do likewise."

If Jesus' instructions to the Jewish people of His day were to love the people they literally hated, then why on earth would anyone think that His instructions to His Church in this day would be any different?

And who is the one group of people the overwhelming majority of the Evangelical Church is united in hating? Clearly it is the modern-day equivalent of the Samaritan people—the LGBTQ community. Incredibly, pastor after pastor has called for the death of all gays on social media. The Evangelical Church in America is beginning to look more like the Westboro Baptist Church than it does Jesus Christ.

The Church has missed the mark in so many areas, and it severely affects our ability to be effective witnesses for Jesus Christ when we espouse values that are diametrically opposed to those He taught in His ministry and in His Word.

The mainstream Evangelical Church has mistaken a man "used by God" for a man "of God." By calling Donald Trump a godly man and refusing to call him out on his immoral, ungodly behavior and giving him unconditional support, the Evangelical Church has done something they have never done in this country before: they have rendered unto Caesar what is God's alone—their undying love, devotion, and … dare I say it? … worship. The actions of the Evangelical Church in America echo the chant of the crowd as they marched Jesus up Calvary's hill, crying, "We have no king but Caesar!"

They've missed the mark by defiantly refusing to love the ones they consider to be the "least of these" when they are, in fact, the very ones Jesus Christ himself says we are to love in His name.

The mainstream Evangelical Church in America is under a spirit of stupor; if we don't break it off, we're going to miss the next great thing Holy Spirit is about to birth upon the earth, and we're going to go down in history as having been on the wrong side of the Gospel … again.

CHAPTER 13
Pro-Life vs. Pro-Birth

IT IS WITH great fear and trembling that I approach such a taboo subject and risk alienating literally every single person who reads this book. This is a subject that very few people take a passive stance on, with most everyone passionately espousing their viewpoint and being unwilling to concede even one modicum of credence to someone with an opposing opinion.

My intention here is to take a look at the issue without taking sides, to point out the hypocrisy of the conservative right while at the same time calling for a balance to both sides. Why do I feel it necessary to shine a light on what I perceive to be hypocrisy on the part of the religious right? Because this book is aimed at exposing anything that would stand in the way of Christians perceiving that the new move of God's Holy Spirit that is coming through the LGBTQ community is truly from Him. And in order to do that, old, wrong ways of thinking have to be broken. Born-again, Spirit-filled Christians on the left will have no trouble perceiving what's coming as being a divine move of God Almighty, as they have been praying for this for literally decades.

Although this could be dangerous ground, someone has to open an honest, compassionate dialogue on the subject of abortion, as it is a "wedge issue," both politically and spiritually. As my personal beliefs on the subject are completely inconsequential and would no doubt get me in trouble with both conservatives and liberals alike, I'll refrain from giving my own opinion and focus instead on how we got here, and what we should do about it.

Please keep in mind that the title of this section is "Pro-Life vs. Pro-Birth," and not "Pro-Life vs. Pro-Choice." I am purposely not addressing the life, health, and agency of the mother, or the dismissal of women in general, because this section is not about choice: it's about birth vs. life. My goal is not to change anyone's mind on this deeply emotional subject; it is to point out that there is a major disconnect within the ranks of conservative Christians when it comes to the welfare of unborn children versus that of children's welfare overall.

Google's online dictionary defines "wedge issue" as follows:

> A divisive political issue, especially one that is raised by a candidate for public office in hopes of attracting or alienating an opponent's supporters.

In researching for this section, I turned to my dear friend Kathy V. Baldock, as her research acumen is light years ahead of anyone I've ever known, both in terms of her ability to dig and find facts that others miss, and in her grasp of what she uncovers.

In her book, *Walking the Bridgeless Canyon* (pages 140–144) Kathy discloses how Jerry Falwell and his newly formed Moral Majority were hired by the GOP to drive conservative Christians to vote for their candidates. Not only was homosexuality purposely identified by the Moral Majority as a wedge issue to drive conservative voters towards the GOP, but abortion was added to the list of hot topics to draw Catholic voters into the fold. John F. Kennedy was considered a truly great president, and he was Catholic, and he was a Democrat. Up until the advent of the so-called Moral Majority, the overwhelming majority of Catholics still voted Democrat. Jerry Falwell, the leader of the Moral Majority, had an unquenchable lust for conservative votes; there was nothing he wouldn't do to get them, including finding ways to turn Catholic members of the Democratic Party to register as Republicans.

Falwell adopted the now infamous slogan, "Get 'em saved, get 'em baptized, get 'em registered."

Unfortunately, this falls short of Jesus' "Great Commission," which we read about in Matthew 28:16–20 (NIV):

> Then the eleven disciples went to Galilee, to the mountain where Jesus had told them to go. [17] When they saw him, they worshiped him, but some doubted. [18] Then Jesus came to them and said, "All authority in heaven and on earth has been given to me. [19] Therefore go and make disciples of all nations, baptizing them in the name of the Father and of the Son and of the Holy Spirit, [20] and teaching them to obey everything I have commanded you. And surely I am with you always, to the very end of the age."

Beyond doubt, Jesus never, never, *never* got caught up in politics! When the religious leaders of His day tried to bait Him with a question about paying taxes, hoping to get Him to answer in a way that would incense the Romans that occupied Jerusalem at the time, Jesus avoided it by telling them to give God what is God's, and to give Caesar what is Caesar's.

> **Matthew 22:17-22 (ESV)**
> Tell us, then, what you think. Is it lawful to pay taxes to Caesar, or not? [18] But Jesus, aware of their malice, said, "Why put me to the test, you hypocrites? [19] Show me the coin for the tax." And they brought him a denarius. [20] And Jesus said to them, "Whose likeness and inscription is this?" [21] They said, "Caesar's." Then he said to them, "Therefore render to Caesar the things that are Caesar's, and to God the things that are God's." [22] When they heard it, they marveled. And they left him and went away.

Following this principle, the forefathers of this amazing country we are so blessed to be able to call home, intentionally built into our Constitution the principle of separation of Church and State. And it wasn't just to protect the Church from the government; it was to protect the government from the Church—and for good reason. Our forefathers had seen firsthand what happens when there's no separation. Our country was originally settled by people who came over from England because they had had their fill of Church dictated by the government. The rest of Europe had governments dictated by the Church (Vatican). Neither of these approaches was the God-established precedent we see in scripture, where kings and priests both had their separate, but equally important, duties to both God and the people.

There was a time in history when the Church ran the Western world, and it was disastrous. Millions upon millions of souls were murdered, martyred if you will, in the name of Christianity. And if the trend we're seeing now continues, this Republicanization of Christianity, a second wave of people being put to death because they don't fit the stereotype of Christianity that the government is setting forth, may not be far behind.

This may seem far-fetched, but on social media we see article after article where this politician, or this church leader, is advocating death to members of the LGBTQ community. The roots of prejudice, bigotry, hatred, and antisemitism run deep in this country, and that's another thing our forty-fifth president was used by God to show us—just how ugly and vile the heart of America actually is.

Given this concern, let's turn our focus to abortion. Prior to the 1973 Supreme Court decision in Roe v. Wade, the Christian Church in America did not have any official position, nor did pastors speak publicly or preach about the issue. As Baldock says, it was not on anyone's radar. Abortion as a controversy was not initially introduced into the American political system as a moral or spiritual issue; it was introduced as a problem several years after legalization, to draw conservative voters away from Democratic candidates and embed them into the Republican Party. It was used to drive a wedge between Catholic voters and the Democratic Party. The problem with this is that when you take something that's intrinsically a medical and/or moral issue and make it political, you've already lost the real battle.

The United States government has never been capable of legislating morality, and it never will be. While I love my country, and there's no place on earth I'd rather live, I recognize that our government has done some pretty messed up things over the past two centuries.

Consider the decision made by top military leaders during our Colonial time to send smallpox-infected blankets to the indigenous people whose land we hand stolen and who were now fighting back (https://www.history.com/news/colonists-native-americans-smallpox-blankets).

Look at the Vietnam War, and the more recent United States invasion of Iraq. Neither of these wars had any motivating factors other than the US military-industrial complex making money and assuaging the fragile egos of weak, morally bankrupt presidents.

Moving forward, let's look at the present situation we find ourselves in. For the sake of this writing, I am remaining completely neutral on the subject, just as, in the recent past, journalists were required to be unbiased in their presentation of the facts. Thanks to our modern-day "every news agency has an agenda" culture, journalists seem to have lost sight of the ability to do this. I am not a journalist, but I am a man of God and a man of integrity who is striving to maintain that integrity.

On one hand, the religious right wants to make all abortions illegal again, and some states have even gone so far as to propose the death penalty for women who have abortions and for the doctors who perform them. So all babies are to be born, regardless of the circumstances, correct? On the other hand, we have Christian leaders like Pat Robertson and others telling Christian parents to disown their children if they come out to them as homosexual. Shocking, yet I've read these statements with my own eyes. And we have multiple so-called "Christian" parents in this country and others, radicalized by brazenly hateful church leaders and pastors such as this one in Arizona, who advocates murdering gays for an "AIDS-free Christmas" (https://www.patheos.com/blogs/progressivesecularhumanist/2014/12/arizona-pastor-wants-to-kill-the-gays-for-aids-free-christmas/). Others have stood trial for actually murdering their own children because they were gay or, in some cases, suspected of being gay. This is a massive disconnect! At what point does a life stop mattering?

We want all babies to be born because all lives have importance; that's understandable. But after they're born, we can throw them away if they don't meet our standards? Are all babies worthy of being saved or not? What if that baby grows up to be gay? What if it turns out to be lesbian, bisexual, or even transgender? By some evangelicals' logic, it would be OK to abort those babies. Surely there has to be a gray area here.

And what about babies born to women in poverty? Babies that weren't planned, weren't wanted, and can't be afforded? Shall they die of starvation or live in abject poverty? If all we're concerned about is the legality of abortion, then we miss the fact that if a society forces a woman to deliver every child she conceives, then that society has an obligation to help her, especially if she is struggling financially, to safely give birth and raise her children. Let me clarify, I am not talking about those rare occasions when people have as many children as possible to increase the amount of money they get from the government. I'm talking about being physically responsible to help raise a child that we required to be born. We have placed great value on the unborn child and very little on the child once it comes into the world, and none on the woman carrying it. There is a huge hypocrisy here, and I believe it breaks the Father's heart.

To see what I'm talking about, you need look no further than the five-thousand-plus migrant children being held in cages and denied proper nutrition and medical care by the same group of people preaching that all babies deserve to be born.

The scenario presented above is the Pro-Life vs. Pro-Birth argument. As a society that claims to be Christian, we cannot be myopic in placing our priority on getting a child born but then abandoning it afterwards. This is assuming, of course, that we do indeed want every child to be born. We have to look at the entire picture and act in the best interest of every child. As stated, this is a complex issue, and my personal views are complex.

Let's take a look at another scenario, assuming that most folks who oppose abortion for any reason do so out of love and compassion for the unborn child. We've discussed how the possibility of the child being LGBTQ or being poor and needing financial assistance should have no bearing on its worth. But what if a child is a minority? Should that baby be aborted? Of course not! God forbid! But what if it's a minority whose parents are caught trying to immigrate to our country illegally? As our system now stands, the so-called "Christian" leaders of our country would force the mother to have the baby and then take it away from her and put it in a cage in a detention center in another state, where it would most likely die, as hundreds of children have already done. Why does a three-month-old immigrant baby not have the same value as an unborn white baby that's still in the womb? Why is any child's life worth less this side of delivery?

If we're not willing to see the value of each and every stage of a child's life, if we're only concerned about the rights of the unborn and are willing to turn our backs on underprivileged, marginalized women and children, then we are pro-birth, not pro-life.

As mentioned at the beginning of this section, the reason I dare broach such a volatile topic is because I'm trying to open an honest, compassionate dialogue about an area where I believe the Church has missed the mark. And that's important because there's a new move of God's Holy Spirit coming to the LGBTQ community that the majority of folks are going to miss because they're so caught up in the enemy's divisiveness.

CHAPTER 14
Methinks the Lady Doth Protest Too Much: A Study of Homophobic Men

AS SOMEONE WHO was bullied mercilessly as a child and teen, I've thought a lot about the roots of homophobia and how to address them so that all people are respected and treated equally. I'm not including this topic as any sort of revenge but because it's imperative that we know where things are coming from so that we can properly discern what to do with them. Remember that scripture has a bearing on the question of where homophobia is coming from:

> **Luke 6:45 (ESV)**
> The good person out of the good treasure of his heart produces good, and the evil person out of his evil treasure produces evil, for out of the abundance of the heart his mouth speaks.

In this chapter, we'll look at how all the nastiness that spews out of some men's mouths is actually a distraction to keep others from seeing what's really hiding in their hearts, behind that vile rhetoric. We'll explore some recent scientific studies that may give us a glimpse into what's really going on inside the hearts and minds of some of the most vocal opponents of the LGBTQ community.

Back in 1996, University of Georgia psychologists reported an intriguing and controversial finding: heterosexual young men with homophobic beliefs were aroused by gay porn, while their non-homophobic straight peers were not.

> "Since the study was published, it has been touted in some circles as proof that many homophobic men are in fact secretly gay themselves."—Ross Pomeroy Real Clear Science Blog "Are Homophobic Men Turned on by Gay Porn?"
>
> "The point is that these men already have this arousal naturally, but that they block it because they do not see it as socially acceptable," Dr. Nathan Heflick, a Senior Lecturer in the School of Psychology at the University of Lincoln, wrote on the study. "So they form extra strong anti-gay attitudes as a means of appearing heterosexual to others, and perhaps trying to convince themselves they are entirely heterosexual."

This study used electrodes attached to the penises of a group of college students to determine arousal to different sexual stimuli. Here is the U.S. National Library of Medicine National Institutes of Health's synopsis of the study, courtesy of the U. S. National Library of Medicine:

> **Is Homophobia Associated with Homosexual Arousal?**
>
> Department of Psychology, University of Georgia, Athens 30602-3013, USA:
>
> The authors investigated the role of homosexual arousal in exclusively heterosexual men who admitted negative affect toward homosexual individuals. Participants consisted of a group of homophobic men (n = 35) and a group of non-homophobic men (n = 29); they were assigned to groups on the basis of their scores on the Index of Homophobia (W. W. Hudson & W. A. Ricketts, 1980). The men were exposed to sexually explicit erotic stimuli consisting of heterosexual, male homosexual, and lesbian videotapes, and changes in penile circumference were monitored. They also completed an Aggression Questionnaire (A. H. Buss & M. Perry, 1992). Both groups exhibited increases in penile circumference to the heterosexual and female homosexual videos. Only

the homophobic men showed an increase in penile erection to male homosexual stimuli. The groups did not differ in aggression. Homophobia is apparently associated with homosexual arousal that the homophobic individual is either unaware of or denies.

Although this study included a limited number of participants and has been highly criticized by conservatives, it's notable that *all* the men in the homophobic group were sexually aroused by images of gay sex, while *none* of the non-homophobic men were. It would appear that openly spewing homophobic rhetoric may be hiding a truth these men aren't willing to admit.

A more recent series of studies published in the prestigious *Journal of Personality and Social Psychology* found higher levels of homophobia in individuals with unacknowledged attractions to the same sex, particularly when they grew up with authoritarian parents who also held homophobic attitudes. In other words, guys who grew up in families where admitting they were sexually attracted to other men was not an option tend to act out in antisocial ways towards the very group of people they secretly identify with. In a *Psychology Today article* by Brian Mustanski, PhD, an associate professor at Northwestern University, Dr. Mustanski graciously gives a link to the synopsis of the studies titled "Is Some Homophobia Self-phobia?" published by the University of Rochester. The UR was the lead in the studies that were conducted in tandem with the University of Essex, England, and The University of California, Santa Barbara.

The following is the overview of the studies as it appeared in *Psychology Today,* also courtesy of the National Library of Medicine, while the UR synopsis in its entirety can be found at http://www.rochester.edu/news/show.php?id=4040.

Are Homophobic People Really Gay and Not Accepting It?

Study finds homophobia linked to unacknowledged attractions to the same sex.

A series of studies recently published in the prestigious *Journal of Personality and Social Psychology* found higher levels of homophobia in individuals with unacknowledged attractions to the same sex, particularly when they grew up with authoritarian parents who also held homophobic attitudes. In the university press release, Netta Weinstein, the study's lead author said, "Individuals who identify as straight but in psychological tests show a strong attraction to the same sex may be threatened by gays and lesbians because homosexuals remind them of similar tendencies within themselves." In the same release, study co-author Richard Ryan added, "In many cases these are people who are at war with themselves and they are turning this internal conflict outward."

Attitudes towards gay and lesbian people are an important part of current political issues like the legality of same-sex marriage and employment nondiscrimination. Yet little scientific research has been done on what drives such anti-gay attitudes.

According to the team of researchers, this study is the first to document the role that both parenting and sexual orientation play in the formation of anti-gay attitudes, including self-reported homophobic attitudes, discriminatory bias, implicit hostility towards gays, and endorsement of anti-gay policies. One prior study used genital measures of sexual attractions and found that homophobic men showed an increase in penile erections to male homosexual male erotica.

What was the study design?

As is typical of papers in this journal, the article includes multiple separate experiments. The experiments were conducted in the United States and Germany, with each study involving an average of 160 college students.

The study focused on measuring participants' explicit and implicit sexual attractions. Explicit attractions are those we are consciously aware of and can provide in a questionnaire. Implicit attractions are those that are more subconscious and may not be detected in a questionnaire and instead are measured using psychological tasks. To explore participants' explicit and implicit sexual attraction, the researchers measured the differences between what people say about their sexual orientation and how they react during a split-second timed task. Students were shown words and pictures on a computer screen and asked to put these in "gay" or "straight" categories. Before each of the 50 trials, participants were subliminally primed with either the word "me" or "others" flashed on the screen for 35 milliseconds, which is too quick to even be consciously perceptible to the participants. They were then shown the words "gay," "straight," "homosexual," and "heterosexual" as well as pictures of straight and gay couples, and the computer tracked precisely their response times. A faster association of "me" with "gay" and a slower association of "me" with "straight" was taken to indicate an implicit gay orientation.

Finally, the researcher measured participants' level of homophobia—both overt, as expressed in questionnaires on social policy and beliefs, and implicit, as revealed in word-completion tasks. For the implicit measure, students wrote down the first three words that came to mind, for example for the prompt "k i _ _". The study tracked the increase in the amount of aggressive words elicited after showing participants the word "gay" for 35 milliseconds.

In these experiments, participants who reported themselves to be more heterosexual than their performance on the reaction time task indicated were most likely to react with hostility towards gay people. In other words, if a participant identified as heterosexual, but showed a reaction pattern consistent with homosexuality, they were more likely to express homophobic attitudes. This incongruence between implicit and explicit measures of sexual orientation predicted a variety of homophobic behaviors, including self-reported anti-gay attitudes, implicit hostility towards gays, endorsement of anti-gay policies, and discriminatory bias such as the assignment of harsher punishments for homosexuals.

This series of studies utilized much more sophisticated psychological methods than simple electrodes attached to young men's penises and had a much larger test group. But the concluding results were the same: men who are overtly homophobic show undeniable signs of same-sex attraction.

In the old days, we referred to these guys as "self-loathing homosexuals," and that's exactly what they are: men who hate who they really are inside and use their vitriolic rhetoric as a smoke screen. Recently, this phenomenon has become so commonplace that the World Health Organization has given it a name: ego-dystonic. They labeled it as not only a sexual orientation but also a mental disorder.

From Wikipedia:

> "Ego-dystonic sexual orientation is an ego-dystonic mental disorder characterized by having a sexual orientation or an attraction that is at odds with one's idealized self-image, causing anxiety and a desire to change one's orientation or become more comfortable with one's sexual orientation. It describes not innate sexual orientation itself, but a conflict between the sexual orientation one wishes to have and the sexual orientation one actually possesses."

There have been many cases in which conservative, "family values" politicians with strong records of voting against legislation benefiting members of the LGBTQ community, and evangelical pastors/Church leaders who have taken a very public stand against gay rights or same-sex marriage, have been exposed for having sexual affairs with other men themselves.

Below is a list of "family values" politicians who got caught on their knees doing something more than praying for their LGBTQ constituents:

> **Jon Hinson.** In 1981, arrested again for performing oral sex on a young clerk in a House of Representatives bathroom. He was charged with sodomy.
>
> **Troy King,** former Alabama Attorney General, railed against homosexuality, calling it "the downfall of society" in a 1992 op-ed about a college LGBTQ group. "The existence of the Gay-Lesbian Alliance on this campus is an affront to the state of Alabama, its citizenry, this university and its students." So it was a bit embarrassing when, in 2008, it was reported he was caught by his wife in bed with a male aide.
>
> **Roy Asburn, a** California State Senator, voted against every piece of LGBTQ rights legislation that ever crossed his desk. Then,

on March 3, 2010, he was pulled over for drunk driving while leaving a popular Sacramento gay club with another man in his car. The arrest sparked nationwide speculation about his sexuality and the hypocrisy of his voting record. Later that same year, Ashburn came out as gay in a radio interview.

Richard Curtis. Washington State Representative Curtis voted against same-sex domestic partnerships and against an anti-discrimination law protecting gay people. But he was eventually outed by a male escort who had been blackmailing him and threatening to tell his wife about their trysts.

Ed Schrock. From 2001 to 2005, Schrock served as U.S. Representative for Virginia's Second Congressional District and stood 100 percent against gay rights. He dropped plans for reelection, though, when a tape of him soliciting sex with men on a gay chat line surfaced.

Jim Kolbe. After Kolbe voted in favor of the Defense of Marriage Act, LGBTQ advocates threatened to out him and others, placing a full-page ad in *the Washington Blade* calling on closeted congressmen to "end your silence and defend your community." Kolbe subsequently came out.

Ralph Shortey, an Oklahoma state senator (R-Oklahoma City) was an early supporter of Donald Trump and served as a coordinator for his campaign in Oklahoma. In March 2017, Shortey, who is married, was caught in a motel room with a seventeen-year-old boy to whom he had offered money for sex.

Wes Goodman, (R-Cardington) resigned from the Ohio House of Representatives in November 2017 after allegations surfaced that he had sex with another man in his office. He was a married, "family values" Republican, who had previous claimed "healthy, vibrant, thriving, values-driven families are the source of Ohio's proud history."

And the list goes on—more than a dozen others, but the point has been made—and this is only the politicians! There are countless pastors and other church leaders, all cut from the same cloth, all passionately espousing an anti-LBGTQ doctrine that diametrically opposes their personal lives.

So the next time you hear a pastor or politician violently defending his hatred for the LGBTQ community, and his personal belief that we should reinstate the death penalty for these "perverts," remember: he's quite possibly the next one to be caught in a men's room or a cheap hotel room with another man—or even an underage boy.

CHAPTER 15
The Dangers of Reparative Therapy, #NotChanged

AS WE CONTINUE examining deadly discrepancies in Christian thought, let's take a look at some statistics and studies concerning the ability of a person to change their sexual orientation, and the inaccurate Christian view that this is a choice, a lifestyle, or a sin. Sexual orientation is a fundamental attraction; it's the way a person is wired.

Before we get into actual statistics and studies, let's dispel this whole "choice" myth. One of the things that non-affirming Christians cling to is their belief that being LGBTQ is actually a choice one makes. The second one is that God "chooses" to turn some folks straight, but not others. We need to address these two erroneous arguments using logic and the Word of God, because they are not only absurd but they are actively damaging the Church, as well as those targeted by these false beliefs.

Rather than taking a hardline biblical stance on everything we've discussed so far, let's switch things up a bit and take a look at the issue of it being a person's choice from a standpoint of logic. Recall the deadly statistics on teen suicide rates among LGBTQ youth. It is hideous and grotesque beyond words that so-called "Christian" parents would reject their kids and drive them to the point of taking their own lives over the rejection of their sexual orientation. If sexual orientation is a matter of choice, why in the world are tens of thousands of teenagers choosing something that literally leads them to take their own lives out of desperation? Why not just choose to be straight? Surely if one can choose to be gay, one can choose to be straight, right?

Let's look again at the statistics behind this heartbreaking situation:

1. 40 percent of homeless youth are LGBTQ— https://truecolorsunited.org/our-issue/?gclid=Cj0KCQj w4s7qBRCzARIsAImcAxZlRyJIgnx80rVgjsVlPaKsS4ZF-6wETnpQaOMKF8xfyVXgBBL6NYr0aAlEOEALw_wcB.

2. Suicide is the second leading cause of death among young people ages ten to twenty-four—CDC, NCIPC. Web-based Injury Statistics Query and Reporting System (WISQARS) [online]. (2010) {2013 Aug. 1}. Available from:www.cdc.gov/ncipc/wisqars.

3. LGBTQ youth seriously contemplate suicide at almost three times the rate of heterosexual youth, and LGBTQ youth are almost five times as likely to have attempted suicide compared to heterosexual youth—CDC. (2016). Sexual Identity, Sex of Sexual Contacts, and Health-Risk Behaviors Among Students in Grades 9-12: Youth Risk Behavior Surveillance. Atlanta, GA: U.S. Department of Health and Human Services.

4. LGBTQ youth who come from highly rejecting families are 8.4 times as likely to have attempted suicide as LGBTQ peers who reported no or low levels of family rejection. Family Acceptance Project™ (2009). Family rejection as a predictor of negative health outcomes in white and Latino lesbian, gay, and bisexual young adults. Pediatrics. 123(1), 346–52.

In reviewing these statistics, does it make any logical sense whatsoever that someone would choose to be rejected by everyone they love and end up on the streets, going through unspeakable abuse and horrors, only to end up attempting or completing suicide? Even the most ardent believer in the "it's a choice" faction must see that this is unreasonable. And if we don't buy the lie of it being a "choice" when it comes to teenagers, why would we believe it would be any different for an adult?

My prayer is that you'll take some time and ruminate on the statistics I've presented and seek the wisdom of God's Holy Spirit on the matter. The lunacy of telling people that they are choosing something that is causing them to want to die has got to stop. And what's worse is that we're telling folks that God's Word backs this insanity.

Before we get into scientific findings on attempts to change one's sexual orientation, let's examine the theory that God chooses to "heal" some people's sexual orientation and not others. It doesn't matter if you use the word "cure," change," deliver," "heal," or some other Christianized jargon, this teaching that a person's orientation can change is not biblical, nor is it supported by any facts.

To start, let's ponder several verses from both the Old and New Testament, paying particular attention to the common thread throughout: that God is no respecter of persons. He does not show partiality; what He does for one He'll do for another.

As you read these verses, keep in mind that some of them are referencing salvation, but as you'll see, they are clear in their message that God refuses to "play favorites" in any situation. Let's start in the Old Testament and work our way forward.

> **2 Chronicles 19:7 (ESV)**
> Now then, let the fear of the Lord be upon you. Be careful what you do, for there is no injustice with the Lord our God, or partiality or taking bribes.
>
> **Job 34:19 (NKJV)**
> Yet He is not partial to princes, nor does He regard the rich more than the poor; for they are all the work of His hands.
>
> **Romans 2:10-11 (NKJV)**
> Glory, honor, and peace to everyone who works what is good, to the Jew first and also to the Greek. [11] For there is no partiality with God.
>
> **1 Peter 1:17 (NKJV)**
> And if you call on the Father, who without partiality judges according to each one's work, conduct yourselves throughout the time of your stay here in fear.

> **Acts 10:34 (NKJV)**
> Then Peter opened his mouth and said: "In truth I perceive that God shows no partiality."

These five verses pass the litmus test we established, that a precept has to be repeated more than once in scripture for us to be able to consider it doctrine. God does not change some people and not others. That would be showing partiality, and we've just read in five different places in scripture that He doesn't do that.

And remember, there's a difference between doctrine and dogma. Google's online dictionary defines the two as follows:

> dog·ma
> /ˈdôgmə/
> noun
> A principle or set of principles laid down by an authority as incontrovertibly true.
>
> doc·trine
> /ˈdäktrən/
> noun
> A belief or set of beliefs held and taught by a Church, political party, or other group.

I absolutely believe that the basic aspects of our faith should be taught as dogma: the virgin birth and sinless life of Jesus Christ, His redemptive work on Calvary, His physical death and resurrection on the third day, and the infilling of Holy Spirit. I think the Church has gotten herself into a lot of trouble over the past two millennia for making things that should have been left as doctrine, a set of beliefs, into dogma, a set of principles laid down by an authority as "incontrovertibly true."

As stated at the beginning of this chapter, one of the problems members of the religious right have in accepting LGBTQ people is that they think that these people *chose* to be gay, or lesbian, etc., and/or they think that God can change them. The big problem with that second non-biblical belief is that believers always put the onus on the person who has *not* been changed, as if it's their fault for not changing.

I spent years hating myself because I couldn't figure out what was wrong with me, and why God wouldn't change me, while He was changing all those guys and gals on the Exodus International conversion therapy posters. I was told I didn't pray hard enough, I didn't want it bad enough, I didn't love Jesus enough; I was blamed for my shortcomings, for the reasons I was still attracted to men—even though I had an amazing marriage, a loving wife, and three beautiful kids! All this was because of me. God "wanted" to change me, but ... *I* was apparently somehow blocking Him.

I won't go into great detail here about my journey, which I chronicle in my next book, *Called, Chosen, and Gay,* but what I will share is that this damnable teaching sent me to the hospital with four separate suicide attempts and a complete mental breakdown.

If wanting to be straight was all it took, I would have definitely been one of the ones that God chose to change. I wanted it so badly that I would have rather been dead than gay, and my stays in psychiatric wards in Tucson, San Diego, and Palm Desert were undeniable proof of it.

Now that we've looked at the difference between dangerous teaching and the reality that LGBTQ people do not choose their sexual orientation or gender identity, now that we've seen that God does not play favorites and does not choose to change people's sexual orientation, let's take a look at the faulty theology that says that being LGBTQ is a sin!

Nowhere does scripture ever tell us that being attracted to, or even making love to another person of the same sex, is a sin. What scripture does tell us, repeatedly, is that any sexual relations between two people who are not in a covenant relationship between themselves and God is a sin. Straight, gay, lesbian, it doesn't matter; it's a sin according to God's laws. And the Church has got to realize that beating a non-Christian over the head with the laws of a God they don't know is futile. What would happen if the Church just loved people into the Kingdom, and let God worry about what was sin and what wasn't?

I think one reason Christians feel compelled to place the blame squarely on the backs of those who haven't changed their orientation is that they know the verses and concepts I've outlined above: God does not show partiality; therefore, they fall into their own trap when they tell someone that God can change their orientation. And for the record, He can. He can do anything; He's Sovereign. But I have never seen an honest case of it yet. I can't tell you how many people I know who once claimed the "changed" label, "in Jesus Name," who have since conceded that they retain their original orientation—and now they want nothing to do with the Church. Or, if they're still active in their walk with Jesus, it's with a same-sex partner by their side.

Why am I so sure that God doesn't play favorites by changing some people but not others? Again, this is another place the religious right shoots themselves in the foot. If just being LGBTQ, whether you act on your desires or not, is a sin, then God would be sentencing innocent folks to hell by refusing to change them. And we've already seen in multiple scriptures that He is no respecter of persons.

I've had folks ask me, "Well, what about healing? God heals some people but not others." That's absolutely true. Again, He's Sovereign. He chooses who, what, when, where, and why. And sometimes our faith does play a part in the healing process, but God not healing a person doesn't send them to hell!

If being LGBTQ is a sin that sends a person to hell, as the non-affirming, religious right tell the LGBTQ community it does, then God is damming people by playing favorites and changing some, but not all.

Here is a simple reminder from the mouth of Jesus himself:

> **John 3:16-17 (KJV)**
> For God so loved the world that he gave his only begotten Son, that whosoever believeth in him should not perish, but have everlasting life. [17] For God sent not his Son into the world to condemn the world, but that the world through him might be saved.

I know there are some who get touchy when someone says "Scripture is clear" on this or that. Some passages aren't clear and need to be studied with the help of Holy Spirit to discern what God is saying, but other passages, like the one above, are indeed very clear. Whosoever: no requirements other than believing, and later we read "confessing with our mouth" is also prerequisite:

> **Romans 10:9 (NKJV)**
> If you confess with your mouth the Lord Jesus and believe in your heart that God has raised Him from the dead, you will be saved.

Nowhere do we read anything about being disqualified because of whom you love or are attracted to. Nowhere do we read of a requirement for any person to change, or to allow God to change them, before they can become His child. Nowhere. Church, stop telling people things that God never said!

Turning to the scientific portion of this section, let's take a look at studies and statistics compiled by professional researchers in the field of conversion therapy. The first study was done in in 2001 by psychiatry giant Dr. Robert Spitzer, a major architect of the modern classification of mental disorders. His study was immediately hailed by ex-gay groups as a major boon to their doctrine of change. Although the study was later discredited and disavowed by its own author, "Christian," anti-LGBTQ groups continue to hail it to this day as proof that people can and do change sexual orientations.

Here is an excerpt from the *New York Times*, published May 18, 2012, that describes Dr. Spitzer's study, reprinted under PARS International license #000090772. The entire article can be read at https://www.nytimes.com/2012/05/19/health/dr-robert-l-spitzer-noted-psychiatrist-apologizes-for-study-on-gay-cure.html.

> He recruited 200 men and women, from the centers that were performing the therapy, including Exodus International, based in Florida, and NARTH (National Association for Research and Therapy of Homosexuality). He interviewed each in depth over the phone, asking about their sexual urges, feelings and behaviors before and after having the therapy, rating the answers on a scale. He then compared the scores on this questionnaire, before and after therapy. "The majority of participants gave reports of change from a predominantly or exclusively homosexual orientation before therapy to a predominantly or exclusively heterosexual orientation in the past year," his paper concluded.

The study — presented at a psychiatry meeting in 2001, before publication — immediately created a sensation, and ex-gay groups seized on it as solid evidence for their case. This was Dr. Spitzer, after all, the man who single-handedly removed homosexuality from the manual of mental disorders. No one could accuse him of bias.

But gay leaders accused him of betrayal, and they had their reasons. The study had serious problems. It was based on what people remembered feeling years before — an often fuzzy record. It included some ex-gay advocates, who were politically active. And it did not test any particular therapy; only half of the participants engaged with a therapist at all, while the others worked with pastoral counselors, or in independent Bible study.

Several colleagues tried to stop the study in its tracks, and urged him not to publish it, Dr. Spitzer said. Yet, heavily invested after all the work, he turned to a friend and former collaborator, Dr. Kenneth J. Zucker, psychologist in chief at the Center for Addiction and Mental Health in Toronto and editor of the *Archives of Sexual Behavior,* another influential journal. "I knew Bob and the quality of his work, and I agreed to publish it," Dr. Zucker said in an interview last week. The paper did not go through the usual peer-review process, in which unnamed experts critique a manuscript before publication. "But I told him I would do it only if I also published commentaries of response from other scientists to accompany the study," Dr. Zucker said.

Those commentaries, with a few exceptions, were merciless. One cited the Nuremberg Code of ethics to denounce the study as not only flawed but morally wrong. "We fear the repercussions of this study, including an increase in suffering, prejudice, and discrimination," concluded a group of 15 researchers at the New York State Psychiatric Institute, where Dr. Spitzer was affiliated.

Dr. Spitzer in no way implied in the study that being gay was a choice, or that it was possible for anyone who wanted to change to do so in therapy. But that didn't stop socially conservative groups from citing the paper in support of just those points, according to Wayne Besen, executive director of Truth Wins Out, a nonprofit group that fights antigay bias. On one occasion, a politician in Finland held up the study in Parliament to argue against civil unions, according to Dr. Drescher.

It needs to be said that when this study was misused for political purposes to say that gays should be cured — as it was, many times — Bob responded immediately, to correct misperceptions," said Dr. Drescher, who is gay. But Dr. Spitzer could not control how his study was interpreted by everyone, and he could not erase the biggest scientific flaw of them all, roundly attacked in many of the commentaries: Simply asking people whether they have changed is no evidence at all of real change. People lie, to themselves and others. They continually change their stories, to suit their needs and moods.

By almost any measure, in short, the study failed the test of scientific rigor that Dr. Spitzer himself was so instrumental in enforcing for so many years. "As I read these commentaries, I knew this was a problem, a big problem, and one I couldn't answer," Dr. Spitzer said. "How do you know someone has really changed?"

Letting Go

It took 11 years for him to admit it publicly. At first he clung to the idea that the study was exploratory, an attempt to prompt scientists to think twice about dismissing the therapy outright. Then he took refuge in the position that the study was focused less on the effectiveness of the therapy and more on how people engaging in it described changes in sexual orientation. "Not a very interesting question," he said. "But for a long time I thought maybe I wouldn't have to face the bigger problem, about measuring change."

After retiring in 2003, he remained active on many fronts, but the reparative study remained a staple of the culture wars and a personal regret that wouldn't leave him be. The Parkinson's symptoms have worsened in the past year, exhausting him mentally as well as physically, making it still harder to fight back pangs of remorse. And one day in March, Dr. Spitzer entertained a visitor. Gabriel Arana, a journalist at the magazine *The American Prospect,* interviewed Dr. Spitzer about the reparative therapy study. This was not just any interview; Mr. Arana went through reparative therapy himself as a teenager, and his therapist had recruited the young man for Dr. Spitzer's study (Mr. Arana did not participate).

"I asked him about all his critics, and he just came out and said, 'I think they're largely correct,'" said Mr. Arana, who wrote about his own experience last month. Mr. Arana said that reparative therapy ultimately delayed his self-acceptance as a gay man and induced thoughts of suicide. "But at the time I was recruited for the Spitzer study, I was referred as a success story. I would have said I was making progress."

That did it. The study that seemed at the time a mere footnote to a large life was growing into a chapter. And it needed a proper ending—a strong correction, directly from its author, not a journalist or colleague. A draft of the letter has already leaked online and has been reported.

"You know, it's the only regret I have; the only professional one," Dr. Spitzer said of the study, near the end of a long interview. "And I think, in the history of psychiatry, I don't know that I've ever seen a scientist write a letter saying that the data were all there but were totally misinterpreted. Who admitted that and who apologized to his readers." He looked away and back again, his big eyes blurring with emotion. "That's something, don't you think?"

This researcher made the mistake of asking research subjects whether they had changed, without validating or in any way confirming actual change. Because he had invested so much time and effort, he decided to publish his findings anyway, and was criticized immediately for his incomplete methods as well as the conclusions that others would draw. Sadly, drawing conclusions and perpetuating incomplete data have led to decades of decisions and opinions based on false information, and decades of pain and grief for those most affected by this study.

It's a sad day when Christians present something as "proof" that they know to be false, or at least should know if they've done their due diligence. It was one thing to jump on the pro-conversion bandwagon when the study first came out, even though all the commentaries published along with the study were negative and denounced it. But it's totally another to continue to espouse something that the very author denounced and apologized for ever writing. It's both deplorable and pathetic. Jesus doesn't need us to lie for Him.

Let's look at the second major study, completed in 2009, which can be found on the prestigious University of California, Davis - Psychology Department website at: https://psychology.ucdavis.edu/rainbow/html/facts_changing.html.

In corresponding with Dr. Gregory Herek, PhD, professor emeritus of UC Davis, he recommended I credit the Task Force directly for this contribution at http://www.apa.org/pi/lgbc/publications/therapeutic-response.pdf

> In response to recent public debates about interventions intended to change individuals' sexual orientation, the American Psychological Association created a Task Force on Appropriate Therapeutic Responses to Sexual Orientation which reviewed the relevant research literature.
>
> In 2009, the Task Force reported that it found "serious methodological problems in this area of research, such that only a few studies met the minimal standards for evaluating whether psychological treatments, such as efforts to change sexual orientation, are effective" (p. 2).
>
> Based on its review of the studies that met these standards, the Task Force concluded that "Enduring change to an individual's sexual orientation is uncommon. The participants in this body of research continued to experience same-sex attractions following SOCE [sexual orientation change efforts] and did not report significant change to other-sex attractions that could be

empirically validated, though some showed lessened physiological arousal to all sexual stimuli. Compelling evidence of decreased same-sex sexual behavior and of engagement in sexual behavior with the other sex was rare. Few studies provided strong evidence that any changes produced in laboratory conditions translated to daily life. Thus, the results of scientifically valid research indicate that it is unlikely that individuals will be able to reduce same-sex attractions or increase other-sex sexual attractions through SOCE" (pp. 2-3).

In addition, the Task Force found evidence to indicate that some individuals experienced harm or believed they had been harmed by these interventions. The Task Force report provides a detailed discussion of this topic and an extensive review of relevant research.

In response to the Task Force report, the APA passed a 2009 resolution that stated, in part, "the American Psychological Association concludes that there is insufficient evidence to support the use of psychological interventions to change sexual orientation" and "the American Psychological Association concludes that the benefits reported by participants in sexual orientation change efforts can be gained through approaches that do not attempt to change sexual orientation.

The article goes on to talk about "ex-gays," NARTH, and the Exodus programs before addressing the issue of reparative therapy:

Reparative Therapy.

The mass media and the Web are filled with claims these days from religious conservatives, orthodox psychoanalysts, anti-gay organizations, and even a professional football player claiming that people with a homosexual orientation not only *can* become heterosexual, but also should do so.

However, claims by the Family Research Council, Charles Socarides, Joseph Nicolosi, and others of "successful" conversions through reparative therapy are filled with methodological ambiguities and questionable results (for reviews, see Haldeman, 1991, 1994; see also Haldeman's 1999 review paper is available on the web in HTML and Adobe Acrobat (PDF) format). They are also ethically suspect. [Bibliographic references are on a different web page]

In many of these behavior-change techniques, "success" has been defined as suppression of homoerotic response or mere display of physiological ability to engage in heterosexual intercourse. Neither outcome is the same as adopting the complex set of attractions and feelings that constitute sexual orientation.

Many interventions aimed at changing sexual orientation have succeeded only in reducing or eliminating homosexual behavior rather than in creating or increasing heterosexual attractions. They have, in effect, deprived individuals of their capacity for sexual response to others. These "therapies" have often exposed their victims to electric shocks or nausea-producing drugs while showing them pictures of same-sex nudes (such techniques appear to be less common today than in the past).

Another problem in many published reports of "successful" conversion therapies is that the participants' initial sexual orientation was never adequately assessed. Many bisexuals have been mislabeled as homosexuals with the consequence that the "successes" reported for the conversions actually have occurred among bisexuals who were highly motivated to adopt a heterosexual behavior pattern. The extent to which people have actually changed their behavior—even within the confines of these inadequate operational definitions—often has not been systematically assessed. Instead, only self-reports of patients or therapists' subjective impressions have been available. More rigorous objective assessments (e.g., behavioral indicators over an extended period of time) have been lacking (Coleman, 1982; Haldeman, 1991, 1994; Martin, 1984).

Some psychoanalysts claim to have conducted empirical research demonstrating that their "therapies" are able to change gay people

> into heterosexuals. Their studies have multiple flaws, including a lack of safeguards against bias and a lack of control groups. Rather than having patients evaluated by an independent third party who is unaware of which patients received the "reparative therapy," these studies are simply compilations of self-reports from psychoanalysts who are attempting to change their patients' sexual orientation (and who are highly motivated to report "success").
>
> And even if we accept these studies' claim that change has occurred, they do not provide any evidence that such change resulted from a particular therapy. Individuals who changed might well have done so anyway, even without therapy."

In summary, there is no evidence that sexual orientation can be changed, and no evidence that reparative therapy does anything to create desire for the opposite sex. It's time for the Church of Jesus Christ to let go of myths and beliefs the Bible doesn't back up, and science not only can't confirm but, in reality, has proven to be false. Science and scripture are not in conflict with each other, as so many of our evangelical leaders would have you believe.

In fact, believing science does not make you anti-Christian; in my research on scientists who were also Christians, I found statistics that blew me away; they can be viewed at: https://en.wikipedia.org/wiki/List_of_Christians_in_science_and_technology.

In the past 900 years, over 160 scientists with major achievements to their credit were also born-again Christians, many of them using science to prove the Bible. As if that weren't enough, there are living among us today, 117 Christian scientists whose fields of expertise range from biology and biomedical sciences to chemistry, physics, astronomy, and earth sciences. Clearly, science and scripture are not at war with each other.

To recap, the entire purpose of this chapter, and the book overall, is to prepare you for a massive new move of God's Holy Spirit that is about to hit this country like a tsunami, and that move is coming through the LGBTQ community. In the next section, we'll get to how it's coming, but I want you to see the areas where the mainstream Church is missing God in the season we presently find ourselves in. The reason this is so important is because if we can't see where we've missed the mark now, we're never going to repent, and lack of repentance will lead to us missing this new move altogether. The easiest way to miss what Holy Spirit is doing is to dismiss it as not being of Him.

Earlier, we reviewed the last three major moves of Holy Spirit the Church dismissed as being "not of God" and missed out on until the moves were almost over. Azusa Street, the Great Charismatic Renewal, and the Jesus People were all disparaged by the mainstream Church in America, who wanted nothing to do with what they condemned as "apostasy" because it didn't look like what they thought a move of God should look like. We didn't even go into the Great Healing Revival that took place in the late 1940s and 1950s, where tens of millions of people were saved as a result of the healings they saw at the hands of men of God like A.A. Allen, Jack Coe, John G. Lake, and others. But once again, the mainstream Church wanted no part of these so-called faith-healers and labeled them as charlatans. The Church has literally fought against every major move of God's divine Holy Spirit because they've dismissed these moves as heretical to their beliefs. Be aware: if we dismiss it, we'll miss it.

In this day and age, Christianity and politics have become intertwined to such a degree that to some folks they're interchangeable, and this is complete heresy. Yehovah God is not a Republican, and He's not a Democrat either. He's the Sovereign King of the Universe. Our eyes have to be fixed on the person of Jesus Christ himself, not a political candidate, a party, or a system if we're going to navigate the raging seas of this twenty-first-century, religio-political environment. Loyalty to anyone or anything before our Lord and Savior is treason and must be treated as such.

We cannot allow ourselves to fall into the trap that was set when professional politicians hired a so-called "man of God" to devise a way to divide our country along party lines by turning a moral issue into a political "wedge" issue.

We can't allow the screams of homophobic men who are condemning an entire group of people to hell to drown out the cry of the Father's heart for salvation and restoration for all of His children.

And we can't believe the lies that tell us people choose to be straight, gay, lesbian, bisexual, or transgender. Not a single man or woman alive has ever woken up one morning and said, "Gee, I think I want to be gay" or "I think I want to be straight," and was able, by his/her own will, to change the way they are sexually "wired." It doesn't work that way. If you're reading this and you're heterosexual, you know beyond a shadow of a doubt that it wasn't a choice you made; it's who God made you.

We have got to stop trying to fix people who aren't broken. Let's focus on telling them how much God loves them—enough to send His one and only Son to die for them, just as they are, and let God worry about everything else.

These are all areas where the mainstream Church has missed the mark. Our focus on politics and people's sexual orientation, and whether God changes them or not, has not drawn one single person closer to Jesus Christ, but it has driven lost and dying souls away from Him by the hundreds of thousands, possibly millions.

The Church of Jesus Christ in America is asleep, deluded by a spirit of stupor, and my admonition to her today is the same as the Apostle Paul spoke to the first-century church at Ephesus:

> **Ephesians 5:14 KJV**
> Awake, O sleeper, and arise from the dead, and Christ will shine on you.

CHAPTER 16
Like Israel, the Church Plays the Harlot, and Makes God Jealous

THE BIBLE IS a beautiful literary work spoken into existence by the inspiration of Holy Spirit, and it's filled with historical accounts of ancient battles, poetry, and symbolism. Some of the most exquisite literary devices found in scripture are in its use of metaphors and allegories to convey God's love and compassion towards His creation. We'll be looking at biblical metaphors and allegories; here's a brief definition of each word taken from Google's online dictionary:

> met·a·phor
> noun
> A figure of speech in which a word or phrase is applied to an object or action to which it is not literally applicable. A thing regarded as representative or symbolic of something else, especially something abstract.
>
> al·le·go·ry
> noun
> A story, poem, or picture that can be interpreted to reveal a hidden meaning, typically a moral or political one.

Without a doubt, the most famous metaphor found in scripture would be "The Lord is my Shepherd" in the 23rd Psalm. The psalms are actually entire chapters of metaphors, and in Psalm 23, we see Jesus Christ depicted as our shepherd, which would portray us as being His sheep. We go on to read, "He makes me lie down in green pastures, He leads me beside still waters, He prepares a feast before me, He anoints my head with oil, my cup is running over;" these are all metaphors for the extraordinary way in which God watches over and cares for those of us who truly belong to Him.

One of the most memorable scriptural allegories is the parable of the Prodigal Son, found in Luke chapter 15, verses 11–32. I love the way Gotquestions.org delineates the story as an allegory in this post, found at https://www.gotquestions.org/Bible-allegory.html.

> In this story the titular son represents the average person: sinful and prone to selfishness. The wealthy father represents God, and the son's harsh life of hedonism and, later, poverty represents the hollowness of the ungodly lifestyle. When the son returns home in genuine sorrow, we have an illustration of repentance. In the father's mercy and willingness to receive his son back, we see God's joy when we turn from sin and seek His forgiveness.
>
> Simply stunning!

The Correlation between Natural Israel and the Church

All through the Old Testament, God uses the metaphor of Israel being His wife. How beautiful, how poignant—poignant when we take a deeper look and see that God repeatedly accuses Israel of being "unfaithful" to Him in the same way a cheating wife is unfaithful to her husband.

The metaphor of Israel being God's "wife" is of paramount importance to this book. I'm going to show you a second, more modern metaphor where I believe God's "bride," the Church, also fits into the story and is guilty of the same sin: worshiping other gods.

Multiple times God calls Israel a "harlot" for the way she, as a nation, chased after other gods that were not her God. According to an online Bible Concordance found at http://bibleapps.com/a/a-whoring.htm, there are thirty-five instances in scripture where God blasts Israel for her "whoring."

That's right, God says that the apple of His eye became a whore. She turned herself out and played the harlot in pursuit of other gods—gods neither she nor her forefathers had ever known. Gods who were not gods at all but mere creations formed by the hands of men.

To illustrate how seriously God takes His people giving their attention and affection to anyone or anything other than Him, look at Hosea: God actually instructs His prophet to marry a prostitute. Why? To show him, and by example all of Israel, the heartbreak of loving someone who just couldn't be faithful. Hosea's wife, Gomer, was a whore—and, in God's eyes, so was Israel.

In the New Testament, we see that although Israel is and always will be the apple of God's eye, the metaphor of Israel being God's "wife" changes to the Church being the "bride of Christ." If God considered Israel, His beloved, to be a whore for chasing after other gods, loving and giving her allegiance to something other than Him—how would He not consider the mainstream Evangelical Church in America a whore as well for giving her allegiance to politics—a politician and a political party—over Himself? Have we not done exactly the same thing in giving our unconditional love and devotion to a mere man? A very, very flawed man, whom the Evangelical Church has placed in a position of veneration that belongs to God and God alone.

I know some of my alt-right friends are insulted by the very idea that I would compare their political allegiances to Donald Trump to that of Israel chasing after other gods, so here are a couple of examples of why I would say that.

On December 20, 2019, evangelical pastor Jonathan Shuttlesworth sent out a tweet to his followers stating that he would "continue to support Trump even if he's found to be running a dog-fighting ring on Mother Teresa's grave while having multiple affairs ..." Earlier, in 2017, Trump supporter Mark Lee told CNN's Alysin Camerota in an interview, "If Jesus Christ gets down off the cross and tells me Trump is with Russia, I would tell him, hold on a second, I need to check with the president if it is true. That is how confident I feel in the president."

Earlier we considered the blasphemous billboard with the picture of Donald Trump, emblazoned with the words from the Gospel of John, "And the Word became flesh and dwelt among us." There's a professionally-printed yard sign, like the kind realtors use, in the front yard of a home that reads, "God bows down to President Donald J. Trump and declares 'He is Perfect!'" Finally, there is a zealot with the back of her hatchback car done as a "shrine" to President Trump, sporting a picture of a glorified Jesus, wearing a crown of thorns, with the words, "Trump: The man who left his great life to be defamed, mocked, ridiculed & humiliated to serve & protect America." The sign below says; "Donald is Mine, Chosen Divine. Stand with Him Before Man & I Will Stand with You Before my Father in Heaven."

These are just a few specific examples of recent outright blasphemy! The Creator of the Universe does not bow down to any man! In what kind of a depraved mind is it acceptable to label any mortal man with the title given to Jesus Christ, Yeshua Messiah alone, "The Word?" And why did the former president's evangelical followers not condemn this publicly instead of encouraging it, allowing it, or ignoring it and hoping it will go away?

As the bride of Christ, our unconditional adoration, veneration, and devotion are to be His, and His alone. Anyone, anything other than Jesus Christ is an idol, and giving our devotion to that one or that thing is idolatry in God's eyes. God called Israel a whore and a harlot when she committed idolatry. If this political adulation isn't idolatry, I don't know what is. As my friend who walked out when the Pastor started screaming, "This is a Trump church," you're either for Jesus Christ or you're not. There were never any "Reagan churches," no "Obama churches." Why in the world would any church identify itself with anyone other than the One True God? In God's own words, these churches, these pastors, and these followers are all whores.

To be clear, I absolutely believe our church leaders should have been praying for our president and laying hands on him if the opportunity arose, but to turn a blind eye to his complete and utter dismissal of any and all godly principles, as Evangelical leaders have done with the former president, is reprehensible. Would they have done the same if Barack Obama had invited them to pray for him? Or would they have required some token of his "repentance" from the things they disagreed with before they would go?

And what about our new president, Joe Biden? Will they run to pray for him and declare him to be God's vessel on earth? What if Pete Buttigieg, who very openly declared his Christian faith for well over a decade before running for the office of president of the United States, what if Mayor Pete had become President Pete? Would our evangelical leaders rush to pray for him unconditionally if he were to ask them? I'm sure they wouldn't. Why? Because Joe and Pete wouldn't be advancing the political agenda of the Evangelical Church, despite the fact that the church was never intended to have a political agenda.

In Ephesians 6:12, we read an allegory describing the warfare we, as Christians, are to engage in:

> For we wrestle not against flesh and blood, but against principalities, against powers, against the rulers of the darkness of this world, against spiritual wickedness in high places.

Jesus Christ called us not just believers, but disciples; as disciples, our battle is not in the earthly realm, but in the heavenly.

According to Billy Graham in an article entitled, "What Does It Mean to Be a Disciple of Jesus?" published by Tribune Media Services and found at https://www.kansascity.com/living/liv-columns-blogs/billy-graham/article77272832.html, "a disciple is someone who believes in Jesus and seeks to follow him in his or her daily life."

As disciples, we are called to change nations through prayer and avocation of the godly values we stand for and live out in our own lives, not to impose our beliefs on those who are not of the same faith as we are. As we noted earlier, Jesus Himself told us to give to Caesar what was his and to God what was His. The two were never meant to be one and the same.

So what was the result of Israel playing the harlot? Scripture repeatedly tells us it made God jealous. Here is a descriptive explanation of the kind of jealousy God felt towards Israel, found in a blog post from Bible.org at https://bible.org/seriespage/jealous-god.

A Jealous God

Jealousy is an ugly word. "It is the green-eyed monster," said Shakespeare in *Othello*. It has overtones of selfishness, suspicion, and distrust, and implies a hideous resentment or hostility toward other people because they enjoy some advantage. It is possessive, demanding, and overbearing, and that is repulsive. It stifles freedom and individuality, it degrades and demeans, it breeds tension and discord, it destroys friendships and marriages. We view jealousy as a horrible trait and we hate it.

We do not read very far in the Bible before we hear God saying, "You shall not make for yourself an idol, or any likeness of what is in heaven above or on the earth beneath or in the water under the earth. You shall not worship them or serve them; for I, the LORD your God, am a jealous God" (Exodus 20:4–5). A jealous God! How can a God who is holy, just, loving, gracious, merciful, and long-suffering possibly be jealous? We need to explore a side of jealousy that may have escaped us.

The Meaning of God's Jealousy

The root idea in the Old Testament word jealous is to become intensely red. It seems to refer to the changing color of the face or the rising heat of the emotions which are associated with intense zeal or fervor over something dear to us. In fact, both the Old and New Testament words for jealousy are also translated "zeal." Being jealous and being zealous are essentially the same thing in the Bible. God is zealous—eager about protecting what is precious to Him.

One thing He views as especially important to Him in the Old Testament is the nation of Israel. She belongs to Him as His special possession, His unique treasure.

For the LORD has chosen Jacob for Himself, Israel for His own possession (Psalm 135:4). In fact, He views her as His wife. Through the Prophet Hosea He said to the nation, "And I will betroth you to Me forever" (Hosea 2:19).

No man with any moral fiber wants to share his wife with another man, and neither does God. He expects exclusive devotion from her. When she goes after other lovers, that is, when she worships other gods and thus commits spiritual adultery, He is said to be jealous. When the term jealousy is applied to God in

Scripture it is usually because His people are worshiping idols. In the second of His ten commandments He warned them not to do that, but they failed to listen to Him. For they provoked Him with their high places, And aroused His jealousy with their graven images (Psalm 78:58).

In 1 Corinthians 10:22, the Apostle Paul, after a discussion about idolatry in the church at Corinth, asks the question, "Or do we provoke the Lord to jealousy?"

There were consequences for the nation of Israel, the Jewish people, for making God jealous: He gave salvation to the Gentiles, which was His plan all along. What will the consequences be for the modern-day Evangelical Church's idolatry? Keep reading; we will soon see.

SECTION V— THE REALITY OF IT ALL

CHAPTER 17
God's Presence Is What Sets a People Apart

UP TO THIS point, the majority of this book has been historical exploration, compilation, and interpretation of data and statistics, and the laying of theological foundations for where we are now headed This groundwork will give us a solid foundation leading to the conclusion I believe Holy Spirit has in store for us.

In chapter 16, we transitioned from history to modern times with a correlation between the nation of Israel, the Jewish people, and today's Christian Church; now we'll take one step further in that correlation to move us towards the conclusion.

The title of this chapter states an immutable truth: the presence of God is what sets a group of people apart from all the other people of the earth.

Moses was the first to recognize this truth, and we read about it in the book of Exodus. In the following passage, we'll see that Yehovah God had delivered the children of Israel out of Egypt and given Moses the Ten Commandments written on stone tablets. Moses had come down from the mountain top, where he had spent forty days meeting with God in person, only to find the people drunk, dancing around an idol they had made in the form of a solid gold calf, and declaring that the calf was the god that had brought them out of Egypt. We already know how God feels about His people worshiping anyone or anything other than Him.

We pick up the story at the point where God has just told Moses to get ready to lead the people into the land He had promised on oath to give to Abraham's decedents.

> **Exodus 33:12-17 (NIV)**
> Moses said to the Lord, "You have been telling me, 'Lead these people,' but you have not let me know whom you will send with me. You have said, 'I know you by name and you have found favor with me.' ¹³ If you are pleased with me, teach me your ways so I may know you and continue to find favor with you. Remember that this nation is your people."
>
> ¹⁴ The Lord replied, "My Presence will go with you, and I will give you rest."
>
> ¹⁵ Then Moses said to him, "If your Presence does not go with us, do not send us up from here. ¹⁶ How will anyone know that you are pleased with me and with your people unless you go with us? What else will distinguish me and your people from all the other people on the face of the earth?"
>
> ¹⁷ And the Lord said to Moses, "I will do the very thing you have asked, because I am pleased with you and I know you by name."

The rest, as the saying goes, is history. The presence of the LORD did indeed go with Moses and the Israelites everywhere they went. Yehovah God, transliterated Adonai in Hebrew and then translated "LORD" in English, went with His people in a very literal way. The pillar of cloud by day and the pillar of fire by night that had guided the people out of Egypt and brought them to Mt. Sinai continued to guide them for the next forty years. Along the way, God did many mighty miracles for His people, including toppling the immense walls of the city of Jericho with only a trumpet burst and the shouts of the people.

There are many other examples in the Old Testament where God went with His servants and they did mighty exploits because of His presence being with them: Abraham, Joshua, Gideon, King David, King Asa, and many others were surrounded by His presence.

Just as God's presence was the distinguishing factor in setting the Jewish people, the nation of Israel, apart from the rest of the people groups in the world in biblical times, so it is this very same presence that sets the Christian Church apart from all other religions and people groups in the world today. Only in the Christian Church do you see people's lives being transformed by the power of the Living God. Only in Christianity do we see and hear about people being delivered from demons, being healed, and even being raised from the dead. Only the presence of the Most High God can accomplish that, and that presence is found in the manifestation of His Holy Spirit.

On a website called truthimmutable.com (http://truthimmutable.com/set-apart-manifest-presence-god/), an author identified as Jude sums it all up beautifully:

> The defining factor of the people of God under the new covenant remains the presence of God. In the Old Testament, the spiritual presence of God was a physically tangible and separate presence. For us, however, it's a spiritually tangible indwelling presence. We are still required to separate ourselves from the world but it's to spiritual separation rather than physical separation. It does not define our position as the people of God. It is His indwelling presence that sets us apart—something the world cannot help but recognize. This is the purpose of God in separating a people to Himself.
>
> The Old Testament principles still apply, though they are now fulfilled in Christ. God's purpose in raising up a people who were His own was to reveal Himself to the world. The purpose of the Jewish nation was to show the rest of the world what it meant to live as people and children of God. They provided a living, visible example of the extraordinary privilege of being set apart for God. This hasn't changed. Our purpose is still to manifest the glory and power of God, and we can only do this when His presence is a reality. If we do not have a recognizable presence of God, we cannot fulfil this fundamental purpose. He does not set

His people apart for the sole purpose of blessing them, though blessings do follow. It is so that He can be perfectly revealed and that others would seek Him as a result.

The words, "God's purpose in raising up a people who were His own was to reveal Himself to the world" went through me like a knife. When I consider what the world is seeing in the Church in America today as she staunchly stands behind one of the vilest figures we've seen in recent history, I can't help but weep and ask for forgiveness on behalf of those too deluded to ask for themselves.

So what does this have to do with God having some sort of "secret agenda" for the LGBTQ community? If it's the presence of God, manifest in, by, and through His Holy Spirit that marks a people as belonging to God, set apart by Him for Himself, then the manifestation of Holy Spirit is what we must look for in any people that claim to be His. Not how they talk, not how they vote, but whether or not there are blatant, visible signs that they belong to God. This same criteria is also how we determine if a "move" is of God or not.

This may be surprising, but God has been manifesting His presence in gay and LGBTQ-affirming churches for years. There are not large numbers of LGBTQ Christians out there walking the walk and talking the talk, but those who are there are Spirit-filled, and Holy Spirit is doing some pretty awesome things in and through some of them.

Many people ask, "How can God's Holy Spirit work through gay men and women?" It's simple, really. There are two spiritual principles at work here. First, God says in His word that He will redeem for Himself members of every people group on the planet.

> **Revelation 7:9 (ESV)**
> After this I looked, and behold, a great multitude that no one could number, from every nation, from all tribes and peoples and languages, standing before the throne and before the Lamb, clothed in white robes, with palm branches in their hands.

The second is this: scripture tells us that God confirms His word with "signs and wonders."

> **Mark 16:17-20 (ESV)**
> And these signs will accompany those who believe: in my name they will cast out demons; they will speak in new tongues; [18] they will pick up serpents with their hands, and if they drink any deadly poison, it will not hurt them; they will lay their hands on the sick, and they will recover.'
>
> [19] So then the Lord Jesus, after he had spoken to them, was taken up into heaven and sat down at the right hand of God. [20] And they went out and preached everywhere, while the Lord worked with them and confirmed the message by accompanying signs.

You see, it doesn't matter to Him who preaches it. As long as they are preaching the unadulterated Word of God, He will confirm it with signs and wonders. It's the Church that has decided that certain people, certain people-groups, are excluded from the kingdom, when in actuality, scripture tells us just the opposite:

> **John 3:16 (NKJV)**
> For God so loved the world, that he gave his only Son, that whosoever believes in him should not perish but have eternal life.

We see this inclusive, impartial God that the mainstream Church is so desperately trying to tell an entire group of people isn't for them. Yes. He. Is. And His Spirit moving among some of our LGBTQ-affirming churches is proof, according to scripture, that whosoever means whosoever.

Some may be tempted to think that these signs and wonders, as demonstrated in gay or LGBTQ-affirming churches, must be false signs sent by Satan to deceive people. First, there is no biblical evidence of Satan ever doing anything to give glory to God! Second, Jesus Himself told us this isn't possible; in fact, He addresses this concern directly:

> **Matthew 12:22-28 (NKJV)**
> Then one was brought to Him who was demon-possessed, blind and mute, and He healed him, so that the blind and mute man both spoke and saw. [23] And all the multitudes were amazed and said, "Could this be the Son of David?"

> ²⁴ Now when the Pharisees heard it they said, "This fellow does not cast out demons except by Beelzebub, the ruler of the demons." [Oh, look! Religious people were doing the same thing back then that they're doing today!]
>
> ²⁵ But Jesus knew their thoughts, and said to them: "Every kingdom divided against itself is brought to desolation, and every city or house divided against itself will not stand. ²⁶ If Satan casts out Satan, he is divided against himself. How then will his kingdom stand? ²⁷ And if I cast out demons by Beelzebub, by whom do your sons cast them out? Therefore they shall be your judges. ²⁸ But if I cast out demons by the Spirit of God, surely the kingdom of God has come upon you."

As Jesus explains, it is impossible for anyone to cast out demons or heal the sick by any spirit other than the Holy Spirit, and God's Holy Spirit dwelling in and manifesting through a group of people marks them as being genuinely God's people—no matter what anyone else says or believes.

Many Christians are skeptical of any ministry that claims to have had supernatural demonstrations of God's Holy Spirit in their meetings, yet I've seen it with my own eyes, experienced it for myself, and heard firsthand accounts of divine and miraculous healings coming from various ministries. Even internationally known evangelical pastor Henry Blackaby in his book, *Experiencing God,* concedes:

> When God spoke to Moses and others in the Old Testament, those events were encounters with God. An encounter with Jesus was an encounter with God for the disciples. In the same way an encounter with the Holy Spirit is an encounter with God for you.

Yes, indeed, Holy Spirit *is* still moving in His Church today.

Yet the Church at large is slow to catch on; we examined three major moves of God's Holy Spirit that took place in the United States during the twentieth century, and the Church discounted every single one of those moves as not being of God. They literally gave credit to Satan for the Azusa Street Revival and the Great Healing Revival, because the Church didn't believe that speaking in tongues or healing was of God, even though scripture clearly tells us:

> **Mark 16:17-18**
> And these signs shall follow them that believe; In my name shall they cast out devils; they shall speak with new tongues; [18] They shall take up serpents, and if they drink any deadly thing, it shall not hurt them; they shall lay hands on the sick, and they shall recover.

Truly, it doesn't matter if you're Pentecostal, Charismatic, Catholic, Episcopal, Baptist, Methodist, straight, gay, lesbian, bisexual, or transgender, if Holy Spirit manifests His presence in and through your life, that is Father God's seal that sets you apart as being His.

Let's address the "false signs and wonders" warned about in Mark:

> **Mark 13:21-23 ESV**
> And then if anyone says to you, "Look, here is the Christ!" or "Look, there he is!" do not believe it. [22] For false Christs and false prophets will arise and perform signs and wonders, to lead astray, if possible, the elect. [23] But be on guard; I have told you all things beforehand.

False signs and wonders will be performed by false prophets to lead people *away* from Jesus, not *to* Him. An LGBTQ-affirming church preaching Jesus Christ and Him crucified, operating in signs and wonders confirming the inclusive gospel of Jesus Christ, is not what Mark is talking about.

Why does all this matter? Because we're on the threshold of a major new move of God, and it's going to come in a way that will cause a lot of Christians to reject it; it will be coming through the LGBTQ community. And to be perfectly clear—it will not be a move in which God changes people's sexual orientation or gender identity so He can use them. It will be a sovereign move where His Spirit saves and fills LGBTQ men and women and uses them to reach others exactly as they are.

CHAPTER 18
The Condition of the LGBTQ Community

The Gay "Lifestyle"

I'll never forget the look on my daughter's face. It was a brisk fall evening. She was in her early twenties at the time, and she and her potential new boyfriend were hanging out in the Jacuzzi at my condo in Palm Springs, just chatting and getting to know each other. I had been inside when she called to ask me to come meet the cute, sweet Christian boy she was with. He was a really nice kid, but typical of so many Evangelicals, completely ignorant and uninformed concerning matters of faith as it pertains to members of the LGBTQ community. That's when "it" happened. We were talking, and somehow the subject of me being gay came up, and he made the massive mistake of thinking he knew who I was based on his perception of gay people. He made a comment that sent me over the edge: "I don't have a problem with gay people," he said, "I just don't approve of the lifestyle."

I looked at my daughter; she had a look of sheer terror on her face because she knew that I was about to light him up like a Christmas tree and there was no escaping for him. I looked at the young man and said, "The what?"

He made his second mistake by repeating himself. I asked him, "Really? My lifestyle?" and he responded, "Well, yes sir, you are gay, aren't you?"

Wow! Mistake number three, and that's when the fireworks went off.

With the intensity of a marine sergeant, I proceeded to drill the young man as to what exactly was it about my "lifestyle" that he disapproved of. Was it my daily Bible reading? Was it the fact that I spent hours a day in worship? Or maybe it was that I fasted and prayed regularly to see God move in my city, to save the souls of the men and women I had grown to love. That must be it. Or maybe it was the fact that I only listened to Christian music and had cut as much of the world's influence out of my life as possible. Was that what he found so reprehensible? Or was it the fact that I ate, slept, and breathed Jesus Christ that made him uncomfortable? I asked him each of these things because I truly wanted to know what exactly he *thought* he knew about me that had caused him to deem my lifestyle inappropriate, because all these things were me. This was my life. For lack of a better term, I was a gay "Jesus Freak."

Of course, I actually knew what he was implying, but he had made the mistake of thinking all gay men lived a stereotypical, hedonistic lifestyle of lust and lasciviousness, consisting of an endless string of one-night stands and dancing half-naked on floats at Pride parades. He was, as I observed, typical of so many Evangelicals, completely ignorant and uninformed concerning matters of faith as they pertain to members of the LGBTQ community. There definitely are gay "party boys" that gave my community that reputation, and in all honesty, I was one of those guys in the years preceding my giving my heart and life back to Jesus Christ. (If you want to know more about my history, read my book, *Called, Chosen, and Gay.*) With the exception of dancing half-naked on parade floats, I was the stereotypical gay guy, and there was no shame in my game: I was proud of who I was.

It took me a lot of years and a lot of therapy to be able to say that, but I was most definitely proud of who and what I was. I have lived "the gay lifestyle." A lifestyle that is the absolute antithesis of everything I was raised to believe and everything I had held dear to my heart for most of my life. I drank, I took drugs recreationally, and I had sex with whomever I wanted, whenever I wanted. I was as far away from the Christian standards I had been raised to follow as one could possibly get, and I was numb to anything that challenged my lifestyle. In the same way being a gay Jesus Freak now defines me, the "gay lifestyle" stereotype that I lived back then defined me at that time.

The honest truth is the "lifestyle" that young man thought I lived is one type of lifestyle that a portion of my community lives. But by no means do all of them live it, and it's probably not as large a percentage as you would imagine if you read any sort of gay magazines. LGBTQ men and women, just like heterosexual men and women, live a variety of lifestyles that can't be relegated to one particular stereotype.

Of course, there are those of my community who have never lived like that. I have friends that have been in stable, monogamous relationships for decades. They've never been to a sex party, never had a one-night stand, never cheated on their spouse—never done any of the things the mainstream Church imagines as the life of every gay man on the planet. (I'm specifically referencing gay men here because we're the ones typically associated with wanton sexual behavior.)

As before, I'm not here to tickle anyone's ears; I'm telling it like it is when I say my people, the LGBTQ community, are a mess. I say it in love, because I genuinely do love them with all my heart, but we, as a community, are a hot mess. One of my Facebook friends made a post the other day that really struck a nerve with me and a lot of his other followers: "The more therapy I do the more I realize how toxic the gay community is," followed by a "sad face" emoji.

I can picture some hardcore Evangelical readers who are probably astounded that I've finally said something they can agree with.

Yes, I've just affirmed something the Evangelical Church has been saying for years: the LGBTQ community is a hot mess. Many of us in the community will agree with that statement if we're really honest, but here is a challenge: regardless of which side of the issue you're on, have you ever asked yourself "Why?" Why are we such a mess? Why does sexual immorality run so rampant? Why do LGBTQ people overall want nothing to do with the things of God? Why do so many literally run from anything that smacks of Christianity?

Once again, we find the answer in scripture:

> **Proverbs 29:18 (KJV)**
> Where there is no vision, the people perish.

At first glance that verse might not seem germane; let's dig a little deeper. A study of different translations reveals just how truly relevant this verse is in describing why the LGBTQ community is in the shape they are in today.

In the English Standard Version of the Holy Bible, which many scholars and theologians consider to be the most accurate translation, this verse reads: "Where there is no prophetic vision the people cast off restraint."

This means that when the Church of Jesus Christ repeatedly tells a group of people that there is no hope, no future for them, those people cast off Judeo-Christian restraints, and societal norms in general, and live life on their own terms. We need to face the fact that the Church's own damnation of the LGBTQ community has caused them to cast off the very restraints the Church condemns them for casting off.

Ever since the late 1970s, when the Republican Party hired Jerry Falwell to use abortion and gay rights as wedge issues to bring Christians to the polls as conservative voters, the Church has had one message to the LGBTQ community: "You're going to Hell!"

The only prophetic vision my community has received from the mainstream Church is one of hellfire and eternal damnation, yet the same Church wonders why most of my people have cast off all restraint and want nothing to do with their God or their version of Christianity.

I challenge you to thoroughly read the Gospels of Matthew, Mark, Luke, and John, where Jesus' words are highlighted in red letters in most translations. I challenge you to find any group of people that Jesus condemned. If you've never read the Gospels for yourself, it may surprise you to find that the only people Jesus ever condemned were the religious leaders of His day. In Matthew 23:27, He calls them hypocrites and compares them to "whitewashed tombs, beautiful on the outside but filled with dead men's bones and every unclean thing." It grieves my spirit immensely to say this, but I thoroughly believe He would use that analogy to describe the leaders in today's mainstream Church.

So if lack of prophetic revelation is what causes people to cast off restraint and subsequently "perish," I want to change that. The purpose of this book is to bring prophetic revelation to the LGBTQ community and to tell the mainstream Church what's coming.

If you've not heard any of the prophecies spoken about a move of God coming to the LGBTQ community, let me be the one to declare it to you. God *does* have an "agenda," a plan, for the LGBTQ community, and it's not for their destruction—it is for their salvation, healing, and deliverance. It's a plan for a hope and a future, and it's about to be birthed in the earth. God has chosen the LGBTQ community for the awesome privilege of stewarding what I believe will be the final move of His spirit before the return of Jesus Christ.

Before we get to why God is moving in this way, I want to address the issue of where LGBTQ-affirming spiritual leaders have missed the mark. I've repeatedly called out the mainstream and Evangelical Church leaders in this book, now it's time to expose the things that are hindering this coming move of God's Holy Spirit in affirming churches.

CHAPTER 19
A Call to Repentance for Affirming Leaders

IN BRINGING CORRECTION in a public format such as a book or from the pulpit, it's important to deal in generalities whenever possible, stating instances and circumstances and not specific names to keep from appearing to attack people. I have kept to this principle in most of this book; however, this chapter will focus on the need to expose sin in the LGBTQ church, for several reasons. First, it's because scripture tells us:

> **Ephesians 5:11 (NIV)**
> Have nothing to do with the fruitless deeds of darkness, but rather expose them.

This was written to the church in Ephesus, so the Apostle Paul was definitely talking to fellow believers in the church. Today, many are gun-shy when it comes to calling out spiritual leaders for things that aren't scriptural because there's been so much abuse in the Church historically, and most LGBTQ Christians have suffered at the hands of non-affirming ministries. This has created an "anything goes" culture in many affirming churches today.

A lot of folks are quick to quote what may well be the only verse they know: "Judge not lest you be judged," Matthew 7:1, but here's the rest of that scripture,

> **Matthew 7:1-2 (NIV)**
> Do not judge, or you too will be judged. ² For in the same way you judge others, you will be judged, and with the measure you use, it will be measured to you.

Rather than thinking it's a "command" not to judge, we need to recognize that this is a warning that we need to have our own house in order before we judge another person's actions. One unidentified Bible commentator put it this way:

> The primary meaning is that we must not judge the sins of others until we have acknowledged and repented of our own sins.

My primary reason for exposing the gross things that go on in some, definitely not all, gay and LGBTQ-affirming churches is to shed light on the "fruitless deeds of darkness." If a thing isn't exposed as wrong, there's little chance that it will be acknowledged and subsequently repented for: and lack of repentance will get you "set on a shelf," so to speak, unable to be used by God in the new move that He's about to sovereignly release on the earth.

The scriptural foundation for that statement is found in:

> **Matthew 9:17 (ESV)**
> Neither is new wine put into old wineskins. If it is, the skins burst and the wine is spilled and the skins are destroyed. But new wine is put into fresh wineskins, and so both are preserved.

In this instance, the "new wine" is the coming new move of Holy Spirit. The new "wineskin" is the lives of men and women of God who have consecrated themselves to God by repenting of anything that would hinder Him from using them in whatever way He sees fit in that move.

Most heterosexual people, and probably even the vast majority of folks in the LGBTQ community, have never been to a "gay" church or an LGBTQ-affirming church. There *is* a difference between the two; I pastor an affirming church, which means that members of the LGBTQ community participate as fully as all other members of the church community. On any given Sunday, our attendance is usually a 60/40 mix of LGBTQ folks and straight folks; that blend goes back and forth depending on the Sunday. Some other churches are "gay" churches that identify themselves as safe places for the LGBTQ community exclusively. I've even heard of some pastors of these gay churches telling their congregations that they don't want straight folks in their church. I don't see this exclusivity anywhere in scripture, and personally, I don't agree with this approach.

The fact that most of American society has never been to a single service in a gay or LGBTQ-affirming church is significant here, because many readers have never been exposed to some of the things that have been allowed to infiltrate these churches in the name of "inclusion."

In keeping with scriptural mandates, I present the third reason we're called to address things that are wrong in the Church and not just overlook them, and that is that by addressing them in love, and our primary motivation *has* to be love, we bring people, churches, and movements to maturity in Christ.

> **Ephesians 4:11-15 (ESV)**
> And he gave the apostles, the prophets, the evangelists, the pastors and teachers, [12] to equip the saints for the work of ministry, for building up the body of Christ, [13] until we all attain to the unity of the faith and of the knowledge of the Son of God, to mature manhood, to the measure of the stature of the fullness of Christ, [14] so that we may no longer be children, tossed to and fro by the waves and carried about by every wind of doctrine, by human cunning, by craftiness in deceitful schemes. [15] Rather, speaking the truth in love, we are to grow up in every way into him who is the head, into Christ.

I had an experience a couple of years ago where a young pastor I was affiliated with was making a move in his ministry that was based solely out of ego. I knew it, the head of the ministry knew it and told me so, but no one would address it openly. Finally one day, in complete frustration, I asked the head of that ministry why he was letting this slide, and his answer absolutely floored me. He said, "Because he's too immature to receive the truth."

That's not an answer based in scripture; in fact, that's the exact opposite of what scripture says. We must affirm that presenting the truth to the immature, in love, brings about the maturity people need to effectively serve God. Now I understand that some of us don't really have a "gift" for being loving. Some folks will rip a person to shreds bringing correction and do way more harm than good. But the man in charge in this instance is one of the most gentle, loving people I've ever known. He's someone that, to this day, I love dearly, but the bottom line was that he didn't want to offend the young man.

If you're going to be a truly effective leader, you can't withhold correction out of sentiment. That's where the love comes in. Scripture tells us in Proverbs that withholding correction from children (natural or spiritual) is bad for them—worse than punishment.

Just as the leader of this immature Christian was reluctant to correct him, I procrastinated on writing this section for over a week, fearing backlash as well as the discomfort of making people mad at me. But I do know Holy Spirit's voice, and He's relentlessly prompted me to say what needs to be said.

The best approach is to recount some of the things I've encountered in gay-affirming churches since I came out a little over twenty-four years ago. My first experience at a gay church was back in 1998. I was living in San Diego at the time, having moved there to be a part of an "ex-gay" ministry called Living Waters. Needless to say, my attempted conversion to heterosexuality was a bust (I share all the gory details, suicide attempts, etc. in my next book, *Called, Chosen, and Gay*). Suffering from severe depression after the realization that there was no changing my sexual orientation, I decided to visit a local church that was part of a "gay denomination."

My first Sunday there was really enjoyable. After the service, I found out that the worship pastor had been an ordained Assembly of God pastor prior to his coming out. Having been baptized with the Holy Spirit in an AG church, I felt at home talking to him. Additionally, I met four really great guys who immediately befriended me and invited me to join them for dinner that evening. Wow! I thought I'd hit the jackpot.

I had dinner with the guys that night and really clicked with one of them whom I thought would make not only a great friend but possibly a boyfriend. It all seemed too good to be true … and it was.

The guy and I talked several times throughout the week, and we went to dinner a time or two. I had come out three years earlier, so I was familiar with the whole gay dating scene, but I really didn't know how the dating game went in gay Christian circles. He was super sweet, though fairly aggressive when it came to wanting sex, but he was respectful and kept inviting me back to church the next Sunday. I liked him and the church, so I went—and got the shock of my life.

I was a couple of minutes late that next Sunday morning, so as I rushed in and sat with my new group of friends, I didn't really notice how anyone else was dressed. Then came Communion time. In this church, they had people go to the front of the church and receive the elements one person, or a couple, at a time. I was just sitting there, listening to the music, waiting for it to be my turn to join the line, when I looked up and saw one of the guys in line was wearing bare-ass chaps! If you're not familiar with chaps, they're the leather pants without a seat or crotch that cowboys or motorcyclists wear over their jeans to protect their legs. But this guy wasn't wearing the jeans under them—only a black leather jock strap. I was in shock. I couldn't believe what I was seeing. I declined Communion that morning and left the service early.

I met my new friend later that afternoon for a long talk and a walk around Hillcrest, the center of gay life in downtown San Diego. He told me I needed to "loosen up" and enjoy my sexuality. During the course of that walk, he also told me that the reason he had been pursuing me was that he and the other three guys that had befriended me had a "club" in which they competed with each other to see who could get the most church visitors into bed, and who could get them first. I was literally numb.

I was no prude; I was sexually active, but I had never taken my sexual orientation to church with me until my visit to this church. I had been raised in very conservative evangelical churches, and even though those churches had made it extremely clear that I was no longer welcome, I still believed some things did *not* belong in church ... and bare-ass chaps and competitions to bed the most guys were definitely two of those things.

I have never stepped foot in another church of that denomination since then, but I've had other equally unsettling encounters with them through other people and religious organizations I've been involved with over the years.

Fast-forward about a decade to an encounter that took place during a non-denominational workshop for people in LGBTQ-affirming ministries, including leaders. The workshop was just one part of a weekend-long event that was, overall, a beautiful experience.

When I'd registered for this weekend conference, I had received instruction to bring some old magazines from home, as we would be cutting out pictures and words from them as part of one of the workshops. I grabbed a couple of *Architectural Digest* magazines and a few other things I had lying around the house and thought nothing more about it, until the workshop started.

We were divided into groups and assigned a large, round table to work at. We were instructed to take out the magazines we had brought with us and share them with the group. We were then instructed to look through all the magazines to find words or pictures that best represented Christian life as we saw it and to cut those pictures and/or words out and paste them on a large sheet of poster board to tell our story. Well, one of the people who had been assigned to my group was a deacon in a church of the same gay denomination I had first visited back in 1998. Not knowing what we were going to do with the magazines, he had brought gay porn. Yes, indeed, there it was in the middle of the table: a stack of gay porn magazines in front of God and everyone. What makes it even more embarrassing is that he and I were the only two guys at the table; the rest were women.

Let me say right here that I know for a fact that porn consumption and even addiction is not by any stretch of the imagination confined to the LGBTQ community. According to a Barna Group study commissioned by Josh McDowell Ministry that included 432 pastors and 338 youth pastors:

> https://www.christianitytoday.com/news/2016/january/how-pastors-struggle-porn-phenomenon-josh-mcdowell-barna.html
>
> Most pastors (57%) and youth pastors (64%) admit they have struggled with porn, either currently or in the past," Barna reported. "Overall, 21 percent of youth pastors and 14 percent of pastors admit they currently struggle with using porn. More than 1 in 10 youth pastors (12%) and 1 in 20 pastors (5%) said they're addicted.

(This article first appeared on ChristianityToday.com in January, 2016. Used by permission of Christianity Today, Carol Stream, IL 60188.)

The Barna Group is an independent Christian company that does research on everything trending in Christian churches in America, and these are statistics taken from straight, evangelical churches.

Please hear my heart in this. My problem is not that this man had an obvious addiction to pornography, but that he, as a deacon in his church, thought it was OK to bring it to a Christian function. I mean, in what other world would this ever be thought of as acceptable behavior?

The leaders of the event were quite put off by the situation I described above, and it was addressed, but in the denomination this man was affiliated with, his actions weren't considered objectionable.

Thankfully, overall the weekend was a beautiful experience, as Father taught me so many things through some of the folks in attendance. And Holy Spirit was definitely present in Sunday morning's worship service in the most amazing way.

On the ride home that afternoon, I had a conversation with the gentleman who had invited me to the conference. He had also invited me to ride with him, as the event was several hours from my home. During the course of that ride, I discovered that he had been a paid staff member in the home office of the gay denomination with which I'd had the two negative encounters. He was surprised that this deacon had brought pornography to the event we had just attended, because the facilitators of the event had been pretty clear in the past about that kind of thing not being acceptable, and this man had been to previous events hosted by this group.

He then went on to tell me of some of the things he had encountered while being a staff member with that ministry for over eight years. He related that although the head of that ministry was in a long-term relationship with another man, the number of affairs the leader had been involved in during the eight years my friend had been with them were too numerous to count. Everyone who worked in the denominational headquarters had been fully aware of this leader's sexual proclivities, which included bringing men to his office for sex.

This is just wrong. I don't think that anyone actually believes that God doesn't have a problem with this, and if they do, it's because, as scripture says, they've had their conscience seared (cauterized, hardened, withered):

> **1 Timothy 4:1-2 (KJV)**
> Now the Spirit speaketh expressly, that in the latter times some shall depart from the faith, giving heed to seducing spirits, and doctrines of devils; ² Speaking lies in hypocrisy; having their conscience seared with a hot iron.

As messed up as the Evangelical Church in America may be, this type of behavior would never be tolerated by any heterosexual leader. When an evangelical leader has fallen, they have been called to repentance for their actions once they're exposed.

Let's explore the connections these three instances concerning this particular "gay denomination" have with each other, and why and how they differ from most non-affirming churches.

Pentecostal and charismatic circles are quite familiar with the concept and term, "the anointing," which is described in the following excerpt from a blog found at compellinttruth.org/anointed.html:

> Anointing was a common ancient cultural practice. Shepherds often poured oil on the heads of their sheep in order to protect them from insects that would burrow in their ears and kill them, contributing to anointing becoming symbolic of blessing, protection, and empowerment. The Jewish people anointed the altar when making sacrifices. Spiritually, anointing was related to the idea of strength or blessing. Priests were anointed with oil, later followed by Samuel anointing both Saul and later David as kings of Israel. This anointing signified a person as a chosen one among other people.
>
> In the New Testament, we are told God anointed Jesus with the Holy Spirit: "The Spirit of the Lord is upon me, because he has anointed me to proclaim good news to the poor" (Luke 4:18). Acts 10:38 adds, "God anointed Jesus of Nazareth with the Holy Spirit and with power." Acts 4:26-27 calls Jesus God's anointed. This was a term used to emphasize Jesus as the chosen one of God.

In addition to Old Testament leaders and Jesus being anointed, the apostle Paul spoke of an anointing of all Christians: "And it is God who establishes us with you in Christ, and has anointed us, and who has also put his seal on us and given us his Spirit in our hearts as a guarantee" (2 Corinthians 1:21).

So the anointing of God's Holy Spirit rests on those who are called into ministry, whether it be in a five-fold (apostle, prophet, pastor, evangelist, teacher) capacity or as a lay minister—one who works in ministry without holding one of the five offices.

The common understanding is that the anointing flows from the head down, as referenced in this passage:

Psalm 133:2 (NIV)
It is like precious oil poured on the head, running down on the beard, running down on Aaron's beard, down on the collar of his robe.

In this we see that the anointing that's on a ministry runs from the head, the leader, down on to everyone else. In the case of the particular group of churches I've been referencing, the problem, like the anointing, flowed from the head down. The sexual promiscuity and total lack of any moral standards had made its way from the denomination's leader down to the folks in the churches in the communities the ministry served.

This is difficult to write, and my goal is not to sit in judgment, but if someone doesn't say, "Hey, this is wrong," then we don't have a chance of changing the behavior. And the three instances I've described aren't the only examples I could have written about with this particular ministry. Without going into detail, I've heard story after story from friends and pastors about the inappropriate sexual encounters they had in this denomination, and I am led to point out that there are some problems in gay and affirming churches that must be addressed: problems that are based in the fact that sexuality has been wantonly incorporated into the church.

This problem isn't confined to just this one denomination. I have friends who have told me stories of being groped in the men's room, or even worse, in the communion line at affirming and gay churches. I've been "hit on" more times than I can count at different churches I've visited over the years, and I will be the first to admit that in the years that followed my first gay church encounter, I was one of the guys hitting on visitors. I had assimilated into the culture so well I had become a part of the problem. When you have a pastor that encourages you to go out and "hook up" if you're really "horny," it's easy to lose your bearings. And that's what my first gay pastor used to tell me to do. Heck, he was doing it. Why shouldn't I?

My pastor had lost his bearings, his moral compass, and so had I. Attitudes and behaviors flow from the head down. When the head of a ministry preaches abstinence to his leaders but then ordains people he knows are sleeping together without being in covenant with each other, he's lost his bearings as well. And I see it happening all around me in LGBTQ-affirming ministries. Why do gay Christian men have such a hard time adhering to the same moral standards as straight Christian men? And yes, straight Christian leaders can and sometimes do commit infidelities, but at least they show some shame and try to hide what they're doing, while so many LGBTQ Christian men seem almost proud that they don't follow traditional moral guidelines. This is wrong, and it's hurting the body of Christ.

To be clear, I am not addressing anyone who doesn't claim to be a Christian; I am specifically talking to LGBTQ Christian men and women who are in positions of leadership. The Christian Church in America needs to stop trying to hold people who do not profess to be Christians to Church standards; however, the LGBTQ-affirming church does need to start holding its leaders to biblical standards.

In Acts 17:30, we're told that in times past God overlooked our ignorance, but now He calls us to repentance. I am 100 percent in favor of making church a safe place for LGBTQ folks. I believe that every single church in America should be that safe place for them and for every other people group that wants to worship or even find God. But it's supposed to be just that: a safe place to come and worship, not to solicit sex.

In other chapters I've called out the Evangelical Church for where she's missed the mark; in this chapter, I've done the same to the LGBTQ-affirming churches. If you're in a position of leadership in an affirming church, I implore you to ask Holy Spirit to show you His heart on the matter, and then repent of whatever He convicts you of.

Holy Spirit will convict of sin, but He will never condemn. My mission with this book is not to condemn either. I say this with all humility: my mission is similar to that of John the Baptist, the voice in the wilderness. I literally live in a desert, calling to my LGBTQ brothers and sisters, and my evangelical brothers and sisters, "Make straight the way of the LORD."

There's a new move of God's Holy Spirit coming, and it's coming to and through my people—the LGBTQ community, but God will not pour Himself out through filthy vessels. It's time for our leaders to repent.

SECTION VI– A WAKE-UP CALL!

CHAPTER 20
God's Gay Agenda: His Plan for the LGBTQ Community

AT LAST, WE have come to the crux of what God's agenda for the LGBTQ community is. In chapter 1, we learned that God said that at the time of Jesus' visitation, the nation of Israel was under a "spirit of stupor," a spirit that kept them from seeing the truth that their prayers for Messiah had been answered. I relayed my belief that the mainstream Evangelical Church in America is under that same spirit of stupor today, keeping it from seeing the truth about where we are as a Church and how far we've fallen from God's plan for us.

In chapter 2, we discussed the necessity for the foundation of any and all spiritual references being based on the truth as outlined in scripture, as originally written, because the truth isn't subjective.

In chapters 3 through 6, we looked at what the scripture did and didn't say about the word homosexual, and in chapter 7, we took a look at Israel's eternal place in God's heart by exposing the false doctrine of Replacement Theology.

Then in chapters 8 through 10, we reviewed three of the five major moves of God's Holy Spirit that have occurred in the United States since the beginning of the twentieth century. We saw how the church was initially on the wrong side of every single move, and how some churches are still condemning these moves of God to this day.

In chapters 11 through 15, we went a few rounds in a no-holds-barred match, exposing where the religious right has missed the mark in our current season. We covered everything from scripture's mandate to love one another to the dangers of reparative therapy.

Chapter 16 shows how scripture used the metaphor of an unfaithful wife to describe Israel's relationship with God, and subsequently charged the modern-day Church with the same sin as Israel. Israel prostituted herself to foreign gods, whereas the Evangelical Church has whored after political power in place of the humility of the Cross.

In chapter 17, we saw that it was the presence of God that set the nation of Israel apart from the rest of the world, how it's the presence of God's Spirit that still sets the Church apart today, and how God's presence is proof to the world that a people belong to Him.

Chapters 18 and 19 expose not only the LGBTQ community's abandonment of godly principles, but the church's complicity in that abandonment. I called for the leadership of affirming churches to get their houses in order and repent of the things they have allowed to pollute the purity, simplicity, and beauty of the Gospel of Jesus Christ.

Turning to the crux of the matter, let's tie it all together and see how this relates to the LGBTQ community. The very end of chapter 16 warns us that Israel's constantly chasing after other gods had consequences. One of those consequences was the invasion and overthrow of the country by foreign powers, and the scattering of the Jewish people all over the world for almost two thousand years. The other consequence was that God gave His salvation, brought through the Jewish people, to the Gentiles. The scriptures supporting that statement are found when the Apostle Paul speaks to the Church of Rome, saying:

> **Romans 10:19-21 (NIV)**
> Again I ask: Did Israel not understand? First, Moses says,
>
> "I will make you envious by those who are not a nation; I will make you angry by a nation that has no understanding."
>
> [20] And Isaiah boldly says,

> "I was found by those who did not seek me; I revealed myself to those who did not ask for me."
>
> [21] But concerning Israel he says, "All day long I have held out my hands to a disobedient and obstinate people."

Moses led the Jewish nation out of Egypt in 1447 B.C., which means that before they ever entered their homeland of Israel, God was already telling them that because of their disobedience, He was going to make them "envious," jealous, by another group of people that neither knew Him nor were seeking Him.

In chapter 9 of Romans, the Apostle Paul gives an impassioned treatise about Israel's spiritual heritage and how in spite of it, God chose to offer salvation to the Gentiles as well as Israel. As we know, some Jews did indeed accept Jesus as their Messiah, but the vast majority did not, and salvation came to the Gentiles as a result of Israel's overall rejection of Messiah.

In the passage above, Paul is quoting Moses and Isaiah; in the following passage, Paul quotes the prophet Hosea, the one God had marry a prostitute, who lived approximately 700–750 years before Jesus:

> **Romans 9:25-26 (NIV)**
>
> As he says in Hosea:
>
> I will call them "my people" who are not my people; and I will call her "my loved one" who is not my loved one,"
>
> [26] and, in the very place where it was said to them, "You are not my people," there they will be called "children of the living God."

God makes it very clear here that He deliberately offered salvation to the Gentile people as a part of His redemption plan for humanity. Up until this time, the Jewish people had been quite arrogant about their election by God as being His chosen people. They were the only ones, according to their understanding, who would inherit salvation. And yet they were wrong. And so has the Evangelical Church been wrong about their belief that they have a corner on the "salvation market."

Let's look again at the passage we opened with in chapter 1:

> **Romans 11:1-8 (NIV)**
>
> I ask then: Did God reject his people? By no means! I am an Israelite myself, a descendant of Abraham, from the tribe of Benjamin. ² God did not reject his people, whom he foreknew. Don't you know what Scripture says in the passage about Elijah—how he appealed to God against Israel: ³ "Lord, they have killed your prophets and torn down your altars; I am the only one left, and they are trying to kill me?" ⁴ And what was God's answer to him? "I have reserved for myself seven thousand who have not bowed the knee to Baal." ⁵ So too, at the present time there is a remnant chosen by grace. ⁶ And if by grace, then it cannot be based on works; if it were, grace would no longer be grace.
>
> ⁷ What then? What the people of Israel sought so earnestly they did not obtain. The elect among them did, but the others were hardened, ⁸ as it is written:
>
> "God gave them a spirit of stupor, eyes that could not see and ears that could not hear, to this very day."

There's that spirit of stupor we talked about at the beginning of the book, and it's in play once again to bring about the same end: to make God's people envious of what He's about to do.

One final verse to seal this subject:

> **Romans 11:11 (NIV)**
>
> Again I ask: Did they stumble so as to fall beyond recovery? Not at all! Rather, because of their transgression, salvation has come to the Gentiles to make Israel envious.

Here is the crux: I purport to you that Father God is about to do it again. He's about to pour Himself out on a group of people who have not sought Him and have not asked for Him: the LGBTQ community.

He is about to call them "His people" who are not His people, and those who are not His beloved He is about to call "His beloved."

In the very place where it was said to them, "You are not my people," there, in the church, they will be called "children of the living God."

I'm not talking about the "remnant" of LGBTQ believers who have been around for the past hundred years or so, I'm talking about a full-blown, divine move of God's Holy Spirit where LGBTQ folks come into the kingdom by the millions!

And by bringing them in, God's going to once again make His people—this time the present day, Evangelical Church, envious. And, most likely, downright angry. Just as the Jews resented the Gentiles receiving salvation, and persecuted the believers, so too will the mainstream Church in America resent what God does when He pours out His Spirit on the LGBTQ community—unless they repent now and align themselves with the new thing Father God is about to do.

As we discussed in chapter 17, when God's presence went before the Israelites in Exodus, it showed the entire world that they were His people, and the nations of the earth were envious of them. In fact, there is animosity to this very day because the Jewish nation still clings to their status as God's only chosen people.

Israel, although arrogant in her divine election, still wasn't satisfied with worshiping the King of the Universe. She wanted to worship "gods" made by human hands, gods that neither thought nor had breath, nor understanding. This caused Yehovah God to become jealous, and in His anger, He sent a spirit of stupor upon the people so that they would not recognize salvation when it came to them. (Yeshua, the original Hebrew name for Jesus, means "Salvation.") Additionally, He not only scattered Israel among the nations but extended His offer of salvation to anyone who wanted it. God extended the offer to "whosoever" believed, and the Gentile Church was born.

God poured out His Spirit upon the new Church on the day of Pentecost and showed the Jewish people and the world that the Church belonged to Him. His presence would no longer dwell in a temple built by human hands but now dwelt in His newly chosen people. The Jewish people became extremely jealous of those newly named "Christians" and persecuted them.

After the first couple hundred years, Holy Spirit was removed from the visible position He had in the early Church, and from that time, the Church, spiritually, went virtually unchanged for close to 1,300 years until the Protestant Reformation. It was at this point that the mainline

Christian denominations were birthed. Then the Church continued virtually unchanged for over four hundred more years until the beginning of the twentieth century, when in a period of about a hundred years, God poured out His Spirit time and time again on the Christian Church. Every single time God did this, the Church fought Him and railed against the new move He was birthing. The Church was content in its religiosity, thinking they had it all figured out. They either didn't want the people God was saving in the new moves, or they didn't like the way He went about it.

Then, a little over fifty years ago, the Evangelical Church began to lust after a new god she had been introduced to by politicians. The god's name was Political Power, and the Church, much like Israel, left her first love to chase after an unholy god. Jesus, the Prince of Glory, the Darling of Heaven, was no longer enough for her; she pursued this new god with reckless abandon. In His anger, Father God allowed the same spirit of stupor that He had sent to Israel to once again fall on His chosen people, the mainstream Church. This spirit kept them from seeing the difference between a man being *used* by God and a man *of* God.

Leaders of the mainstream Church in America have sold their souls for political power, abandoning the most basic principles of their faith, along with every shred of decency and morality. They claimed it was in exchange for the appointment of Supreme Court Justices, to set the nation back on the road to righteousness, but the root of their idolatrous treason was money and power. How can I say that? Because not even a fool would believe that a godless, morally-bankrupt man could lead a people back to godliness.

God's "Heads-Up"

If you're not a member of the LGBTQ community, or are not involved in an affirming church, then the news of God sending a revival to this community may be surprising or even shocking to you. In reality, those of us who are involved in affirming ministries have known for three decades that it was coming; we just didn't know how or why.

By "why" I mean, why would God choose the LGBTQ community to lead His next, and very possibly last, divine move?

We read in scripture that God always announces His plans beforehand through people with prophetic gifts. Chapter 7 affirmed the fact that the gifts of God's Holy Spirit are the same today as they were for the early Church, and the fact that Holy Spirit is still active today, and so are His gifts, including prophecy.

> **Amos 3:7**
> Surely the Sovereign LORD does nothing without revealing his plan to his servants the prophets.

There are many people in Spirit-filled churches in this day and age who possess prophetic gifts, and there are those today who walk in the five-fold office of prophet. Please understand that the prophets of today are not the same as prophets in the Bible. In scripture, prophets heard the audible voice of God; therefore, if they prophesied something that didn't come true, they were put to death. That's because they were to only repeat what they actually heard God say, not their own thoughts.

I'm only aware of one man, in India, who actually hears the audible voice of God and receives daily direction in that manner. The rest of today's prophets, and those with a prophetic gift, rely on their ability to discern what Holy Spirit is speaking, and they don't always get it right. Sometimes they "hear" Holy Spirit speaking to their spirit, and sometimes they see visions and interpret their meaning.

In his writing to the church at Corinth, the Apostle Paul confirmed that prophets in the New Testament weren't infallible. In that writing, he states that what we know, what we prophesy, is "in part:"

> **1 Corinthians 13:9-12 (KJV)**
> For we know in part, and we prophesy in part.
>
> [10] But when that which is perfect is come, then that which is in part shall be done away.
>
> [11] When I was a child, I spoke as a child, I understood as a child, I thought as a child: but when I became a man, I put away childish things.

> ¹² For now we see through a glass, darkly, but then face to face: now I know in part, but then shall I know even as also I am known.

As we discussed in chapter 7 in the section on cessationism, the "perfect" that Paul references is not the canonization and subsequent printing and distribution of scripture in the form of the Holy Bible; it's the physical return of Jesus Christ. This is clearly spelled out at the end of the passage where Paul says that at that time, we'll see face to face.

So modern-day prophets do exist, but they aren't infallible; they do the best they can according to the gifting of Holy Spirit operating within them. With that in mind, let's explore why those of us in the LGBTQ community who are born-again Christians, who are involved in ministry, have known that God had a plan for us, for the LGBTQ community, for at least the past three decades.

On December 31, 1989, at Orlando Christian Center, Benny Hinn gave a series of prophecies of things that were going to happen. Unfortunately, Pastor Benny put time frames and dates on the things he prophesied, and those dates were not correct. As one who, on occasion, walks in the prophetic, I can tell you that giving dates is one of the most dangerous things you can do. It's very easy to get a feeling in your spirit as to timing and be completely off. The dates of his prophesies being off has caused scores of people to brand Hinn as a false prophet.

I was in the service that New Year's Eve, and I heard everything Benny Hinn prophesied with my own ears. I experienced the power of God's Holy Spirit as He swept through that auditorium and left people scattered like matchsticks in His wake. Holy Spirit did that—Pastor Benny never left the platform. He may have gotten the timing wrong, and even missed completely on a couple of items, but for those of us who were there, the presence of God in that meeting was one of the most powerful things we've ever encountered. The prophecy that night was the longest I've ever heard, lasting, from what I recall, about ten to fifteen minutes.

During that time, Pastor Benny gave those of us in the LGBTQ community our first glimmer of hope. At this time, I was married with three young children and was hiding in the closet, telling people I had been "delivered" from homosexuality "in Jesus' name." ("In Jesus' Name" is what Charismatic Christians say after saying something that isn't true. It's supposed to mean that it's happened in the "Spirit," but just hasn't "manifested" in the natural/earthly realm yet.)

Pastor Benny prophesied that God was going to "destroy" the homosexual community in America, and the congregation went wild with applause. My heart sank in my chest as I felt the crushing weight of their applause, aghast at the excitement of five thousand of my Christian brothers and sisters applauding what they assumed was going to be the death of an entire people group. I'm tearing up just remembering it—my friends in that room wanted me and my kind dead. But then Pastor Benny continued, telling them it would not be as they suspected (which I took to mean AIDS), but it would be by the fire of the Holy Spirit.

In the common Christian parlance known as Christianese, "the fire of the Holy Spirit," as used in that sense, meant that God was going to make them His own. They would no longer find their identity in their sexual orientation but in their adoption into the Kingdom of God. Orientation doesn't change; how you identify does. I identify as a born-again, Spirit-filled Christian who happens to be gay—not a "gay Christian," and there is a huge difference.

As mentioned, Pastor Benny gave a lot of prophecies that night with dates attached to them that didn't come to pass. This prophecy about God sending His Spirit upon the LGBTQ community was one of them: he gave a timetable for this particular prophecy of 1994 to 1995 at the latest. It may help to know that Pastor Benny had been asking God about what was going to happen in the 1990s, so he may have assumed that's what God was giving him. It was a tumultuous time: communism was collapsing, and under pressure from the United States, Soviet president Gorbachev had finally torn down the Berlin wall just fifty-two days earlier. I've read transcripts of the entire prophecy from that night, and many of the things that Pastor Benny prophesied did come to pass; they just didn't do so within the time parameters he assigned to them.

As we've seen, if you can't find something in the Bible in more than one place, you're on dangerous grounds to apply it as a spiritual principle or look to it as a promise. As 2 Corinthians 13:1 says, "In the mouth of two or three witnesses shall every word be established." The same is true with modern-day prophesy: God always confirms His word so we can know it's a valid word spoken by Him.

Many people have very strong feelings about Benny Hinn; whether it be positive or negative, most people are passionate about the way they feel about the man I still call Pastor Benny, and I love him dearly. Do I agree with him on every point? No. Do I agree with any man or woman of God on every point? No. But that's the beauty of the Kingdom. We're all different; we all have our strengths and our weaknesses.

Let's look at a couple more prophetic words about the revival to come in the LGBTQ community, coming from two different sources, both of whom are well respected in charismatic, evangelical circles.

The first one I'd like to present to you was released by author and internationally recognized prophet, Lana Vawser, of Lana Vawser Ministries. The word was released on her Facebook page in June, 2015. Lana is one of those prophets that not only hears from Holy Spirit but has dreams and sees visions that are allegories of what God is planning. The following is the entire "word" as it appeared on her page:

> I had a dream where I saw "nets" being cast on a "different" side of the boat than "normal" for many and suddenly the nets were being pulled out of the water full and overflowing with what looked like rainbow trout.
>
> I woke up feeling the Lord say even though it may feel like what the Lord is asking you/prompting you to do is completely opposite to what you thought or expected and you may not understand it. But be encouraged that your obedience and faith is going to bring in an overflowing harvest of His manifest promises, provision, and increase, which will also result in many being impacted by your testimony and coming to know Him. Because this "step of faith" is completely "outside" what you would ever do normally, your testimony will shout "ONLY GOD DID THIS!!!!" and His Glory will shine!
>
> Don't let fear keep you in the "familiar." Step out! He's leading you into new ways and new waters of faith and seeing His faithfulness.

Truly, I have no idea if Lana knew what this vision meant, but I certainly did! My heart leapt within me as I read her words over and over again that June morning. I shared this word with everyone I knew in the affirming church.

The next prophetic declaration came about six months later by a gentleman named Doug Addison. Doug is the founder and President of InLight Connection and is a recognized prophetic speaker, author, and coach. I was not able to find anything about this particular word on the internet, and that's probably because it was not released on social media but to a group of people in a conference setting. This was not a popular word when it was released to a large group of evangelical pastors, and Doug received a lot of backlash for it. Doug Addison, like Lana Vawser, is heterosexual, and neither of them is in an affirming ministry.

I originally heard about this prophetic word through a dear friend, Zoila Aguilar, who was at the meeting where this all took place in January of 2016. Zoila originally told me about it a week or two afterward, when she ministered in my church in Palm Springs, CA. I asked her to write, in her own words, what she heard Doug say that afternoon, and she gave me the word to the best of her ability:

> I attended one of Joan Hunter Ministries' conferences in January 2016 and Doug Addison was one of the speakers. What a pleasant surprise when he got on the platform and said (and I'm paraphrasing of course because unfortunately I didn't record it) he said: "I'm going to say something to the leaders of churches right now that has hurt my ministry, speaking engagements, and finances. The Supreme Court's ruling on gay marriage was the LORD's doing!
>
> "Some of you here are believing for revival in your churches and territories. Revival will not come unless you stop judging people-groups that are not like you, especially the LGBTQ community.
>
> "There's a remnant in that community that worship God in spirit and truth, and angels visit their services. I know because I have seen it myself. They speak in tongues—prophesy and healing flows through them. Some have even been taken to heaven. They

are most certainly saved and going to heaven. God has a special plan to use them."

Then again he said, "I'm not afraid to lose friendships and money over this because God told me." You could hear a pin drop in that place. No one clapped and I just sat there in awe.

Most certainly, this is a major move of God's divine Holy Spirit coming to the LGBTQ community, and it will not, cannot, be stopped. The first prophetic announcement came to the church thirty-two years ago this past December 31, then a second in June of 2015 and a third in January of 2016. The message that it's coming isn't new; what I'm bringing to the table is God's motivation behind it—to make the Evangelical Church envious that what she has rejected, what she has hated so deeply, the LGBTQ community, is now become the object of His affection, and to wake them from their spirit of stupor.

SECTION VII– SOMETHING TO THINK ABOUT

CHAPTER 21
One New Man?

AFTER I PREACHED the message, "Does God Have a Gay Agenda?" on February 17, 2019, Holy Spirit prompted me to write this book. To be sure I was actually hearing from Him, I did what Christians call "throwing out a fleece." This is taken from the Book of Judges, chapter 6, verses 36 through 40, where we read the story of God telling Gideon to fight against two of the enemy armies that were oppressing the nation of Israel. Gideon, not being a warrior, was having a hard time believing that God would actually choose him for such a task. The story goes that Gideon asked God for a sign that he had really heard from Him, and that he would be victorious over Israel's enemies. The sign Gideon asked for was that he was going to lay a fleece, a sheep's skin, on his threshing floor. If God was going to give Gideon the victory, the fleece would be wet with dew the next morning, and the ground around it would be dry. God did as Gideon asked. Gideon asked for a second sign, a second fleece, and God answered Gideon according to what He had told Him.

In the same manner, I was eager to know that I was being led by Holy Spirit, not my own imagination, because this book is a prophetic revelation to the church and the LGBTQ community regarding God's plan for them. I decided to throw out this fleece: knowing how reluctant my dear friend and respected author, Kathy Baldock, is to associate herself with anything she isn't 100 percent sure of, I prayed, "If this is You telling me to write this book, then Kathy Baldock will have to agree to write the foreword for me." Kathy had already watched my sermon on the subject a few days earlier on my YouTube channel. I called her and told her that I believed Holy Spirit was speaking to me to write this book, and she enthusiastically agreed that she believed it needed to be written. Not mentioning anything about my fleece, I asked her if she would be willing to write the foreword. Her response almost floored me. Without hesitation, she replied, "It would be my honor." I knew then and there that God was in this book and I had to write it.

Several months into the writing process, I began feeling a stirring in my spirit that there was something Holy Spirit wanted me to see, something I had overlooked. This "stirring" came in the form of a passage of scripture that Holy Spirit dropped into my spirit. I kept ruminating on it, and I just couldn't get it out of my head. I didn't know what it was He was trying to show me. Then he added a second passage to it, and I began to see something that I had never seen before, and something I'd never heard any preacher preach. The first passage was this:

> **Matthew 22:23-30 (NIV)**
> That same day the Sadducees, who say there is no resurrection, came to him with a question. [24] "Teacher," they said, "Moses told us that if a man dies without having children, his brother must marry the widow and raise up offspring for him. [25] Now there were seven brothers among us. The first one married and died, and since he had no children, he left his wife to his brother. [26] The same thing happened to the second and third brother, right on down to the seventh. [27] Finally, the woman died. [28] Now then, at the resurrection, whose wife will she be of the seven, since all of them were married to her?"
>
> [29] Jesus replied, "You are in error because you do not know the Scriptures or the power of God. [30] At the resurrection people

will neither marry nor be given in marriage; they will be like the angels in heaven."

Take a look at the end of Matthew 22:30, where it says there will be no marriage in heaven because we will all be like the angels. What does that mean? I was perplexed as to why this would be what Holy Spirit was speaking to me as I was writing a book about God's plan for the LGBTQ community.

Let's take a look at scripture where people encounter angels and see how it might relate to this book.

There are over a dozen times in the Old Testament and an equal number or greater in the New Testament where ordinary human beings encounter angelic visitors. Not one scriptural account of an angelic encounter describes a female angel. Every single time it's a male. Am I saying that we'll all be male in Heaven? No, absolutely not; however, according to this passage, that is a possibility. What I am saying is that angels are always portrayed as male. The pictures we've all seen of the beautiful angels with golden locks of hair, wearing magnificent flowing gowns, are man's depiction of what we imagine them to look like, but it's completely against scripture. Scripture most often depicts angels as either messengers or warriors.

Several weeks after I was given this passage, Holy Spirit added a second passage, and it all started to make sense, as I had preached on this passage and referenced it multiple times but had never looked at it in the way Holy Spirit was now showing it to me.

The key to the meaning and message of this chapter is in the second passage:

> **Galatians 3:26-28 (NIV)**
> So in Christ Jesus you are all children of God through faith, [27] for all of you who were baptized into Christ have clothed yourselves with Christ. [28] There is neither Jew nor Gentile, neither slave nor free, nor is there male and female, for you are all one in Christ Jesus.

Speaking through the Apostle Paul, Father God tells us that once we're born again into His Kingdom, He no longer sees Jew or Gentile, slave of free, male or female. We are all one!

In the Old Testament there were dozens of restrictions as to who could enter Yehovah God's temple. A woman could not go into the temple, and neither could a man who still had his foreskin. God was extremely rigid in His requirements as to what was acceptable in His eyes if you wanted to be called "His." This was the same dispensation of time in which all of the Old Testament laws were in full force, where two men couldn't have penetrative sex together because it was not only unclean, but one of the ways pagans of that time worshiped their gods. But everything changes with the appearance of Messiah.

Ponder this if you will: Father God no longer sees gender once a person is born again. If at the point of our acceptance of Jesus' atoning work on Calvary—where Jesus Himself said He came to fulfill the law—if at that point all Father sees is our spirits, that part of us that will dwell with Him for all eternity, as neither male nor female, how then can intimacy between two born-again human beings who have made covenant with their Heavenly Father be unacceptable in his sight? Once we're washed in the blood of Jesus Christ, He does not see our gender. Our sexual identity is a non-issue, and we are one in His sight.

The mainstream Evangelical Church has been condemning and damning an entire group of people to hell based on the mistranslation and misinterpretation of a few passages of scripture, when scripture very clearly says that for those of us under the New Covenant, the covenant of grace, which was sealed with Jesus' own blood, gender is a non-issue with God. Instead of screaming that they're going to hell, the church should be doing its best to show the love of Jesus to those two boys who walk into church together. That sweet lesbian couple needs to be told that Jesus loves them and died for them too. We need to be expressing the love of God, letting Him convict folks of what *He* considers sin, instead of trying to shove our misguided dogma down their throats.

Think about this. Pray about it. Is the reason Jesus Christ said absolutely nothing about same-sex relationships in His time on earth because He knew and understood the principle that Paul would later espouse? The principle that it didn't matter because once we're born again, our earthly gender, and the expression of that gender, became null and void—that Father only saw us in the Spirit from that point on?

If there is no male or female in the Spirit, as the Apostle Paul clearly says in the passage above, then there can neither be gay nor straight in the Father's eyes either, as these are both expressions of a sexuality that no longer exists.

Think about it. Pray about it. And remember as you do that there are countless souls on the line.

SECTION VIII – WHAT'S NEXT?

CHAPTER 22
A Word from an Intercessory General

IN MARCH OF 2019, I received an extremely important word from an intercessory general, but before sharing it, let's take a look at the meaning of the term "intercessory general."

Intercession wasn't a term I grew up with in the Baptist Church, so let's look first at what intercession is, using the definition from Google's online dictionary:

> in·ter·ces·sion
> /ˌin(t)ərˈseSHən/
> noun
> 1. The action of intervening on behalf of another.

Intercession is intervening on behalf of another person, and in a spiritual sense, intercessors intervene on behalf of others in prayer. But there's an even deeper level to it than just praying for other people, and it is beautifully described in a blog post from https://www.tishasledd.com/blogposts/2017/03/the-difference-between-prayer-and:

> Prayer is to our lives what fuel is to an engine. We will not go very far in life without a healthy prayer life. Intercession is a step up from prayer.
>
> Intercession is praying God's heart into a specific situation or standing in the gap on behalf of a person or region who is in need of mercy and grace.

Now, if intercessory prayer is "praying God's heart into a specific situation or standing in the gap on behalf of a person or region who is in need of mercy and grace," what exactly is an intercessory general?

Although you won't find the actual term "general" as referring to anyone in scripture, you will read about the patriarchs of the faith in the Old Testament (kings, priest, prophets, judges), and apostles in the New Testament. These are the kind of people we would refer to in today's vernacular as "generals" of the faith: people who achieved great things for the kingdom of God.

The Christian faith has had modern-day "generals" for the past couple of hundred years, but they weren't really recognized as such until the early 1990s, when Dr. Roberts Liardon coined the phrase with the release of his first book about the lives of some of these men and women of God, entitled *God's Generals*. The book was an instant success, and over the decades has turned into a series of six books, selling millions of copies, containing over 2,200 pages chronicling the lives of such great men and women of God, like John and Charles Wesley, who founded the Methodist Church; Jonathan Edwards, who led the Welsh Revival; William and Catherine Booth, who founded the Salvation Army; Smith Wigglesworth, William J Seymour; Aimee Semple McPherson, Kathryn Kuhlman; and modern-day legend and evangelist, the late Billy Graham.

While most of the folks I've named above are well known in evangelical circles as "generals," there is another group of people who are not that well known, and those are the "intercessory generals." These are the largely unsung heroes whose prayers were the backbone of every major move of God's Holy Spirit the world has ever seen. And they do what they're called to do quietly, without any fanfare or acknowledgement. Most intercessors don't like being recognized publicly and shun any kind of attention you might try to give to them and their vital calling. Before I share the word I received from an intercessory general, let's take a look at an example of how intercessory generals help change the world.

As someone who absolutely loves to read about and study past revivals and moves of God, I have delighted in a favorite story of intercessors Peggy and Christine Smith. Peggy was eighty-four years old and blind, and her sister Christine was eighty-two and crippled with arthritis when these two Scottish sisters prayed in one of the greatest revivals the British Isles has ever seen: the Hebrides Revival, 1949–1952. It's reported by church historians that at the close of this amazing move of God every single person living in the Hebrides Islands confessed to having accepted Jesus Christ as Lord and Savior and being a Christian. But nothing happened before the sisters began to pray.

According to the church historians, in their advanced years, Peggy and Christine Smith began to get a real longing in their spirits to see the churches of their forefathers on the island of Lewis filled again and the young people of the island living for God. The sisters got a hold of the verse in Isaiah 44:3 that says,

> For I will pour water on the thirsty land, and streams on the dry ground; I will pour out my Spirit on your offspring, and my blessing on your descendants.

The sisters were just precocious enough to believe that God meant what was written in His Word, so they began earnestly bombarding the throne room of God for a sovereign move of His Spirit for their town and for the Hebrides islands.

The story goes that the two women agreed to pray two nights a week from 10:00 in the evening until 3:00 or 4:00 in the morning, on their knees. Though these two women were eighty-two and eighty-four years old, one blind and one with crippling arthritis, they were hungry to see God move in their lifetime.

After several weeks of praying like this, Peggy had a vision of her church being crowded with young people, and an unknown minister preaching from the pulpit. She immediately sent for the parish minister to come talk with her and her sister. After sharing Peggy's vision with the minister, the sisters asked him to gather together some of the church deacons and elders to pray with them for God to send the revival Peggy had seen in the vision.

Through a series of events, the unknown minister Peggy Smith had seen in the vision did come to the Island of Lewis, and God did pour Himself out on the island. It was one of the most spectacular moves of Holy Spirit the world has seen since the day of Pentecost, and it lasted nearly three years.

I recount this because I want my readers to understand that no move of God will take place in any people-group without people first being willing to pay the price in intercession. Intercessors are vitally important to the church even today. Remember, this happened less than eighty years ago!

Peggy and Christine Smith would be considered intercessory generals. They not only paid the price for the revival themselves, but they brought others into the fold to pray with them for God's plan to manifest, and they didn't stop praying until they saw it with their own eyes.

There are intercessory generals amongst us today who have been tasked with praying in the next, and possibly final, move of God's Spirit on the earth, as well as "birthing" new intercessors to join with them in their divine call. These people look just like you and me, but they don't act like us. They see things in the Spirit we don't see, and God speaks to them things we can't begin to fathom. They're consumed with prayer and won't allow anything to stand in the way of it. Intercessory generals will even go so far as to move to remote parts of the country, or even the desert for a season, so as not to be distracted from their prayer by the things of this world. They're few, they're far between, and they're precious beyond words. And I happen to be blessed enough to not only know one of these divine creatures but to call her my friend.

Typical of most true intercessors, my friend doesn't like attention being brought to her unless it's in a setting where she's using that attention to further the Kingdom of God, such as training up others with the call of intercession on their lives. I think the only thing this woman loves as much as prayer is imparting her passion for prayer to others who have the same calling. This is what's meant by the idea of "birthing" intercessors. My intercessor friend has imparted her passion and gifting for prayer to so many people over the years that her close friends and ministry partners lovingly refer to her as "Mama," because she has given "birth" to so many intercessors. She's a tiny little thing, but in the spirit realm she packs the equivalent of a nuclear warhead.

Mama was trained in her gifting as an intercessor as a part of one of the largest, most famous television ministries in the world. She asked me not to mention the name out of respect for that ministry, and her incredible humility. Additionally, she has a regular weekly prayer call with another Christian leader who heads a huge international ministry. Mama is truly a general.

At the beginning of 2019, I felt Holy Spirit urging me to have Mama come to Palm Springs and spend some time with my church's leadership and "core" group. The core are those folks without whom the church wouldn't be able to function properly—the ones a leader knows he or she can always count on.

The first of March, 2019, Mama came and spent a weekend ministering to my folks, teaching them the deep aspects of prayer and intercession. While she was with us, I told her that Holy Spirit was calling me to write this book and that I had already started it. That's when she shared a word with me that she had received from the Lord. This entire chapter is leading to one main point: the word she shared with me.

Mama knew my history. She knew that I had been a part of Benny Hinn's church in Orlando back in the day; she knew that I had been a volunteer on his crusade team, and that Pastor Benny had prophesied over me numerous times that God was going to give me a "double portion" of his healing anointing. Mama told me that while she was in prayer just a short time before she came to Palm Springs, Holy Spirit had spoken to her during one of her extended prayer times saying:

> "It's time for those who have sat at the feet of generals in the past season to rise up and take their place as generals themselves in the new move that's coming." He went on to say, "Everything they needed to complete their calling has already been deposited in them, and it is time to begin to walk in it."

This may not seem meaningful to those who have never sat at the feet of a great general of the faith, but to those of us who have, it's a word that brings life and direction to us as individuals, and a new sense of meaning and urgency to our ministries. For those who *have* sat at the feet of generals but are not currently involved in ministry and have been crying out to God, asking Him, "When? When will it be my turn?" you will understand how I'd felt. For years I questioned God, asking why He had spoken so many promises to me through great men and women of the faith only to forget that I was even alive. At least that's how it felt—like He had totally forgotten about me.

Some Christians are currently sitting at the feet of generals and don't even realize it! Don't let someone's age fool you; you don't have to be eighty years old to be a general—you just have to have been willing to pay the price to be used by God in whatever way He sees fit. Benny Hinn, T.D. Jakes, Steven Furtick, Daniel Kolenda, Heidi Baker, Joyce Meyer, Shirley Arnold, Bill Johnson, Roberts Liardon: these leaders are all generals. If you're currently a part of their ministries, absorb as much as you possibly can from these amazing men and women of God. And if you're blessed enough to actually be involved in ministry with these folks, praise God and realize you're there for a reason. There is no such thing as chance in the Kingdom of God. Avoid getting hung up on a certain aspect of a leader's doctrine that you may not agree with; there's still much to be imparted through God's generals to those who are teachable and hungry for the next move of His Holy Spirit.

This is important, so take heed: there's a brand-new crop of generals about to appear on the scene. Men and women who've sat at the feet of some of the greatest spiritual leaders of the twentieth and twenty-first centuries. Men and women who up until now have felt overlooked, passed over, and in many cases, invisible. Men and women who have been on the verge of giving up when in actuality they're the very ones God has prepared in advance to steward this next move of His Spirit.

If you're a born-again Christian member of the LGBTQ community, and you're one of the people I've described above, one who thought you had missed God's timing for His call on your life, or felt that you couldn't possibly do anything for the Kingdom of God because of your sexual orientation or gender identity, I'm here to give you hope. It's not too late, and He hasn't forgotten about you. As was the case with Queen Esther of old, you *were* brought into the Kingdom for such a time as this.

If you're a born-again Christian who hasn't come out as LGBTQ and are hiding in the closet of some mega-church out of fear of being rejected if people find out who you are, this is a word of hope for you too. You have a part to play in the coming move. Learn as much as you can, absorb as much as you can, and when Holy Spirit tells you it's time to move on, do so knowing God has you and will direct your steps if you put your full trust in Him.

As Mama's word encouraged and re-energized me for what's coming next, may you also be encouraged and energized. What's coming is going to be glorious, folks.

Get ready!

CHAPTER 23
The Dinner Bell to Salvation

WHEN I BEGAN writing this book, I wondered what this divine new move of God's Holy Spirit coming to the LGBTQ community is going to look like. All I knew was that Father had put it in my heart that He was going to bring my people into the Kingdom in unprecedented numbers in a supernatural display of His sovereignty; however, as I've written and pressed in to hear Father's heart on the matter, I started sensing His direction and began hearing Him in my spirit. I believe He's allowed me to hear what He's speaking concerning that which is coming to America and will then, as in other moves of His Spirit, spill over to the other countries of the world.

A few years ago, I spent several months studying the life and ministry of Kenneth "Dad" Hagin. Hagin's friends and ministry partners began calling him Dad later on in his ministry, after he was dubbed the "Father of the Faith Movement." His life story tells of an amazing man with an even more amazing call of God on his life.

When Dad Hagin died on September 19, 2003, at the age of eighty-six, he was considered one of the greatest healing evangelists of all time. Church historians rank him with the likes of John G. Lake, Aimee Semple McPherson, Smith Wigglesworth, Kathryn Kuhlman, and Oral Roberts. Having been miraculously healed from a fatal heart condition at the age of sixteen, he always believed in and preached healing. However, it wasn't until one evening, when he heard a preacher by the name of Raymond T. Richey, that his ministry changed and transformed into one of the most incredible healing ministries, with souls being brought into the Kingdom of God.

Here's Kenneth Hagin's story of that evening in his own words, taken from a blog found at: http://agbabo.blogspot.com/2017/12/healing-is-dinner-bell.html

> As a young pastor, just before my twenty-fourth birthday, I remember hearing Rev. Raymond T. Richey (a man who was used mightily by God in the area of healing) say, "Divine healing is the dinner bell." I knew exactly what he meant when he said that.
>
> At that time people living out in the country had a big bell on their back porch, and when dinner was ready, someone would ring the bell to let everyone in the fields know it was time to eat.
>
> When I heard Rev. Richey say that, I wasn't having healing services at my church on a regular basis. But I said to myself, "I'm going back home, and I'm going to start ringing the dinner bell."
>
> We had Wednesday night, Saturday night, Sunday morning, and Sunday night services. I told the congregation, "Every Saturday night is divine healing night. I'm not going to preach on anything but divine healing." So I started ringing the dinner bell.
>
> Initially, the crowd on Saturday night became smaller, and, as far as I could ascertain, no one was getting healed. I would anoint them with oil and lay hands on them. I would have a healing line every Saturday night.
>
> Still, no one was getting healed. But I kept on ringing the dinner bell! Finally, after six months, things started happening. People started getting healed.
>
> I didn't understand it then, but I know now that when I first began teaching on healing, I was planting seed. I had to keep watering that seed, and that takes time. I could have become discouraged and stopped holding healing services. Or I could have resigned the church and left. But when the harvest came, I wouldn't have been there to enjoy it.

Raymond Richey became famous for his "dinner bell" statement, but there was actually more to it than what Dad Hagin repeated in his story above. The whole statement was, "Divine healing is the dinner bell to salvation … ring it and they will come!" By "ring it" he was saying if you preached that God was still in the healing business today, that God would heal folks, and when He did, they would get saved. Healing would be the catalyst to salvation, and it worked!

In a condensed biography on Richey I found at https://healingandrevival.com/BioRTRichey.htm, the author says that it was believed that over one million people answered Raymond Richey's call for healing and/or salvation. Keep in mind that this was in the early twentieth century, and the ability to track numbers wasn't nearly as sophisticated as it is today.

By the end of reading the short biography, I was in tears. God poured Himself out through that man's ministry in such a spectacular, supernatural way that I was deeply moved. It's imperative to grasp the magnitude of what God did in this move, so here's a brief excerpt:

> Then God called them to hold a citywide revival in Houston, Texas in 1921. They did not have the money for it but pressed on. They started in a tent but it was too small. They moved to the City Auditorium and filled it. The revival went forty days and they saw 5,000 conversions. People came out of wheelchairs, deafness, tuberculosis, arthritis, blindness, and other diseases were healed. 40,000 people had received healing prayer. At one service 13 people were brought in on stretchers and 12 walked home. Richey then held meetings in Galveston and San Antonio … In Forth Worth the auditorium was too small and when people were refused entrance they climbed the walls to sit in the windows to hear. They went back to Houston twice in 1923. After one of the revival meetings a parade was held for those who had been healed. It was 13 blocks long! In a meeting in Tulsa there were 11,000 conversions and a truck was piled high with crutches and other medical supports that had been left behind.

This incredible move, this is what I believe is coming to the LGBTQ community: a healing wave that will make anything like it ever seen before on the earth pale by comparison. A virtual tsunami, if you will, of God's miraculous healing power, only this time it will be poured out not only *on* the LGBTQ community but through the LGBTQ community, and people will come into the Kingdom by the millions.

As we saw in chapter 20, Prophet Doug Addison said there was a "remnant" in the LGBTQ community that belonged to God:

> "There's a remnant in that community that worship God in spirit and truth, and angels visit their services. I know because I have seen it myself. They speak in tongues, prophesy and healing flows through them. Some have even been taken to heaven. They are most certainly saved and going to heaven. God has a special plan to use them."

Remember the story of Elijah from 1 Kings, where Elijah told God that he was the only one in Israel worth saving, because the rest had turned away from Him and deserved to die? What was God's response?

> **1 Kings 19:18 (NKJV)**
> I have reserved seven thousand in Israel, all whose knees have not bowed to Baal, and every mouth that has not kissed him.

These seven thousand people were God's "remnant," people who had stayed true to Him in spite of everything. Throughout history, God has always had a remnant! In every "nation, tribe and tongue," there is a remnant that belongs to the sovereign LORD and they bow their knee to no one else but Him—and the LGBTQ community is no exception.

That remnant consists of men and women in the LGBTQ community who have not "bowed their knees" to the things the mainstream Christian Church thinks all gay, lesbian, bisexual, and transgender people have given themselves over to: men and women who have sat, or are currently sitting, at the feet of God's generals— generals who would never affirm them if they knew they were LGBTQ. Those men and women are about to rise up and steward the greatest move of God's Holy Spirit the world has ever seen. It will be a healing revival in and through the LGBTQ community that will leave the mainstream, non-affirming, Evangelical Church not only absolutely aghast but, as the old saying goes, "green with envy."

It's important to understand the purpose in God making the Evangelical Church envious, jealous—not to frustrate them, but to compel them to repent and turn away from their idolatry in giving their unconditional love, adoration, and allegiance to a politician and a set of political ideals. It is to get them to once again return to their first love and have no other God before Him. Jesus, not a politician or a political party or an "agenda," is to be the lover of our souls. Our allegiance and devotion belong to Him, and Him alone.

CHAPTER 24
Same Spirit, Different Administrations

WHEN I FIRST sat down to outline this book, I felt a very strong urging in my spirit that, in addition to providing a background in Church history and foretelling the details of the next divine move of God's Holy Spirit, I was also to honor some of the men and women of God for the works they have already established. These are ministries that are vital to the LGBTQ community, whose growing acceptance of the true Gospel of Jesus Christ is due in no small part to these men and women, as is the fledgling acceptance of LGBTQ Christian folks by mainstream churches.

There are many, many other ministries beyond those we'll explore in this chapter, but these are the ones Father God laid on my heart to present to you. One of the major reasons behind my affection for these ministries and their leaders is that these ministries have each had an enormous impact on my personal life, as well as the LGBTQ community in general.

My intention here is to give honor to men and women who have lovingly, tirelessly labored to bring hope, healing, and freedom in Jesus Christ to the LGBTQ community. Their inclusion in this book is in no way an endorsement of every single theological and/or doctrinal stance that these wonderful people hold, as I've never met anyone with whom I agree 100 percent. So please hear my heart as I attempt to follow scripture and "give honor where honor is due," Romans 13:7. Please keep in mind that the ministries acknowledged below are completely independent of each other, are in no way affiliated with each other, and are not to be misconstrued as anything other than independent ministries each doing their part to bring healing and wholeness to a broken world.

While writing this chapter, I felt Holy Spirit give me a green light to also include some information about the ministry He's entrusted to me. My prayer in presenting all of these ministries to you is that you might catch the vision of one of them and do whatever Holy Spirit puts in your heart to be a part of that ministry and help it grow to its full potential.

Bishop Randy Morgan and the Covenant Network.

Of all the ministries in this chapter, I am most familiar with Bishop Randy's, and I have a deep-seated love for this amazing man of God.

Bishop Randy Morgan is the senior and founding pastor of New Covenant Church of Atlanta, and the presiding bishop over the Covenant Network. The Covenant Network is an affirming, full-gospel, word-faith, Apostolic/Prophetic network of churches and ministries with over a dozen locations in the United States, Mexico, Puerto Rico, and Australia, with a virtual online campus as well.

This impressive, expanding global ministry had its humble beginnings on July 23, 2000, in the clubhouse of the Doraville, Georgia apartment complex where Bishop Randy and his husband, Johnny Layton, lived. As the congregation grew over the years, the church had numerous temporary homes until their eighteenth year of ministry, when they finally settled in a beautiful complex on three acres located at 1600 Eastland Road SE, Atlanta, GA 30316. Here's the link to the church website https://www.newcovenantatlanta.com. Check them out and definitely stop in and visit if you're ever in the Atlanta area.

I asked Bishop Randy to tell me, in his words, what the mission of New Covenant Church of Atlanta (NCCA) was. His response was both simple and stunningly beautiful:

> To become a place where the Spirit of God is poured out on all people: all people, regardless of race, gender, gender identity, or sexual orientation. A place where people can come in and experience the presence of God and be equipped for ministry. A place where everyone becomes a minister in some way.

NCCA is open to anyone and everyone who desires a personal relationship with Jesus Christ, with their primary outreach being to the LGBTQ community.

The Covenant Network (CN) is a group of likeminded churches whose primary outreach is to the LGBTQ community. It's a group of churches who believe and consequently speak the same things. Their motto, or guiding principle, is found in scripture:

> **2 Corinthians 4:13 (ESV)**
> Since we have the same spirit of faith according to what has been written, "I believed, and so I spoke," we also believe, and so we also speak.

Bishop Randy describes the Network as:

> An independent group of churches that is "presence-driven," five-fold led and equipped, faith-oriented, Word-based, and Jesus-centric, whose primary goal is to establish churches and ministries throughout the world that carry the presence and word of God into all the world.

In keeping with the goal of continued expansion, the Network is open to new affiliations, but they can only begin through relationship, in accordance with the scriptural mandate set out in 1 Thessalonians 5:12, where the Apostle Paul admonishes the church:

> And we beseech you, brethren, to know them which labor among you, and are over you in the Lord, and admonish you.

Bishop Randy said they were always happy to meet new people who have a love for the ministry and that reaching out to a CN leader was the first step in establishing a relationship with them. Anyone may reach out to a member who has an active ordination within the Network; it doesn't have to be Bishop Randy himself.

The list of CN churches and leader contact information can be found at the CN website, https://www.thecovenantnetwork.com

I have personally seen and experienced things at the CN Immersed Conference, held every summer in Atlanta, that I haven't seen outside my time at Benny Hinn's church in Orlando. The Spirit of God is definitely moving in that place. One weekend at Immersed demonstrates what Prophet Doug Addison was talking about.

Matthew Vines and The Reformation Project

My interview with Matthew Vines was one of the highlights of researching and writing this book. I was blown away by what an incredible young man of God he is, embodying intellect, charisma, passion, and integrity, and at such a young age.

Matthew was born in Wichita, Kansas in 1990 into a conservative, Evangelical Christian home, where he says his parents' number-one priority was to share their faith in Jesus Christ with him, which they lovingly did. They did it so beautifully, in fact, that Matthew's first memory as a child is of him quietly asking Jesus into his heart one Sunday morning in the back seat of the family car as they headed home from church. He was three years old. Matthew loved going to church, and he loved Jesus, and every year for several years after this he would ask Jesus back into his heart, just to make sure He was really there. (I love the innocence of that, only a child.)

Matthew had pretty much the perfect childhood for a white American Christian boy with a great family life: he was smart, likeable, and fit in perfectly at the conservative Presbyterian Church his family had attended since before he was born. Everything was wonderful ... until he got to high school, where he met the first openly gay kids he had ever known, and these kids identified as Christian!

Up to this point, Matthew had never even met anyone who openly identified as lesbian, gay, bisexual, transgender, or queer (LGBTQ), let alone LGBTQ and Christian. This was problematic for him, as these kids were nothing like what his church had taught him about LGBTQ folks. They were loving and kind and gentle, and this caused Matthew no small amount of internal tension. The more Matthew got to know these kids, the bigger the disconnect became between his church's stance on LGBTQ relations and working to be loving and Christ-like towards people. This was something Matthew would struggle with all through high school.

The American Dream that Matthew was living just seemed to keep getting better as he packed up in the fall of 2008 and headed off for Boston, to Harvard University. It was here that he got involved with Intervarsity (IV), a conservative campus ministry that took a hardline stance against same-sex relationships. This led to increasing discomfort for Matthew, which finally resulted in him starting a small Bible study within IV, including other students who shared his feelings, or were at least open to conversation.

In this small study group, Matthew discovered that although he definitely didn't have anywhere near all the answers, the subject was not as black-and-white an issue as it had been presented. What he was seeing for the first time was that there was room for complexity in understanding the passages dealing with same-sex behavior.

After a time of living in a state where same-sex marriage was legal, on a campus where LGBTQ people were open about who they were and were treated the same as everyone else, the non-affirming position Matthew was raised with made less and less sense. In addition, seeing the negative impact it was having on LGBTQ people made it seem just morally wrong to him. And the more he studied the subject, the clearer it became that the non-affirming stance the church had taken was not well rooted in scripture—and scripture was everything to Matthew; in fact, I have never met a person with a greater love and respect for scripture than Matthew. A lot of the passages required him to ask questions about how applicable they were to the LGBTQ Christians.

By the end of his freshman year, Matthew had moved from a position of neutrality on the subject of LGBTQ inclusion to feeling extremely passionate about it as an issue of justice and dignity. This newfound passion led him to do some serious soul-searching and to ask himself some extremely hard questions about his own sexuality. Matthew relayed to me that he was "not very pleased" with the answers.

Knowing his parents' non-affirming stance on the subject, Matthew told me he felt like his entire world was coming undone. To deal with the crisis he now found himself in, he took a semester off from Harvard and went home to do the thing every Christian LGBTQ kid dreads the most—come out to his parents.

Like most heterosexual Christians, Matthew's parents hadn't had any reason to actually get into scripture and really "study" it on this particular subject until it became a matter of personal importance. All of a sudden, this wasn't just another issue their church took a stance on. This was real life. This was a matter of where their precious son would spend eternity. Believing their son's very soul was on the line, they desperately wanted to know what scripture actually had to say about same-sex behavior.

Matthew's parents reacted in the most beautiful way imaginable to his revelation: they spent that semester studying scripture with their son to see what Holy Spirit was speaking in God's Word. The result? They completely changed their stance on LGBTQ inclusion.

Matthew and his parents worked through the six "clobber passages" that we looked at in chapters 3 through 6 and came to the realization that although some same-sex behavior was definitely condemned in scripture, there was absolutely nothing that even hinted that a loving, committed, monogamous relationship between two people of the same sex was anathema, as the Church universal claims it to be.

Matthew and his parents came to the realization that Christian preachers and teachers are using one broad brush to paint a picture of same-sex behavior when, in fact, there are many aspects of it scripture doesn't cover. This is why studying the origin and evolution of the words found in scripture is so important. As we'll see later in this chapter, Kathy Baldock, who makes researching her life's work, has shown how languages have evolved so much even over the past 150 years that there's no way a word could mean something in scripture today that it didn't mean 2,000 years ago.

I cannot overemphasize the need to study. Study, study, study—not a cursory reading of scripture, but deep and broad study of the scriptures. Jesus said, "You shall know the truth and the truth shall set you free." The truth is found when we study. Freedom, therefore, comes when we study.

The experience of studying scripture with his parents that semester left Matthew full of hope that non-affirming Christians could come to see the topic of LGBTQ inclusion differently if they were engaged in the right way. Matthew believed that approaching the subject from a place of love, relationship, and a true desire to uphold the authority of the biblical text would bring people to a better, more nuanced understanding of scripture. The approach so many had tried of dismissing scripture as outdated just wasn't working, and unfortunately, this was the rhetoric a lot of conservative churches were hearing from progressives on the subject of LGBTQ inclusion. Growing up in a conservative home, Matthew knew how off-putting this was and that it rarely, if ever, led to a meaningful dialogue.

After a period of time, Matthew realized that there were only so many of the two thousand people in the church where he had grown up who were even willing to engage him. He also realized that the greatest challenge LGBTQ youth faced when coming out to their family and loved ones was not having resources that were accessible to put into the hands of their parents or pastors or youth leaders. Coming out was daunting enough without having to defend yourself or try to do all the research yourself.

Matthew's foray into affirming ministry came when he accepted an invitation to speak about the Bible and same-sex relationships at a local Wichita church in 2012. The hour-long talk was videotaped, and the video went viral with over one million views. It created such a stir that the *New York Times* did an article about it, and Matthew was offered a book deal to flesh out the arguments he was making in his now-famous video. His book, *God and the Gay Christian,* was published in 2014.

The two years following his now-famous talk in that Wichita church were an amazing, hectic time for Matthew. Not only was he writing his book, but he was being inundated with feedback from people everywhere telling him how much the video had helped them in reconciling their faith with their sexuality, or in accepting their child's sexuality. All this was extremely exciting, but Matthew found it deeply troubling that while hearing how much he had helped so many people, they were still struggling with feeling alone, isolated, and invisible in their own churches. Matthew had been there; he knew that feeling.

The need for more organizational support for LGBTQ people to be able to come out and still stay in their churches was obvious. Out of this need, and the need for change in the mainstream churches, The Reformation Project was born in 2013.

The Reformation Project, commonly known as TRP, is a non-denominational ministry whose purpose is to empower and equip Christians who are LGBTQ-affirming with theological knowledge and tools and the network they need to be effective advocates of an affirming perspective within their own congregations, thereby helping those churches change their policies and procedures.

The three main values set forth by TRP lay the foundation for the remainder of their beliefs. They are 1. Love for God, 2. Love for the Bible, and 3. Love for the Church. You can read more about these core values at https://reformationproject.org/values/.

Building on these, TRP adds in Monogamy and Covenant, and Diversity and Inclusion. Rather than trying to put their values into my own words, here is the value statement from their website:

> **On Monogamy and Covenant:**
>
> As a Christian organization with a deep love for the Bible, we believe that our values about sexuality must be shaped by Scripture, the communion of saints, and the Christian tradition. We honor the link that Scripture and the Christian tradition make between sex and lifelong commitment, and therefore, we embrace the principle that we should seek to say with our bodies what we are able and willing to say with the rest of our lives. That is why we are specifically asking churches to bless monogamous, covenantal same-sex relationships. (See Bible, Gender, Sexuality by Dr. Jim Brownson to learn more about our understanding of Scripture and sexual ethics.)
>
> As churches assess their teachings on sexuality, we encourage church leaders to move away from shame-based teachings about sexual ethics that communicate that a person's value or worthiness as a future spouse is tied to their virginity or their sexual history. These teachings have caused significant harm to both LGBTQ and straight people and have undermined the church's credibility on sexual ethics across the board. No one is damaged goods, and no one should be treated as if they are.
>
> **And on Diversity and Inclusion:**
>
> Jesus's life and ministry were marked by his love and concern for people on the margins of society, and as a Christian organization,

we believe we are called to follow Jesus's example by prioritizing diversity and inclusion in our work. LGBTQ Christians have too often experienced the pain of exclusion from the church, and that reality compels us to care about and address the ways in which the church has also fallen short of honoring other marginalized people as equal image-bearers of God.

We embrace the Bible's teaching that if one part of the body suffers, every part suffers with it, and if one part is honored, every part shares in its joy (1 Corinthians 12:25–26). This biblical principle is why we're committed to having a diversity of voices in our leadership and programming, and it is why we strive to foster belonging and inclusion for everyone regardless of their race, ethnicity, age, class, gender, gender identity, sexual orientation, or disability.

Some evangelical Christians have extremely critical words towards Matthew and TRP, but it's hard to understand how anyone can reject their core values, and thereby their message, when they echo the very words of Jesus Christ and so beautifully mirror His teachings.

TRP offers several exciting opportunities for everyday people to serve and thereby become equipped to join them in their mission of bringing LGBTQ inclusion to mainstream churches in America and the world. The first of these is TRP Cohort program.

Cohorts are core leadership teams of Christian people who have gone through three months of intensive study and training with the sole purpose of learning how to help shift churches, and other Christians, in their local areas from a non-affirming to an affirming stance on the issue of LGBTQ inclusion. TRP currently has cohorts in eight different locations in the United States, as well as a chapter in Sydney, Australia and a virtual chapter in Latin America comprised of people from several different countries.

Another program TRP offers is called Parents in Process. This is a fairly new program for parents who are wrestling with the news of their child's sexual orientation or gender identity. This program offers those parents a vital lifeline of love, support, and resources to better understand what their children are going through, and to help equip them to support their children in this crucial time. Anyone can learn more about this program by contacting TRP at the link above.

Pastors in Process is TRP's program for pastors of non-affirming churches who are seeking to lead their churches into becoming more inclusive and affirming of LGBTQ people in a way that strengthens, rather than weakens, their church's commitment to the authority of scripture and orthodox Christian values and beliefs.

These programs are all tied together by the TRP National Conference held each year in the fall. The 2019 conference in Seattle saw over nine hundred attendees, and while the 2020 Conference was canceled due to the pandemic, the 2021 conference in Phoenix, AZ is expected to have a record turnout—and I intend to be there.

Acknowledging the complexity of the scriptural witness, TRP is very specific about what they're asking churches that become involved with them to endorse. As stated in the section on Monogamy and Covenant, they are "specifically asking churches to bless monogamous, covenantal same-sex relationships." The "anything goes as long as it's between two consenting adults" philosophy of many affirming churches is not held in TRP because it doesn't mesh with scripture; it's actually antithetical to it, asserting that the Old Testament "tolerated" a lot of things that it did not "teach," for example, polygamy, which was later taught against in the New Testament.

Sexual ethics from a scriptural standpoint are based in the belief and acceptance that as born-again Christians, our bodies are the temple of the Holy Spirit and that we were bought with a price. Freedom in Christ does not mean the freedom to have sex with whomever we want, wherever we want, as long as it's consensual. This is a horizontal perspective only taking into account our responsibility towards each other and leaving out the vertical aspect, which is our responsibility towards God, the one to whom we belong.

Covenant takes priority in understanding sexual ethics as outlined in scripture. If we truly believe that we are Holy Spirit's temple, His dwelling place, and that Father God bought us for Himself at the cost of His son's life, then it is not solely up to us to determine how we should order our sexual lives. This goes for every true Christian, regardless of their sexual orientation or gender identity.

I had heard something about Matthew that really intrigued me, so I asked him if I could be so bold as to ask him an extremely personal question. He graciously said "yes," and I was completely overwhelmed to hear straight from his mouth that as the head of TRP, Matthew practices what he preaches. He personally is sexually abstinent, waiting until God sends him the man he knows he's to be in covenant with. God has honored Matthew's commitment and given him a boyfriend of over two years, who shares the same values and passions that he does.

On a personal note, this gave me great hope, as abstinence, although preached from many a pulpit, is almost unheard of in practice in any church. I can count on one hand the number of people I know practicing it, both gay and straight. I know several leaders of affirming ministries who claim to require this of their leaders but turn a blind eye when they move from one "partner" to another, while others just say, "It's none of my business." I disagree—it is your business how your leaders live, because their effectiveness suffers when they disobey God.

In summary, TRP plays a vital role in developing a culture of inclusion and affirmation in mainstream churches both in the United States and abroad, while adhering firmly to the authority of scripture.

If you or a loved one is a born-again Christian who identifies as LGBTQ and doesn't have an affirming church to go to, I suggest contacting TRP to see if there's a cohort program in or planned for your area. If you are or know of a pastor from a non-affirming church who is searching for the truth and scriptural clarity on same-sex behavior and relationships, contact TRP.

I am a major believer in TRP and a huge Matthew Vines fan. Together they are working to bring love, hope, and inclusion to LGBTQ folks everywhere, and that's a beautiful thing. It's a "whosoever" thing, and it's such a God thing.

You can reach TRP at https://reformationproject.org/

Pastor Stan Mitchell and the Everybody Church

Pastor Stan Mitchell is an amazing man of God, one whom I've been following for the past three years and, with the writing of this book, one with whom I have become personally acquainted. I now have the immense honor of calling him my friend.

Pastor Stan grew up in the United Pentecostal Church—the UPC, as it's known in church circles—and was a rising young star. By the age of nineteen, he was an ordained evangelist in the denomination, and it seemed as though there was no stopping his burgeoning career. As the saying goes, "But God…" It seemed Father had other plans for him. Through a series of events divinely orchestrated by Holy Spirit, Stan found himself growing further and further away from the exclusionary, non-inclusive doctrine of the denomination that taught that hell awaited anyone not of their flock. Not only were they a "my four and no more" type of denomination, but they followed the cult-like practice of "shunning" anyone who dared wander from what they deemed "the straight and narrow." To leave the UPC was tantamount to death; you simply ceased to exist.

By the age of twenty-six, Stan had grown so disillusioned that he turned in his papers and left the church. A year and a half and an immense amount of soul-searching later, Stan joined a mega-church in Nashville, called Christ Church, as their teaching pastor. It was a great fit, as the senior pastor there was also formerly UPC. Stan was with Christ Church from 1995 until 2002. After a brief sabbatical, he founded GracePointe Church in Nashville in 2003. GracePointe is an inter-denominational church that is currently open and affirming to the LGBTQ community, but it wasn't always that way.

Holy Spirit had been doing a slow, subtle work in Pastor Stan since his days in the UPC. What started out as questioning the exclusionary doctrine of a denomination slowly transformed into questioning the exclusionary doctrine of mainstream Christianity when it comes to the LGBTQ community.

GracePointe had reached a "sweet spot" where gay folks attended the church and were loved and accepted with their sexuality, shall we say, overlooked. By 2012, things were going beautifully, with the church even attracting some Nashville celebrities, including country-western superstar Carrie Underwood. And that's where our story really begins.

While in London for a concert, Carrie Underwood did an interview for the BBC. Being very vocal about her faith as a Christian, Carrie was asked about her church. She exuberantly gushed about the wonderful church home she had found and, having a huge LGBTQ fan base, how she loved the fact that her church was "gay friendly." That's when the proverbial shit hit the fan. What was meant to be a loving endorsement of a place of worship where she felt at home ended up thrusting GracePointe Church into the international spotlight, and the crosshairs of the Westboro Baptist Church. Picketing ensued.

In light of where they now found themselves, Pastor Stan, his board of directors, and the congregation had no choice but to make a formal determination as to where they stood on the issue of LGBTQ inclusion. Being led by Holy Spirit, the church entered into a two-and-a-half-year "time of discovery," starting in July of 2012. During this time, the pastor, board, and congregation fervently sought Holy Spirit's direction on the matter but seemed to be at a stalemate until December of 2014.

During Pastor Stan's time at Christ Church, he had become very dear friends with the worship leader he served alongside. In the years since he had left Christ Church, that worship leader, who was every bit a Nashville celebrity in his own right, had come out as being gay. Needless to say, the world this man had known his whole life completely imploded. After a lengthy, complicated, and painful divorce, Stan's friend was now in love and planning to marry the man of his dreams, who enjoyed national celebrity from numerous appearances on reality television.

It was December 2014, and the wedding was all set: three hundred guests at the Country Music Hall of Fame. Then the unthinkable happened. Bowing to pressure from Evangelical Christians, the pastor who was scheduled to officiate the wedding cancelled on the guys two weeks before the big day. This is where Pastor Stan explained to me the reality of what he experienced in his journey of inclusion in the most beautiful metaphor I've heard outside of scripture:

> Once it moves from black letters on a white page to flesh tones of human life it reads completely differently.

When Pastor Stan heard the news that his longtime friend had been so deeply wounded, he did what any loving friend would do; he called and asked him if he needed a pastor to officiate the ceremony. Tears ensued.

After two and a half years of seeking Father's heart on the matter of LGBTQ inclusion, the whole issue became a moot point. Pastor Stan had officiated the most highly publicized gay celebrity wedding the country had ever seen, and there was no turning back.

The following month, January of 2015, Pastor Stan officially announced that he and GracePointe Church were 100 percent open and affirming to the LGBTQ community. Chaos ensued.

Nine out of twelve members of the GracePointe Board of Directors resigned that morning. The flourishing congregation, with an average Sunday attendance of nine hundred, immediately dropped to around five hundred to six hundred, and continued to spiral out of control until there were only about seventy to eighty people left. The entire evangelical world was watching as the amazing ministry that had once been GracePointe Church was in the throes of death, and all Stan Mitchell could do was mourn.

GracePointe did recover and began to grow again around the end of 2018, and it is now running three-hundred-plus in their Sunday services, but this isn't the focus of our story; everything we've explored about Pastor Stan and GracePointe has been to provide the context and background of this man's journey. Everything Pastor Stan went through in his progression to full inclusion of the Gospel was to bring him to the ministry he is now involved in: saving lives on social media, one life at a time. And this is where our story gets exciting.

During the season Stan Mitchell was mourning the death of GracePointe as he knew it, he became active on social media, sharing his journey on Facebook. Things were going along smoothly, not really anything exciting from a ministry standpoint, until one fateful evening in November of 2017 when Pastor Stan received a private message on his Facebook page that would change his life and the lives of countless others.

The message was from a teenage boy in Idaho who was from a very conservative evangelical family. The boy was sitting at a desk playing with his father's handgun, contemplating putting it to his head and taking his own life. There was a computer on the desk and somehow the gun bumped the mouse, and the computer came on. When it did, there on the screen was Facebook, open to Pastor Stan's page with a recent post. The boy read the post and immediately sent Stan a message telling him where he was and what he was planning to do. Even though it was late at night, Stan was up and read the post. Overwhelmed, Stan Mitchell did the first thing he could think of—he shared the situation with his Facebook family, telling them the boy's story and asking his followers to pray for the young man. By the next day, there were over a thousand responses.

Pastor Stan's Facebook friends not only prayed for the boy, they sent their love and blessings. They shared stories of their own journeys—of both sorrow and victory. Messages of hope and solidarity flooded in from around the world. The response was as overwhelming as the conundrum our pastor had found himself in just hours before, and an unintentional ministry was birthed out of the realization that there was power in stories—stories the everyday people he ministered to could relate to. How could he have missed it? Jesus used stories; they were called parables. There was power and healing in the telling of people's stories. After all, hadn't the story of Cornelius, found in Acts 10, been a crucial part of his own path to inclusion?

Today, young people around the globe who are struggling to reconcile their sexuality with their faith, or the faith of their families, turn to Pastor Stan by reaching out to him on Facebook. Parents who know their kids are struggling and are willing to put their children's lives and well-being ahead of their dogma, but don't know where else to go, turn to Pastor Stan, even though they know they'll be ridiculed and condemned by their evangelical friends and other family members. They'll be accused of "compromising" when in fact they aren't compromising at all: as Pastor Stan puts it, "parents of LGBTQ kids don't compromise illicitly, they are the bona fide players in this because they have flesh in the 'game'; the rest of us are just abstracting."

So the stories keep coming, and Pastor Stan keeps sharing them. Not all of them are young people and parents anymore. People of all ages, from all walks of life and all social standings, have found Pastor Stan's Facebook page a place of safety. The results have been quantifiable as hundreds of people now look to Stan Mitchell for spiritual guidance through virtual means, and that brings us to Everybody Church.

Everybody Church is a church with a virtual campus where people who are, as Pastor Stan puts it, "religiously disenfranchised and spiritually deconstructed" can call home. Pastor Stan's vision for the ministry is that actual brick and mortar churches will come to life in areas where there is a concentration of believers who are affiliated with Everybody Church and are willing to do what's necessary to bring that vision to reality.

One of the stories found on Stan Mitchell's Facebook page is particularly inspiring. This one isn't from a young person or a concerned parent; it's from an adult man who, for the majority of his life, has been right where that teenage boy from Idaho was. This post begins with Pastor Stan's introduction:

> Every day, I receive private messages from people who longingly circle this community. They do so without officially joining it, looking in from the periphery—silently, fearfully, without scarcely clicking the like button. They are a part of us. Today, I received the message below from one such person.
>
> "A month ago, as I lay in bed at the end of a long day, I wake-dreamed about contracting Covid-19. Unable to sleep, my mind raced, playing out multiple scenarios. The scenarios my mind created were not ones in which I avoided the dreaded contagion but instead were 'opportunities' by which I could be stricken. As morbid and disturbed as that may sound, it describes a way of life for me; you see, that night was only one of a thousand more like it—interminably long and tormenting nights where I have thought of, fantasized about, and longed for death. The truth is, I am a faithful coward who has prayed countless times for God to take me, to do for me what I can't do for myself. This, mostly because I have always feared if I took my own life I would be forever damned. Though ritually lapsed as a Catholic, internally I am still a scared child, pathologically concerned by a reward and punishment model of the afterlife. Mostly it's punishment.
>
> "I write this letter to you for a couple of reasons. The first is to say thank you. A few weeks ago, I was introduced by a young priest in my parish to your Facebook page and Everybody Church. (I suspect him to be a fellow struggler though we have never spoken of the matter.) Since that time, I have immersed myself in reading your posts, your friends' loving and supportive comments, and watching hours of your talks. It all has been salve for my soul and

opened a small window of hope inside of me. For that I am grateful. The second reason I write is to offer my story (at least part of it) as an example of the millions of us who carry within the incalculable and often fatal damage created by religious fear, dare I say 'abuse.' You see, I am not a child, a teenager, or young adult, all of whom reasonably lack the psychological tools to process such internal dissonance. On the surface, I possess the years of life and the developed brain necessary to process such an existential dilemma. I am a university provost, lifelong educator, former two-term congressional member, and MD/PhD in my late sixties. In spite of all this, as I plodded slowly through hundreds of your posts, I was reduced to tears again and again by the raw and emotionally unedited words of those who have vulnerably laid bare their hearts to you. Especially the young. One young person in particular so adeptly captured my story that it took my breath away. I ended up reading her words at least a dozen times that first night. She pointedly said, 'I live my life between two hells; one is the life my parents and church say I must live if I am to please God and the other is the hell I will go to if I live out the life that has been inside of me as far back as I can remember.' As I reflect even now on her words, 'I live my life between two hells...' I shudder with resonance. And I so want to say to her, to help her know—the horrible space she so vividly describes exists only in her mind and not in reality. It is ludicrous and cruel and ungodly, this horrid ideology responsible for forbidding so much love and life. And as I tell her this in another of my waking-dreams, I realize I am speaking to the lonely and scared child that still lives so desperately inside of me.

"And so we keep posting stories, stories that give voice to the experience of millions of God's children who have lived before, are now living, and are yet to be born. Until these stories no longer exist."

Pastor Stan can be reached at https://www.facebook.com/stan.mitchell.58.

Kathy V. Baldock and Canyonwalker Connections

Kathy is a classic example of what happens when God disrupts the happy, peaceful life of a heterosexual evangelical by bringing them face-to-face with the inconvenient truth that His Gospel truly is meant for everyone: Whosoever!

As Pastor Stan Mitchell so exquisitely expresses it, "everything changes when black letters on a white page take on flesh tones and become a real person." For Kathy, those "flesh tones" came in the form of a Native American woman she encountered on one of her daily hikes in the Sierra Nevada Mountains. Unlike the overwhelming majority of Kathy's friends, this woman was not a Christian, and she was a lesbian! With time, what at first had seemed like a "chance" meeting became apparent for what it truly was: a divine encounter. As they became friends, Kathy began to see that the teaching she'd received about LGBTQ people was completely different from the reality of this friendship. She sincerely listened to her friend as she shared her journey as an LGBTQ person of color who had been so rejected by the Christian church that she was convinced that God didn't love her! By this time, she and Kathy had been friends for over a year, and Kathy was overcome with grief at the pain her friend had been subjected to. This friendship was the beginning of Kathy's ability to see the effects of evangelical prejudicial messages about the LGBTQ community.

That winter, after a heavy snowfall made it impossible to receive her daily *New York Times* delivery, Kathy went online to do the crossword and happened across a story about an upcoming conference in Seattle, led by Justin Lee, founder of the Gay Christian Network. Kathy was completely shocked to see the words gay and Christian in a headline; she had never even considered that a gay person would or could be a Christian! Her curiosity was piqued, and she decided to attend the conference.

Standing at the back of the auditorium on the first night as the attendees began to sing and worship, Kathy was overwhelmed by the Spirit she felt in that place. She fell to the floor, weeping in agony as she realized what the church had done by excluding these precious souls from fellowship with the Body of Christ.

Kathy is an incredibly bright woman with an engineering degree from Rutgers University; she has an unquenchable thirst for knowledge and a dogged curiosity, and she was determined to find the source of the disconnect between what she had always believed the Word of God said about LGBTQ people and the reality of what she had experienced in Seattle. Out of that unquenchable thirst for truth, a new ministry was born:

> Canyonwalker Connections—where faith and scholarship intersect—exists to repair the division that exists between social and Christian conservative and the lesbian, gay, bisexual, and transgender (LGBT) community through education, training, and dialogue in both secular and religious environments.
>
> "Loosen the chains of injustice, untie the cords of the yoke, set the oppressed free and break every yoke. Then you will be called Repairer of the Breach." Isaiah 58
>
> www.canyonwalkerconnections.com

During my interview with Kathy, she made a profound statement:

> I'm an Evangelical Christian and I want people to hear about the goodness of God. All this nastiness was never God, never God.

Canyonwalker Connections is multi-faceted, consisting of a blog; a very active Facebook page; links to Kathy's first book, *Walking the Bridgeless Canyon* and her upcoming second book, *Forging a Sacred Weapon: How the Bible Became Anti-Gay*; and ongoing international seminars entitled Untangling the Mess, wherein Kathy does an extensive demonstration of how the words we use today and words found in scripture have evolved over the last two thousand years.

In her seminars, which run from two to six hours or more, Kathy uses a timeline on butcher paper that stretches some forty-plus feet to illustrate the timing and history of scriptures, cultures, politics, medicine, and language: what certain words meant at different intersections of time, and how they've slowly morphed to what they mean today. For me, as a born-again Christian who is also gay, seeing this demonstration literally changed my life. It was Kathy's timeline that confirmed what Holy Spirit had been speaking to me for years: I was OK just the way God made me, and His plan for my life didn't include changing me into something I was never meant to be.

Kathy describes her ministry as "the meeting place between faith and accessible academics," where she sets things forth in such plain language that even her ninety-year-old mother can understand the very long, very slow progression of semantics that the Apostle Paul could have never imagined.

Kathy takes centuries of information on human sexuality out of books and puts it hand-in-glove with her faith so that people can see where God and humans interact. She presents it in a way that the majority of folks can understand that the damage that's been done to scripture, and consequently the LGBTQ community, wasn't done by God; it was done by people.

Kathy strings together really complex pieces of academic information in her timeline with no gaps, and she makes them accessible from a position of faith. In seeing this, people begin to realize that with what we thought 150 years ago about human sexuality and what we now know, the Apostle Paul couldn't possibly have thought 1,900 years ago what we've been telling people he was thinking and saying. Kathy lays it out clearly and flawlessly, so that even someone who has never studied the historical documents, let alone the Bible, can grasp it. All it takes is an open mind and a teachable spirit.

By combining accessible academics with faith, and taking a slow crawl through history, we see where, when, and how things changed, and we come to the inevitable conclusion that God never got it wrong; people did.

Kathy's perception is that people of faith don't ask where these ideas or perceptions of "perversions" actually came from. They just marginalize LGBTQ people based on what they think they know, on what they think scripture says, when the problem isn't what God says about sexuality; it's what people say about it. God never says the thing people say He said; it's what people have done to the Bible that's the problem.

Kathy V. Baldock is one of the most brilliant people I've ever had the privilege of not just knowing, but of calling my friend. And as beautiful as her mind is, her heart is even more beautiful. That beauty shone like a finely-cut diamond when she let me see a glimpse of what's inside.

Kathy closed out our time together saying:

I am so sad, because I know the power faith can have in a person's life in terms of healing and blessing, and the opportunity for that has been taken away from LGBTQ people. I'm not trying to drag anyone back to church; I am just so sad that the door has been shut to them. My work is a way that people can find the comfort and healing in life that has been completely taken away from them. I know how much my faith has done for me, and I want it to at least be available to them. I want the faith I've found to be an option on the table for everyone. Rather than them saying, "OK, I can go to counseling, I can take drugs to medicate, or I can go on long runs every day because I certainly can't go to church and find healing from God," I want that to be one of the options LGBTQ people have.

Kathy can be reached at Canyonwalkerconnections.com

Reignite Ministries International, Reignite Palm Springs, and RISSM

Reignite Ministries International is a small network of Spirit-filled, affirming churches and ministries that has no agenda other than to see Holy Spirit make the name of Jesus famous throughout the earth. Our vision is to reignite the fire that once was Azusa Street—only this time it burns for everyone!

We are an Apostolic/Prophetic ministry, believing in the restoration of the five-fold offices of apostle, prophet, evangelist, pastor, and teacher in these last days. We are Word/Faith-based; having a strong Messianic foundation, we acknowledge and ordain the office of rabbi as well as teacher, with a strong understanding of Messianic theology being the difference between the two offices.

> **Acts 1:8**
> But you will receive power when the Holy Spirit has come upon you, and you will be my witnesses in Jerusalem and in all Judea and Samaria, and to the end of the earth.

This is the founding verse for the ministry God has entrusted to me, and we view it through a twenty-first-century, American lens. For us, the commission Jesus gave His disciples would read, "You will be my witnesses in Palm Springs and the West Coast and the entire United States, and then to the ends of the earth." Our vision encompasses a Reignite Church in every major city that has a substantial LGBTQ population.

That being said, we are not a network of "gay" churches, and we are not a network of straight churches. We are a network of churches that love and affirm everyone who seeks a relationship with Yehovah God through His son, Jesus Christ, Yeshua Messiah. In South America, we operate under the Iglasia Nuevo Amiento banner, under the undaunted leadership of Apostle Marlene Vieta. Apostle Sven Verbeet is the founding and senior pastor of Gateway of Hope—Houston, as well as the apostle over Gateway of Hope in the Philippines and India, whose churches operate orphanages as well, and joined the RMI Network in April of 2019.

My intention here is not to promote "my" ministry (it's not mine; it's God's ministry), but to simply affirm that we exist and what our vision is. In addition to multiple church locations, we also have a vision to establish a Christ-centered recovery program, "Reignite Recovery," that accepts God's LGBTQ children as they are and doesn't consider their sexuality something they need to "recover" from. It is our vision to make this program available to every affirming church in America, to help them with their congregants who struggle with any type of addiction.

Holy Spirit has given us various cities where we have a burning desire to see Reignite Churches established, and I want to share that vision with you. If you live in one of these cities and don't have a Spirit-filled, affirming church that's preaching the unadulterated Word of God, pray about establishing a relationship with us and helping us birth a church in your city. We expect to have our "virtual campus" up and running under the direction of an amazing man or woman of God by time this publication reaches your hands.

Our vision currently includes:

Los Angeles, CA   Tampa, FL
San Diego, CA   Miami, FL

Oceanside, CA Jacksonville, FL
Long Beach, CA Washington, D.C.
Sacramento, CA New York, NY
San Francisco, CA Vancouver, Canada
Fresno, CA Tel Aviv, Israel
Phoenix, AZ Reykjavik, Iceland
Las Vegas, NV Pattaya, Thailand
Reno, NV Hong Kong, SAR
Portland, OR New Delhi, India
Seattle, WA

Reignite Palm Springs

Reignite Palm Springs (RPS) is the flagship of the RMI Network and where the ministry is headquartered. We are a small group of believers with a massive vision and unrelenting faith.

To read more, visit us at: Reignitepalmsprings.com

RISSM

RISSM is the acronym for Reignite Ministries International School of Supernatural Ministry, and upon establishment will be the crown jewel in the RMI Network. Modeled after a school in Redding, CA, it will be the first and only school of its kind that teaches how to walk in the supernatural gifts of the Holy Spirit and is open and affirming to all sexual orientations and gender identities. A personal relationship with Jesus Christ and a desire to go deeper into the things of God will be the only spiritual requisites for acceptance into RISSM.

At RISSM, in addition to being taught the Bible and Christian ethics, students will be taught how to flow in the supernatural gifts of Holy Spirit as outlined in 1 Corinthians 12:8–12. Those gifts are: the word of knowledge, the word of wisdom, the gift of prophecy, the gift of faith, the gifts of healings, the working of miracles, the discerning of spirits, different kinds of tongues, and the interpretation of tongues. Those who are not of the Pentecostal/Charismatic belief may be skeptical or hesitant, but these gifts are biblical, they are for real, and they are most definitely still for today.

We have a vision to see a new generation raised up and trained in how to operate effectively in these gifts, according to the Word of God.

The RISSM campus will be located in Palm Springs, fulfilling a promise Father God made to me when we started the church here, that if I would be obedient and follow where He led me, Palm Springs would become known as a place where the presence of God dwells.

The vision the RMI leadership has for ministry is not only massive—it's completely unobtainable without the supernatural help of Holy Spirit. RPS is a very small church, and it's going to take hundreds of people dedicated to the ministry for RISSM to become a reality. But we serve a really, really big God, and it was prophesied to us multiple times when we first started the church here that God would cause people to move from every part of the country to lock arms with us to build the vision Father God gave us, and that people would come from all over the world to experience the worship at Reignite Palm Springs. RISSM will be a direct product of the overflow of that worship.

If you feel Holy Spirit may be leading you to join us in our vision for Palm Springs, RISSM, or any of the locations God has laid on our hearts, please pray about it and then reach out to us. Every church, every ministry, starts the same way—by establishing a relationship. We don't ordain anyone we don't have a relationship with, so please, take the first step and get to know us. We envision people in every aspect of ministry: spirit-filled worship leaders, musicians of every sort, psalmists, deacons whose heart is to serve, ushers, parking lot attendants, folks who know ASL and can lead a Sign Choir, intercessors, and people operating in every other gift and office. Our vision is HUGE. I encourage everyone to ask God if you're one of the people He would send to Palm Springs. Our prayer is that hundreds or thousands will catch the vision, catch the fire, and come be a part of what God is building.

For more information about RMI check out our website at Reigniteministriesinternational.com

You can watch our sermons on our You Tube channel at https://www.youtube.com/channel/UCwws2Qb5LLlpNYdzlUze4pw

My Podcast, "West Coast Fire" is available on our You Tube channel, Apple Music, Google Podcast, Spotify, Pocketcast and all other live-streaming platforms.

You can also follow me on Twitter @PastorBrianKing and Instagram @PastorBrianKingOfficial. As my personal Facebook page has reached a maximum of five thousand friends, I have set up a new public page, Pastor Brian King. I invite all who would like to keep up with where God is taking me in ministry to connect with me.

SECTION IX— GOING FORWARD

CHAPTER 25
The Cry of the Father's Heart

IN THIS FINAL chapter, I want to set some direction as to what to do with all the information we've covered thus far. First of all, and most importantly—pray. Pray like you've never prayed before. Pray as the Apostle Paul instructs the Church in Ephesus, for a "Spirit of wisdom and of revelation" (Ephesians 1:17). Then, remembering what we read in Hosea 4:6, "My people are destroyed for lack of knowledge," ask Father God what He would have you do with the knowledge you now have. In the following pages, I've broken down what Holy Spirit has been speaking to me for three different groups of people, as to what the next move should be for each of them, and thus in closing this book, I leave you with what I hear as the cry of the Father's heart to these three groups.

To the Evangelical Church—Repent

The Evangelical Church in America is certainly quick to call for repentance and pronounce imminent judgment on any and everyone but herself. Evangelical leaders pronounce judgment on America for any number of reasons: gay marriage, abortion, the way Hollywood celebrities live, environmental activism, and even "drag queen story hour" at the local library.

Natural disasters such as hurricanes, floods, tsunamis, and volcanic eruptions are often lauded as God's judgment for any of the things evangelicals condemn.

Even as I was writing this book, evangelical author, pastor, and self-proclaimed "Voice of Evangelism," Perry Stone, declared all over social media that the COVID-19 pandemic, which has caused global suffering and death, is the work of God. He said God "allowed" it to "deal with the 'abominations'" … the gays. Interestingly, very few gay folks have died so far, but thousands upon thousands of ordinary, heterosexual people have. Ironically, Perry Stone has been removed from his pulpit for inappropriate sexual behavior with multiple staff members. This sounds familiar; he should have removed the log from his own eye before trying to look for specks in others' eyes.

The Evangelical Church would have you believe that God hates all the things they hate. Bestselling Christian author Anne Lamott put her keen observation in her now-famous saying:

> You can safely assume you've created God in your own image when it turns out that God hates all the same people you do.

Seeing as how the Evangelical Church calls for judgment on those she hates, it's a pretty good indication that she, the Church, may have fallen victim to this very practice. To her, the object of God's wrath, the reason America is being "punished" is always someone else. The biggest problem with that is that it doesn't fit into scriptural constructs.

All through the Old Testament, we see examples of God's judgment. He literally rained it down on the entire world in the flood of Noah's day because of the gross depravity of the people. We read how Sodom and Gomorrah were destroyed for their depravity and their threats to the out-of-town visitors. That first instance was before God had established a "chosen people" and given them His standards for a chosen people to live by. After that, judgment was usually reserved for Israel. But why? Why, when God says that she, Israel, was the "apple of His eye" was she always the reason He brought judgment in scripture?

Again we find that because she was the apple of His eye is precisely why she was judged; because she belonged to Him, and she knew better. God had statutes and laws the rest of the world didn't know anything about, but Israel did. God had made a covenant with Israel, and therefore she was held to a higher level of accountability and was subsequently judged when she violated that covenant.

The Church of Jesus Christ is no different today than Israel was in scripture. The Church has been grafted in, as we saw in chapter 7. She is now included in being the apple of His eye under a "new covenant" and, once again, held to a higher standard than the rest of the world. Therefore, she, the Church, bears the brunt of any judgment that might come:

> **1 Peter 4:17 (KJV)**
> For the time is come that judgment must begin at the house of God: and if it first begin at us, what shall the end be of them that obey not the gospel of God?

It is an absolute possibility that God would use natural disasters to judge a country, but according to what we just read, it wouldn't be until after He judged His Church. I see no sign that God has judged His Church in America…yet. But trust me, it is most certainly coming.

Whether you believe God is currently judging the United States of America or not, I think we can all agree that our country is in a state of brokenness, and there is a scriptural remedy for that. It's found in:

> **2 Chronicles 7:14**
> If My people who are called by My name will humble themselves, and pray and seek My face, and turn from their wicked ways, then I will hear from heaven, and will forgive their sin and heal their land.

His people, called by His name: these are the ones whose actions can bring about judgment from God—not the heathens. They are also the only ones that can bring healing to the land. That scriptural promise was given to the Jews but also applies to the Church today. Doesn't God say that we, the Church, are His people? The name Christian means "little Christ." Isn't that literally being called by His, Jesus Christ's, name?

Yes, God wants everyone to turn to Him, but punishing the Philistines for their ways in biblical times wasn't any more His priority than punishing the nonbeliever is today. His priority, His passion, has always been Israel/the Church. This is not to dismiss or ignore that we have Heaven to gain and Hell to shun, but we're not talking about eternal judgment; we're talking about judgment in the here and now. The onus of repentance, to turn God from judgment to healing, is on the believer.

Church, stop looking for God to judge a group of people that don't know Him, and take responsibility for the condition of the country you claim to love so much. Scripture says it's we who need to turn from our wicked ways.

The first thing God calls for His Church to do in the passage above is to humble themselves. Then pray, then seek His face and turn from their wicked ways. Unfortunately, if there's one thing the mainstream Evangelical Church in America cannot be accused of, it's being humble. Just look at her highest profile leaders: proud, arrogant, boastful, lovers of political power, oppressors of the poor and marginalized, pronouncing judgment on fellow human beings, and the list goes on.

The next steps we're told to take all follow in line: pray, seek His face, and turn from our wicked ways. And yes, scripture tells us that as God's chosen people, those of us who call ourselves by His Name, we are capable of walking in wicked ways. Church, God considers your pride, your turning your backs on "the least of these," your lust for political power, and giving your adoration to a politician above Him, wicked.

In calling for the repentance of the Evangelical Church, Holy Spirit spoke three different scriptures to me that I outlined in this chapter. The first was from the book of Revelation, in Jesus' charge and admonition to the Church of Laodicea:

> **Revelation 3:14-22 (NIV)**
> To the angel of the church in Laodicea write: These are the words of the Amen, the faithful and true witness, the ruler of God's creation. [15] I know your deeds, that you are neither cold nor hot. I wish you were either one or the other! [16] So, because you are lukewarm—neither hot nor cold—I am about to spit you out of my mouth. [17] You say, "I am rich; I have acquired wealth and do not need a thing." But you do not realize that you are wretched, pitiful, poor, blind, and naked. [18] I counsel you to buy from me

> gold refined in the fire, so you can become rich, and white clothes to wear, so you can cover your shameful nakedness, and salve to put on your eyes, so you can see. Those whom I love I rebuke and discipline. So be earnest and repent.

Dozens of online articles by respected theologians and teachers all agree that Holy Spirit is speaking this word, not only to the Church of Laodicea, but to the Church in America. As discussed in chapter 7, it's quite common for scripture to be speaking to more than one situation at different times. This was written to an ancient church but was also speaking prophetically to the Church that would come in the last days. It's speaking to us. We *are* that church, and Jesus Christ, Yeshua Messiah Himself, is rebuking us and calling us to earnest repentance, because "discipline" is coming.

But repentance doesn't begin with the folks in the pews; it falls on the leaders of the Church to set the pace. Remember that the anointing "flows from the top down." Everything in the Church always starts with the leaders and then flows down to the rest of the people. The Prophet Joel stated it beautifully in the second of the three passages Holy Spirit gave me for this section of this chapter:

> **Joel 2:17 (NKJV)**
> Let the priests, who minister to the Lord, weep between the porch and the altar; let them say, "Spare Your people, O Lord, and do not give Your heritage to reproach, that the nations should rule over them. Why should they say among the peoples, 'Where is their God?'"

Church leaders, whether you're mainstream Evangelical or affirming, it's up to you to set the standard and bring repentance to the Body of Christ. Your congregations will not do anything they don't see you doing personally and hear you sincerely preaching consistently.

This brings us to the final passage Holy Spirit gave me for this section, and it has to do with us as leaders being sincere about our repentance. Coincidentally, it also comes from the Book of Joel in the passage just preceding the one we read above:

> **Joel 2:13,15 (NKJV)**
> So rend your heart, and not your garments; Return to the Lord your God, for He is gracious and merciful, slow to anger, and of great kindness; And He relents from doing harm. [15] Blow the trumpet in Zion, consecrate a fast, and call a sacred assembly.

In biblical times, the way people showed remorse or grief was to "rend their garments," to literally tear their clothes as they wept out loud. Here the prophet is telling us that when we're repenting on behalf of the people that our hearts should be torn in two, not our clothes. He tells us to "consecrate a fast" and call a special meeting of all our people. What God is saying here is that He takes our need to repent seriously, and we should too.

It is imperative that the mainstream Church repents, not only so she can be restored and be a part of the new move God is about to bring to the earth, but because there aren't that many truly Christian affirming churches out there, and there isn't the depth of spiritual maturity in enough of them to shepherd the masses of LGBTQ folk that are about to come into the kingdom.

Will God bring this move without the mainstream Evangelical Church? Absolutely! But the cry of His heart is for the Church to repent, and for once, be on the right side of church history.

To the Affirming Church—Press in and Rise up

The previous section is primarily addressed to the Evangelical Church, just as an exhaustive section of chapter 19 was devoted to calling out the leaders of the Affirming Movement for the things they've allowed to come into their churches, because "It's time for our leaders to repent!"

Once sincere repentance has taken place, what do we, as affirming leaders, do next? What is Holy Spirit's directive for the days ahead?

Having spent more than two years reading, writing, researching, praying, fasting, and waiting on God, I can tell you the cry of the Father's heart to the Affirming Church in America is two-fold: "press in" and "rise up!"

Press in to Him like you never have before, like the very souls of our people are at stake— because they are. Press in beyond the superficial, carnal things of not only the world but of the Church, because there is most definitely a carnality that's crept into the Affirming and Evangelical Church. Repenting of it is the first step, ridding our churches of it is the second, and the third is pressing in to the High Call of God. What exactly does that look like? It looks like following the admonition of Jesus Christ:

> **Matthew 16:24-26 (ESV)**
> Then Jesus told his disciples, "If anyone would come after me, let him deny himself and take up his cross and follow me. ²⁵ For whoever would save his life will lose it, but whoever loses his life for my sake will find it. ²⁶ For what will it profit a man if he gains the whole world and forfeits his soul? Or what shall a man give in return for his soul?"

Take up your cross—what does that mean? It means dying to the things of the flesh, to the things of this world that we get so wrapped up in, and living for the things of the Spirit. The things of this world are temporal; the things of God are eternal. We have to press in to God to learn not only His deeds but His ways, and there's a huge difference. Knowing His ways only comes from spending time with Him in the "secret place."

What is the secret place? It's both a time and a place: it's when you and God spend time alone. It's that time and place where it's only you and Him; nothing else in the world matters. It can be in your bedroom with the door closed, or a private spot on the beach. It can be a special place in the mountains, or it can be on a boat in the middle of a hidden lake. It's that place that only you and God know about. It's that place where He's not only the King of the Universe but your "Abba" Father as well, your "Daddy," your "Papa." If you've never experienced that place of intimacy with Him, I have to tell you that once you do, you'll never want to leave.

Scripture references the secret place several times; here are two of my favorites:

> **Matthew 6:6-7 (NKJV)**
> But you, when you pray, go into your room, and when you have shut your door, pray to your Father who is in the secret place, and your Father who sees in secret will reward you openly. ⁷ And

when you pray, do not use vain repetitions as the heathen do. For they think that they will be heard for their many words.

And,

Psalm 91:1 (NKJV)
He that dwells in the secret place of the Most High shall abide under the shadow of the Almighty.

I love the second passage because it talks about not only going into that place of intimacy with God but dwelling there. That's when you've spent so much time alone with Him that you not only know His ways, but your very heartbeat begins to align and beat in sync with the rhythm of His.

Many people reading this may never have experienced what I've just described; it must sound like fantasy, delusion, or something so ethereal that you don't believe it's obtainable—but it is. Press in and ask Father for it. Don't just ask once and expect something "magical" to happen. Scripture tells us that "God is a rewarder of those who diligently seek Him" (Hebrews 11:6).

The second part of Father's heart's cry to the Affirming Church is "Rise up."

Rise up and take your place in the glorious move of His Holy Spirit that is about to sweep over our community and the world like a spiritual tsunami. Those of you who have sat at the feet of great generals, rise up! Rise up and become the generals you've been trained to be and lead us as we wage war in the spirit against the enemy of mankind's soul, the enemy that has held our people hostage for far too long. Rise up against the lie that God has no place for us in His Kingdom. Rise up against the lie that stereotypes us as vapid, soulless drones dancing to the beat of the drums of lust and perversion. Rise up to your identity in Christ. Rise up to be the men and women of God Jesus Christ spilled His blood on Calvary for you to be. Rise up to your destiny. *Rise up!*

To the LGBTQ Community—Come Home

As I sit here pondering my journey over the last twenty-four months, I can't help but be somewhat overwhelmed with emotion as I conclude this book. My prayer is that reading this book changes you as much as writing it has changed me. I can happily, humbly say that I am not the same man I was a year and a half ago. Everything about me has changed to one degree or another: the way I preach, the way I pray, the way I minister, the way I love, heck, even the way I dress.

As a pastor, I have an almost overwhelming passion to see people who have never known Jesus Christ come into relationship with Him. As a gay man, I have a burning desire for members of the LGBTQ community to be among those new Christians. For far too long, the mainstream Evangelical Church has not only turned her back on my people, but she's condemned them so vehemently that at times it seemed her next move would be to physically hunt us down and kill us … and some evangelical leaders have actually endorsed such a heinous act.

But that's not the Father's heart. Death and destruction have never been His heart towards any people. Father's heart is always towards restoration and redemption. So it's here, in this final section of the final chapter, that I share with you Father's heart for my people. To the LGBTQ community of America and the world, the cry of Father God's heart is—come home!

We've seen that all spiritual truth has to line up with God's Word to be considered truth, and two of the most beautiful examples of the Father's heart being towards restoration and redemption can be found in Jesus' own teachings: His parables. Thus, it's appropriate that we close by looking into these two parables. Let's stop and pray for just a moment and ask Holy Spirit to give us eyes to see, ears to hear, and a heart to receive what He's speaking in this, His Word.

The first parable exquisitely shows us the heart of the Father as it relates to those of His children who, for one reason or another, have wandered away from their faith. Consequently, to them He is just a distant memory—someone they "used to know." That story is of course, that of the prodigal son:

> **Luke 15:11-32 (NIV)**
> Jesus continued: "There was a man who had two sons. ¹²The younger one said to his father, 'Father, give me my share of the estate.' So he divided his property between them.

¹³ "Not long after that, the younger son got together all he had, set off for a distant country and there squandered his wealth in wild living. ¹⁴ After he had spent everything, there was a severe famine in that whole country, and he began to be in need. ¹⁵ So he went and hired himself out to a citizen of that country, who sent him to his fields to feed pigs. ¹⁶ He longed to fill his stomach with the pods that the pigs were eating, but no one gave him anything.

¹⁷ "When he came to his senses, he said, 'How many of my father's hired servants have food to spare, and here I am starving to death! ¹⁸ I will set out and go back to my father and say to him: Father, I have sinned against heaven and against you. ¹⁹ I am no longer worthy to be called your son; make me like one of your hired servants.' ²⁰ So he got up and went to his father.

"But while he was still a long way off, his father saw him and was filled with compassion for him; he ran to his son, threw his arms around him and kissed him.

²¹ "The son said to him, 'Father, I have sinned against heaven and against you. I am no longer worthy to be called your son.'

²² "But the father said to his servants, 'Quick! Bring the best robe and put it on him. Put a ring on his finger and sandals on his feet. ²³ Bring the fattened calf and kill it. Let's have a feast and celebrate. ²⁴ For this son of mine was dead and is alive again; he was lost and is found.' So they began to celebrate."

This whole story is extremely deep and indeed has been the subject of many books. Here, let's focus on the father, because he's a representation of God as depicted by the Son Himself. We all know the story; the son is greedy and rebellious, given to riotous living with drunks and whores. This was definitely me before Jesus came into my life.

As I come from a Jewish family on my mom's side, I have done a lot of study and research on Jewish culture, and I will point out a few things that some people miss in a cursory reading of this story.

At the beginning of the story, Jesus gives us a clue to the financial status of the father when He says the younger son wanted his portion of the estate. The father wasn't a poor farmer barely getting by; he was a wealthy estate owner. This would make sense, as he is a metaphor for God the Father. In Hebrew culture, a wealthy estate owner would have been a very dignified, even pious, man, a man revered and well respected in the community. Now let's look at the father's actions to see who he was when it came to his son.

In verse 20, "while he was still a long way off, his father saw him." He saw him, *from a long way off.*

Think about that for a moment. Here we have a wealthy estate owner, busy about his daily affairs, taking care of all the things the owner of an estate would do in the course of a day. Do we really think that he would have just casually glanced up and noticed someone a long way off, and it would have meant anything to him? I don't buy that for a moment: I own a small landscape construction company, and when I'm on the job, I'm not paying attention to people coming down the road. No, I propose that the reason the father recognized the figure walking towards him was because he was keeping vigil, constantly watching that road, staring at times, in hopes of one day seeing his son coming home. He was a father; his son was gone, and his heart was broken. He was hoping, he was praying, and He was watching for his son's return.

Next we see that the father was filled with compassion for his son. Although the boy was still a long way off, the father recognized that it was his son coming towards him—the son who had been gone long enough to burn through a rather hefty inheritance. His last job had been feeding pigs. Pigs are dirty. They wallow in mud mixed with their own filth. The boy had traveled to a "distant country," which means the trip home had been a long one. The boy was covered in filth and dust; hair disheveled; clothes dirty, ragged, and probably torn; beard matted—he was a mess. He hadn't eaten in a long time; remember, he'd wished he could eat what the pigs were eating. He was thin and weak, most likely stumbling, barely dragging himself down that road, but his father recognized him and had compassion on him.

As a father, I totally get it. Even though his son had been gone for quite some time and was most likely unrecognizable to anyone else but his mother, his father knew him so intimately that even under wretched conditions, he recognized him from a long way off. He knew that was his boy coming down that road, and his heart melted.

What did the father do next? He ran to his son! This is where a little lesson in Hebrew culture comes in. A wealthy estate owner in that time would not have run anywhere, especially not to a son who had humiliated and disgraced him. According to Hebrew law, a boy like this man's son should have been taken to the elders of the city and stoned outside the city gates for the way he treated his father. We must recognize the severity of what this young man had done: demanding his share of the estate while his father was still alive was the ultimate act of disrespect. In essence, what he had done was to tell his father, "I wish that you were dead!"

But the father ran to him. This wealthy, dignified estate owner hiked up his robes like a young boy and ran to his son. This father laid aside his dignity, all decorum, Hebrew law, and all the social edicts of his time, and he ran to his son. Truly, this is Father God's heart towards *all* His children, LGBTQ folks included.

So many of us have been bludgeoned with a diametrically opposing narrative by the Evangelical Church. I wish I could proclaim that they meant well, but the honest-to-God truth is that they've sent a lot of beautiful souls to hell and left countless others without hope in the world.

Please understand: it doesn't matter if you're LGBTQ, or any other letter of the alphabet, Jesus Christ's death on Calvary was for us! For all humankind. There is no qualifier for "whosoever." If you're one of those people, like me, who had a relationship with Jesus Christ only to be disowned and abandoned by the Church when you came out, leaving you battered, bruised, rejected, and feeling all alone without hope, you need to know that just like the loving father of the prodigal son, Father God is keeping vigil, watching and waiting for you to make the decision to come home. And as soon as you take those first steps towards Him, you'll see Him running, arms open wide, towards you. I can tell you from personal experience that it's the most glorious reunion you'll ever encounter.

The last thing to recall before we move on to the second parable is that when the father embraced the boy, he didn't receive him back as a servant, which was the boy's hope when he set out to return home. No, he received him as the son he always was:

> ²² "But the father said to his servants, 'Quick! Bring the best robe and put it on him. Put a ring on his finger and sandals on his feet. ²³ Bring the fattened calf and kill it. Let's have a feast and celebrate. ²⁴ For this son of mine was dead and is alive again; he was lost and is found.' So they began to celebrate."

He put the best robe on him. It doesn't even say that the servants were ordered to clean him up first; they were ordered to clothe him in the robes worthy of his place in the father's house. A ring was put on his finger, signifying his status as a son, and new sandals were put on his feet. In the father's exuberance at having his son back, he couldn't bear to see his boy take one more step in those old, ragged sandals. No, his son took the final steps home dressed as though he had never left. And that's what's waiting for us when we yield to Father's voice and come home.

The second parable we're going to look at shows the Father's heart as it relates to those who have never known Him. This is the parable of the lost sheep. I think this story is particularly poignant and relative to the LGBTQ community because we can so clearly see the Evangelical Church as represented by the Pharisees.

> **Luke 15:1-7 (NIV)**
> Now the tax collectors and sinners were all gathering around to hear Jesus. ² But the Pharisees and the teachers of the law muttered, "This man welcomes sinners and eats with them."
>
> ³ Then Jesus told them this parable: ⁴ "Suppose one of you has a hundred sheep and loses one of them. Doesn't he leave the ninety-nine in the open country and go after the lost sheep until he finds it? ⁵ And when he finds it, he joyfully puts it on his shoulders ⁶ and goes home. Then he calls his friends and neighbors together and says, 'Rejoice with me; I have found my lost sheep.' ⁷ I tell you that in the same way there will be more rejoicing in heaven over one sinner who repents than over ninety-nine righteous persons who do not need to repent."

To put this into context, the Pharisees were the religious leaders of Jesus' day: the Jerry Falwells and Franklin Grahams of their time, place, and Jewish faith. Their attitude towards Jesus and those He associated with was much the same as the present-day Evangelical Church's attitude toward the LGBTQ community: they were disgusted and criticized Him for associating with such undesirables. Sound familiar? Not only did Jesus socialize with them, but He ate with them! In Jewish culture that was a major taboo. As a side note, I've seen posts on social media claiming Jesus "partied with sinners." While the intent may be to make Jesus more accessible to modern sensibilities, that He partied is absolutely not true. Jesus ate and fellowshipped with them; He did not partake with them in their debauchery.

The next thing we see Jesus doing is what Jesus does best—He tells them a story in the form of a parable, a story with a moral to it, one they can relate to. He asks the question, "If you had a hundred sheep and one of them was lost, who of you wouldn't leave the ninety-nine who were safe and go find the lost one?"

Every man, woman, and child in Israel knew the value of a sheep and knew they would do whatever it took to get a lost one back. They would go to any lengths to find what was theirs! Though many do not realize it, we are Father's; we belong to Him, and He has paid the ultimate price to get us back.

Let's focus closely on the next part. What does the shepherd, Jesus, do when He finds that lost sheep? Does He beat it with His staff and berate it for being lost? Does he build an altar there on the spot and sacrifice it to God because it is evil? No! Scripture tells us He "joyfully puts it on his shoulders and goes home." Yes, He lovingly picks it up and carries it.

What does He do next? He calls his friends and neighbors together and says, "Rejoice with me; I have found my lost sheep." The shepherd doesn't get on his phone or make a post on Facebook; He goes from house to house, telling His friends and neighbors that He has found His lost sheep, and inviting them to celebrate with Him! In our culture that might seem a little excessive, a little "extra," but to God, it's a big deal, and Jesus tells us so in the next verse.

> I tell you that in the same way there will be more rejoicing in heaven over one sinner who repents than over ninety-nine righteous persons who do not need to repent.

According to this, there is a celebration in heaven every time a sinner repents and comes to Jesus. The word translated as "sin" in this passage is the Greek word *hamartia*, which, according to Strong's Concordance, means "to miss the mark." People get all weird and defensive if you call them a sinner, but Romans 3:23 says "All have sinned and fall short of the glory of God." We've all missed the mark.

What is baffling in this story is how Jesus could relate the Pharisees to someone who didn't need to repent, given their unkind behavior. The one thing I can come up with is they kept the law, so in that sense they were righteous and weren't like the people Jesus said He was there to save. They were so full of themselves, and so full of the law, that they thought they were safe. They didn't realize they were lost and weren't open to hearing the truth.

Much of the Evangelical Church is the same way today. At the beginning of this chapter, I issued a passionate call for them to repent, even as Jesus issued the cry to the Church of Laodicea. Unfortunately, very few will heed that call. How do I know that? First, Church history shows a disappointing trend of the established church dismissing, ignoring, and even persecuting those who are a part of a new move of Holy Spirit. Second, the fact that Holy Spirit revealed to me that the reason Father God has chosen the LGBTQ community to be the recipient of this new move of His Holy Spirit is to make the mainstream Church jealous of His extravagant display of love towards a group of people they literally hate—in the same way the Jews hated the Gentiles.

This parable is subtly different from the one about the prodigal son. Jesus says this parable is about the sheep that have never known Him, because he talks about the celebration when one of them is found. In this story, the shepherd, Jesus, goes out looking for the lost sheep. In the story of the prodigal son, we see the father, God, patiently waiting for the son to come home. In both cases, the cry of the Father's heart is the same: Come home!

It doesn't matter if you're a son or daughter. It doesn't matter whether you wandered away or stormed off in a fit of anger. It doesn't matter if you walked with the Father for twenty years or if you've never met Him. The cry of His heart is the same: Come Home!

Yehovah God, Creator and King of the Universe, wants a relationship with you so badly that He sent His only son, Jesus, to die on a cross in your place, in my place, to give us the opportunity to have that relationship with Him.

If you're LGBTQ, I am so, so incredibly sorry for the way the mainstream Church has treated you. I'm sorry for the way you've been maligned, mistreated, and downright abused. I'm sorry for the hatred you've endured, for the venom and vitriol that has been spewed at you in Jesus' name. But I promise you the Spirit of God is not the spirit behind any of this, and those operating in that wretched spirit will have a severe price to pay for the damage they've done to our people—and I have the scripture to back that statement up:

> **Jeremiah 23:1-2 (ESV)**
> "Woe to the shepherds who destroy and scatter the sheep of my pasture!" declares the Lord. ² Therefore thus says the Lord, the God of Israel, concerning the shepherds who care for my people: "You have scattered my flock and have driven them away, and you have not attended to them. Behold, I will attend to you for your evil deeds, declares the Lord."

And in the New Testament we read:

> **Luke 17:1-2 (NIV)**
> Jesus said to his disciples: "Things that cause people to stumble are bound to come, but woe to anyone through whom they come. ² It would be better for them to be thrown into the sea with a millstone tied around their neck than to cause one of these little ones to stumble."

The Church will pay for her sins, but that's up to God to deal with in His time, and in the manner He sees fit. Our concern has got to be with our standing with Father God in the here and now.

So what is your standing with Him? Are you an Evangelical Christian who's been an ally to the LGBTQ community? Are you one of the ones working to bring healing and salvation to a group of people the church has so maliciously maligned over the past forty years? If so, thank you. We love, honor, and appreciate you so very much for everything you're doing for the Kingdom. I pray you remain strong in the power of His might and continue to fight the good fight.

Are you one of the Christians who have done damage to the Kingdom of God due to your lack of knowledge of both the meaning of scripture and of the true nature of Father God's heart? If so, realizing that most non-affirming Christians never intended to hurt anyone, I pray I've given Holy Spirit the ammunition to convict you strongly enough for you to get things right with God in this area of your life. I pray you become an integral part in this new move of God that's about to be released on the earth.

Are you a born-again Christian who's also LGBTQ and a part of the Affirming Movement? If so, my prayer for you is that you'll press in and rise up! I pray that you'll find your primary identity in Jesus Christ and will continue, or begin, walking in the power and integrity of the call Father God has on your life. If you're one of those people who has sat at the feet of generals, I pray that you rise up and take your place in this new move.

Are you a prodigal son or daughter? Are you one who, like me, walked away from your faith because you believed the lie the Church told you when they said you were no longer welcome at Father's table? If so, my prayer for you is that you'll hear His heart's cry and come home. He's waiting. All you need to do is ask for forgiveness, and you'll find Him literally running to embrace you and restore you to the place of an honored son or daughter.

Or are you one of those precious souls that, like a lost sheep, Jesus has been looking for? Are you one of those LGBTQ folks that never even considered a relationship with God through His son Jesus Christ, because you believed the lie that His sacrifice wasn't for you? Or that you somehow had to be "good enough" before He would love you? Or that He was angry with you, or that He hated you because you were some kind of "abomination?" I'm here to tell you, as a bishop, a pastor, a father, and a child of God, those things are all lies—lies the enemy of your soul has spoken and ignorant people have repeated—lies straight from the pit of hell. My prayer for you is that you will get alone with God and ask Him to show you if I'm telling you the truth or not. Ask Him if He loves you and then open your heart for His answer, because it's going to be a resounding yes.

> **John 3:16-17 (NKJ)**
> For God so loved the world that He gave His only begotten

> Son, that whoever believes in Him should not perish but have everlasting life. ¹⁷ For God did not send His Son into the world to condemn the world, but that the world through Him might be saved.

I pray that you'll ask Him to forgive you for your sin: for all the times you've "missed the mark." I pray you'll find not only forgiveness but new life in Jesus Christ as you ask Him into your heart to make you a child of God. Scripture tells us "If you declare with your mouth, 'Jesus is Lord,' and believe in your heart that God raised him from the dead, you will be saved. ¹⁰ For it is with your heart that you believe and are justified, and it is with your mouth that you profess your faith and are saved" Romans 10:9–10 (NIV). I pray that you become my new little brother or sister in Christ, and I pray that you grow strong in the might of His Spirit and become a powerful force for God's Kingdom in our community.

The reason I pray all these things for each of you, regardless of which group of people you're a part of, is because God most definitely does have a "Gay Agenda," and there's a part for you to play in the coming move, but it's up to you to accept it.

Will you accept it?

CPSIA information can be obtained
at www.ICGtesting.com
Printed in the USA
BVHW061547221221
624600BV00010B/1108